CW00631840

# SATELLITE REPAIR M

Written
by
Martin Pickering

Printed by Arlon Stationery Printers Ltd., Paradise Ind. Est.,
Wood Lane, Hemel Hempstead, Herts. HP2 4TL
Tel: (01442) 243719

PRINTED IN GREAT BRITAIN

First edition 1992
Second edition 1993
Third edition 1995
Fourth edition 1996
Fifth edition 1998

This book is dedicated to the memory of my friend, David Poole of Davenham Satellites, who lost his fight against cancer in June 1997.

Grateful thanks to all those nice people who contributed to this book.

Original cover design by Lou Franklin of CBC International, modified by me and image-set by Dave Brooke of DMB Reprographics.
Everything was done on computer – real Apple Macintosh computers, not Pee Cees

# DISCLAIMER

The book contains information about faults which have been observed in the workshop. There are also details of faults and modifications which have been provided by the respective manufacturers. However, nothing in this book may be construed to imply that the manufacturers condone or authorise repairs or modifications listed.

*Use of information in this book could invalidate your warranty. Do not attempt to repair or modify a unit which is under warranty. Take it to your authorised dealer.*

Although some receivers may have a large number of faults listed, this does not imply that the respective receivers are more prone to failure than any other similar equipment. Where a large number of faults is listed, this is principally because an enormous number of these receivers has been sold and those exhibiting a fault represent a tiny proportion of the total number. Indeed, the more popular the receiver, the more likely we are to have amassed a large amount of information about it.

Bear in mind, too, that a large amount of information has been supplied to us in the form of technical bulletins by the manufacturers and that most of this information represents faults found in the factory, not in equipment after sale.

**Where we list "modifications" or "upgrades" the reasons are as follows:**

• Experience has shown that users abuse the equipment (by blocking air vents or by applying short circuits or connecting external equipment not recommended by the manufacturer). In this case, the modification helps to eliminate problems caused by such abuse.

• Due to advances in technology or because of popular demand, the manufacturer has been able to improve the operation or functions of the equipment.

• Facilities available as standard in models of higher specification at extra cost may be added to less expensive models.

• The provision of additional channels on newer satellites has made other facilities or functions desirable.

**Any suggestion that a particular fault is prevalent or likely in equipment listed in this book is unintentional.**

**Neither the author, contributors nor the publisher can accept responsibility for any loss, damage, death, injury or litigation which arises directly or indirectly from the use of information presented in this book.**
All information has been given in good faith and is believed to be correct at the time of writing (December 1997 to March 1998). *Yes, it took a long time!*

## About the author

Martin Thomas Pickering was born in Middlesbrough in 1951.
He became a "thirteen plus" graduate from Stokesley County Modern school and attended Guisborough Grammar school (now Prior Pursglove College) until age nineteen. Being an absolute glutton for learning (or afraid of earning an honest living) he went on to spend three beer-swilling years at Liverpool University – a waste, since he didn't drink.

Having graduated with a degree in Electronic Engineering, he worked for ten months at GEC Stoke works in Coventry as a circuit board designer. He transferred to GEC Aycliffe (to be married) designing telephones and related equipment for twelve years then organising Reliability testing for two years.

On moving to Congleton in Cheshire he joined the Quality Assurance department of Siemens Ltd where his knowledge of German language came in handy, if only to make them laugh. After three years he joined Brother Industries in Wrexham as Quality Assurance Manager, moving sideways to Technical Manager after a year.

When the Recession hit, he had the offer of a handsomely paid management job with a large company in Croydon but turned this down in favour of working for Eurosat Midlands Ltd. because it was closer to home.

Now pleading temporary insanity and desperate to earn a crust, he writes books, magazine articles, runs his own repair business and also supplies kits and spares for most satellite receivers.

Contacting him is easy! Send email via the INTERNET to:
repairman@netcentral.co.uk (preferred) or 100613.2105@compuserve.com
You can also write to SatCure, P.O. Box 12, Sandbach, CW11 1XA, England.
Be sure to enclose 2 x 1st class stamps (UK) or 2 x International Reply Coupons (outside UK) if you want a reply/prices/information.

Visit the web site at: **http://www.netcentral.co.uk/satcure/**
Packed with "FAQ" information about common faults and cures for ailing satellite receivers and decoders. Repair kits, upgrade kits, surplus components plus links to other satellite information sites.

# CONTENTS

# Model Cross-Reference and Page Index

I've attempted to list every satellite receiver ever made, with a cross-reference to its nearest equivalent if there is one. I *might* have missed some! Obviously, the bias is towards UK models, since that's what I see but there are lots of European equivalents which are almost identical except that they have no internal decoder.

Some models are not mentioned because

1. Still under warranty so I don't see it
2. Not sold in my part of the UK
3. Ultra-reliable (hah!)
4. You didn't tell me about it
5. Totally and utterly obsolete
6. No service information available

# Introduction

This is the fifth edition of the Satellite Repair Manual but with a new name. It's not such a major revision as edition 4 in terms of new faults because of "diminishing returns" — that is, the more repairs I carry out on a given model, the less new faults come to light in the long term. And I'm modest, too.

However, there is a lot more information about newer models such as Pace MSS models and BT SVS250/300 which had only just "hit the market" when edition 4 was being finalised. There is also more information for the beginner which makes the book more useful to the hobbyist, as well as the professional.

It's inevitable that there will still be errors and omissions. I apologise in advance for any inconvenience but please refer to the manufacturers' Service Manuals. I've done my best to provide correct information but I won't accept any responsibility for problems caused by mistakes. This is intended to be a guide for people who already know what they are doing, with a few useful bits thrown in for those who don't!

Thanks to all who contributed and a big raspberry to those who didn't.
(Some people refuse to divulge useful information. That's why this book has still only a few hundred pages!)

I would be grateful for any information which could be used in future editions. I am happy to barter! You can reach me at SatCure (enclose 2 x 1st class stamps if you want prices / information / reply) or (preferably) by e-mail at:
**repairman@netcentral.co.uk**

Please DO NOT mail me with a question until you have checked the latest information at my Internet web site. I keep this information updated continually so, if this book doesn't answer your question, the web site files just might.

In addition, I offer an information update service by email only. Contact me for more information about this. If you still don't have email, well....

*Martin Pickering*

**SatCure, P.O. Box 12, Sandbach, CW11 1XA, England.**
**http://www.netcentral.co.uk/satcure/**

# Forward

### Electronic Design Reliability

Designers make mistakes. If it were not for that fact, you and I would not be seeing the volume of repairs that we do. I thought it would be a useful introduction to this manual if I discussed some of the problems that designers face. The knowledge is useful because it allows us to carry out repairs more effectively if we understand why the circuits failed.

I began to design circuits using transistors at age 10, back in 1961. At that time, everybody "knew" that germanium transistors were susceptible to damage by heat and voltage. This had to be true because it was widely publicised that you had to use medical clamps, or similar, to sink the soldering iron heat away from the transistor wires. However, I never bothered to do this and most of my transistors survived.

A similar thought process exists with modern semiconductors. Static Electricity is largely misunderstood and ignored because failures can't be traced to it. In fact failures of any sort are, thankfully, quite rare. However, this is often more by luck than good practice. The damage caused by electrostatic discharge is often insidious. It weakens the internal structure of the device so that its tolerance to surges or high voltages or currents is lowered. Failure can come much later.

This sort of information is well documented because lots of manufacturers make mega bucks by selling Electrostatic dissipative or shielding materials. Where there's money to be made, the message gets through by advertising – mostly – although there are still suppliers who pack semiconductors in ordinary plastic bags.

Other information is less often passed on through designers. I've watched successive generations of designers follow me through the same mistakes that I made thirty years ago. There seems to be no central reference of "well known failure modes". No system of training within companies with the result that the lesson is learned the hard way time and time again. In particular, this sort of information is not fed back to educational institutes.

This discussion is simply a compilation of notes. Much of it comes from my head; some of it is remnants of long-ago memories.

### Electrolytic Capacitors

My first indication that *All Might Not Be Well* with capacitors was at age fourteen when a large electrolytic exploded in my father's face! I'd built a valve superhet radio from plans in a magazine but I'd connected a 32 micro Farad capacitor the wrong way round on a 350 volt supply. It did not survive but, luckily, my father did. This example is an extreme. The usual problem comes when the circuit designer doesn't do his sums and also doesn't take measurements to confirm them. I've seen several examples of circuit design where an electrolytic is "the right way round" but experiences a reverse bias voltage. The more often it occurs, the sooner the capacitor will fail. Designers often don't check this.

I've also seen circuits where an electrolytic is expected to pass a pulse current of several hundred milliamps. It will - for a while.
There are electrolytics manufactured with a low ESR (Electrical Series Resistance) that are more suitable for pulse applications. They are widely used in switch mode power supplies but are sometimes needed elsewhere. There is a finite limit, however, to the rate of change of current that an electrolytic will accept. The internal impedance, inherent in the design, is simply too great. In this case a different type of capacitor would be more appropriate.

A prime example of the wrong type of capacitor can be found in old magazines which published designs for car electronic ignition systems. Invariably, a one micro Farad capacitor was charged then discharged through the coil. The capacitor specifed was often a wound polyester component. Nobody checked the dV/dt specification and, as a result, the capacitor would suffer "punch-through". The effect was self-healing for a while but misfiring would occur, followed by failure. The answer was to use a sandwich construction capacitor such as those made by Siemens. This device has a specified dV/dt (change of voltage with time) which is quite low – around 7 volts per microsecond as I recall – but I had some samples from STC which were rated at *four hundred* volts/μS.

Tantalum capacitors have a high capacitance to volume ratio and a lower impedance than an electrolytic. However, an old "Post Office" (now British Telecom) design rule stated that a tantalum capacitor must never be used unless its voltage rating was at least double the average supply voltage. Tantalums experience failure if their working voltage is exceeded and this rule provided a good safety margin.

Electrolytics can safely be worked closer to their rated voltage but, if size and cost are not of the essence, a higher voltage rating will improve reliability.

A problem with electrolytics is their leakage current. A certain amount of direct current will always flow. Low leakage types are available but they cost more. The designer often overlooks the problem of leakage current. Unfortunately, it can become worse with age and temperature but, of course, it doesn't show a problem in the design prototype.

Temperature is something else to watch out for. If an electrolytic is rated at 85 degrees Centigrade for 20,000 hours, that is a typical value, beyond which you can expect problems. 20,000 hours is just over two years. If the capacitor experiences a lower temperature, it will last longer. If higher, it will fail sooner. Try blocking the cabinet vents (as a typical consumer would do with a magazine or book!) Then measure the temperature rise of each capacitor. You will find local hot spots that will kill capacitors in a few months.

The design of an aluminium electrolytic capacitor is ingenious. It consists of two thin strips of aluminium foil with an insulating layer of oxide formed on the anode foil. The whole lot is coiled into a tube shape and both strips of foil are attached to wires. The aluminium anode foil is etched to increase its effective surface area and the separating paper is impregnated with an electrolyte which acts as the cathode. All of this serves to produce the maximum capacitance value in the minimum volume.

Unfortunately, the complexity of the design gives plenty of scope for failure. The wires have to be bonded to the aluminium - not the easiest material for welding. The whole thing has to be sealed to prevent the liquid electrolyte from escaping. It has to be squeezed into a tiny can. Failure is often mechanical. It is not unusual to find an electrolytic which has parted company with a wire. I've also seen them damaged by component insertion machines.

Finally, the tolerance of an electrolytic capacitor is usually quite wide. It used to be plus 80%, minus 20%. Nowadays, manufacturing control is better and you can get much narrower tolerances (at a price). However, don't expect to obtain anything better than about plus/minus 10%. If you want accuracy in a timing circuit, for example, forget electrolytics.

**Multi layer Ceramic Capacitors**
These devices are widely used but seldom understood. Let's start with the manufacturing process. I wonder how many readers understand how they are made? There are two principal methods:

The more common method is to make a sandwich with alternate layers of ceramic paste and silver. The sandwich is then heated to a high temperature to "fire" the ceramic (like making pottery) and cut into little oblongs. The odd layers of silver are bonded together at one end and the even layers at the other. This is performed by deposition of a metal alloy such as silver palladium. A layer of nickel may be added to increase resistance to leaching during soldering.

The other method is to make a sandwich of ceramic paste layered with plastic film. After firing, the plastic has burned away so molten lead can be forced at high pressure into the interstices to form a lead-ceramic sandwich.

The resultant capacitor has a medium capacitance to volume ratio; higher than the old ceramic disc capacitor but lower than the electrolytic. It also has a low impedance at high frequency, making it ideal for passing fast rise time pulses.

The drawback is that, although the apparent tolerance can be low, it suffers from wide changes of capacitance with temperature. Better ceramic materials are used to combat this effect but cost more. In addition, their capacitance to volume ratio is not as good as that of the cheaper materials.

In the 1980s, some manufacturers were having problems with these capacitors. The fault would occur with capacitors of 47nF or 100nF which were used to decouple a 5 volt rail. The capacitor could glow white hot and even burst into flame. I saw circuit boards which had been so badly burned that there was a hole right through.

Plastic housings also caught fire. As far as I know, the failure mechanism was never fully explained. We found by experiment that, for the fault to occur, the 5 volt supply had to provide at least 80mA and the capacitor would measure around 8 Ohms dc resistance as failure began. You probably read this paragraph too quickly for the full implications to sink in. Let me emphasize: a multilayer ceramic capacitor connected to a 5 volt supply where 80mA or more is available has been known to burn like a torch!

The problem may have been caused by micro fractures in the ceramic allowing silver migration. (Silver can grow dendrites or whiskers under certain conditions). We were able to precipitate failure repeatedly by connecting one of these capacitors across a 5v dc supply then applying a brief 2kV pulse. A test using methanol is used by capacitor manufacturers to weed out faulty batches. This test shows up unwanted interstices in the capacitor structure. However, mechanical damage to capacitors during PCB assembly or soldering is possibly more likely to cause failure than is faulty manufacture.

There has been a long debate about whether nickel plating the end terminations of surface mount capacitors is necessary. It definitely resists leaching of silver during soldering. If you have nickel plated terminations, don't waste money on silver-loaded solder. However, some authorities blame the nickel for cracking of the capacitors. I disagreed with this hypothesis and did tests to investigate.

The problem with surface mount capacitors and resistors is that they are brittle and can crack under stress. The simplest way to prove this is simply to bend a printed circuit board and listen. You can hear the cracking sounds! The problem may be worse with paper-phenolic board material which flexes more easily but this is not necessarily the case if you follow simple design rules.

I set up a series of test boards, roughly 75mm by 50mm. Capacitors were soldered between pairs of pads of varying sizes along the length of the boards. The capacitors were heated by the crude method of holding over a soldering iron, then the board was plunged into cold water. The capacitors could be heard to crack as they entered the water.

A jig was set up to apply pressure along the central axis of a fresh board to make it bow. As pressure increased, the capacitors were heard to crack. In both cases the damage was confirmed by measurement. It is worth noting, however, that most of the capacitors measured all right until they had been subjected to humidity.

However, on one set of boards, no damage occurred. The difference between this board and the others was that the capacitors were soldered directly to the copper tracks without wide solder pads.

Further tests were performed and it was established that failure did not occur at all, provided that the width of the solder pad was no greater than 75% of the width of the end termination of the capacitor. It is likely that the solder joint is narrow enough to flex so that tension forces are no longer exerted on the end terminations of the ceramic component. In military and aircraft use where vibration is a problem, it may be that this type of joint would be prone to stress fracturing. However, for domestic equipment it gives much improved reliability.

Designers still throw up their hands in horror at this suggestion which defies all the design rules ever invented. Interestingly, such pad widths gave no wave soldering problems and used only half the amount of solder that would normally have been used. Another advantage is that there was less obstruction to tracks, making the layout easier. You can do these tests yourself at very little cost.

Obvious though it might seem, you should never mount a surface mount ceramic component in line with the longest axis of a board. Flexing is far more likely to crack it than if it is oriented along the shortest axis. Amazing how few designers think of this. I've seen several boards designed with capacitors near the long edge of the board. This is where flexing is likely to be greatest. Worse - the board was designed to mount on plastic pillars and, to fit the board, heavy finger pressure had to be applied directly above the capacitors!

Another failure mechanism has been seen: where capacitors are placed on the PCB by an automatic machine, this machine must be programmed with the thickness of each capacitor. It needs this information so that it can avoid putting too much pressure on the device. I have personally seen instances where machines have been programmed for a 0.6mm device but the Purchasing Department has ordered in a lower

cost device measuring 1.2mm in thickness. The result was that the placement machine tried to force each device through the PCB. The problem
was not seen until field failures occurred and we had to back-track
through weeks of production to trace the cause. This type of failure is
often the most easy to detect. In our case, the placement head used a circular cross-section plunger. Some of the damaged devices exhibited a
circular fracture mark on the surface, clearly visible under microscopic
examination.

**Resistors**
For the first time ever, I've had equipment in the workshop that has
failed because tiny resistors have gone high in value. The equipment is
imported from the Far East. The failure is unusual in that the resistors
which fail are carrying negligible current. They die without any apparent cause. This is probably a case of equipment being "built to a price".
Of course, failure is much more likely if the resistor is required to dissipate a lot of heat.

Another problem which has appeared, recently, is the use, in switch
mode power supplies, of resistors which need to have a high voltage rating – but don't. The conventional type of spiral-cut resistor is prone to
arcing between the spirals. If a resistor will be subjected to a high voltage it is sensible to specify a suitable resistor (wattage alone is not sufficient). These have become quite rare with the demise of valve-based
equipment. Beware, if replacing a power supply resistor, that it might be
safety critical and have a specified voltage rating or it may have to be a
non-flammable or fusible type. Mains powered equipment normally has
type-approval. If you fit parts other than those specified, you may efec-
tively set aside this safety approval and leave yourself vulnerable to
prosecution. Apart from that, your use of inappropriate components
could lead to damage to equipment or injury to the user. Think about
this before you replace a 0.5 Watt fusible resistor with a 5 Watt ceramic
type!

**Glue**
One possible cause of resistor failure is that, in many cases, a petroleum
solvent-based glue had been applied to secure wires and other components. This glue was often found on the failed resistors. In addition,
where the glue had been subjected to a high temperature, it had carbonised and formed a conductive path which created intermittent fault

symptoms. Look out for glue: it can trap heat inside a component, cause corrosion and conduction.

## Heat

I mentioned the susceptibility of electrolytics to failure caused by heat. Well, *all* components will fail if they become too hot. In many designs, heat is the last thing to be considered and often there is a token gesture of putting a few narrow slots in the lid in the hope that heat will get out! Sorry, guys, but it doesn't work that way: if you want warm air to come out of the top you have to let cold air go in at the bottom.

The problem is that modern equipment has very little room inside. Everything has been miniaturised in the extreme. There's a simple rule to understand when dealing with heat. To escape, it requires air movement. OK the purists will argue that it can be lost by direct radiation but that effect is quite small. Air movement is required.

Hot air will expand so a little air escapes from the hot box; but in order for more hot air to come out, cold air must go in. In many designs this can't happen so the only cooling effect is that of cold air moving across the surface of the box and cooling the air inside by conduction. Not very effective and even less so if the box is plastic or inside a cabinet.

In the old days of rack-mounted units, an effect called "the chimney effect" was sometimes used to cool the equipment. Cold air was drawn in at the bottom by hot air flowing out at the top and the effect was self-sustaining without a fan. However, the effect is only reasonably self-sustaining when the height of the box exceeds one metre! You can't rely on it for cooling modern units just 50mm high.

Back in my design days I worked long and hard on this problem. I ended up with a box just 300mm high. The entire base was slotted and covered with mesh, having a 60% effective flow area. So was the top, but it had a false roof supported by 20mm pillars, open at sides and back but closed at the front for cosmetic reasons. All boards inside were mounted vertically. The false roof prevented upwards movement of air but smoke tests showed that air was going in the bottom and coming out of the side slots at the top.

Now, we fitted thermocouples inside and connected them to a chart recorder. The resultant graphs were extraordinary. During the day, when the central heating was on, the temperature rose less than at night! The reason was that, at night, nothing moved; no doors opened and no people walked by. We proved this by experiment. In order for the cooling to be most effective, there had to be air moving sideways in the room. This wafted through the top side slots and shifted the hot air, allowing cool air to rise from the base. The gap beneath the base had to be a minimum of 20mm high, otherwise the cooling effect was less efficient.

However, the design was satisfactory, giving less than 15 degrees rise in temperature with a power supply generating 300 Watts, even in a closed room. No fan was needed. The false roof had no slots so it didn't matter if newspapers were laid on it. The entire inside top and bottom was covered with insect-proof mesh which also kept fingers out. Cosmetically the box looked good.

Television cabinets can be designed in a similar fashion. VCR cabinets can have fans at little extra cost (although they make the dust problem worse). Satellite receivers, however, still have problems. They tend to be small in size and have a tuner, power supply and decoder unit, all of which dissipate a lot of heat. In addition, there is often one large circuit board which covers the entire base. The box is not high and any slots in the top get covered by magazines (or cats!) To make matters worse, the receiver is often installed right on top of the TV or VCR and put inside a "Hi-fi" cabinet with the doors closed!

**Connectors**
Probably the least reliable component in any electronic equipment is the connector. You will see this problem especially in little-used switches, plugs and sockets used for power supply connection, decoder connection and even in the form of "dry" solder joints which fail from various causes including poor factory soldering process, vibration embrittlement and poor solderability of the actual wires or tracks. The problem is made worse if the male and female contacts are not of identical metal – in fact I laugh when I see people using gold-plated plug contacts with tin-plated socket contacts! Electrolytic action takes place between dissimilar metals and results in oxidation which can act as an insulator.

## Overview

This has been a very brief overview of just a few of the problems which designers leave for us to sort out for the customer. I hope that my explanations make sense and allow you to understand the problems facing you a little better than before. Now that you know that the first items to fail are usually connectors, the second are electrolytic capacitors and the third, resistors, you can dig into that "dead" unit with more confidence! (Semiconductors come well down the list. This is especially surprising when you know the complexity of some ICs!) Also bear in mind that more faults occur in power supplies than anywhere else. In fact, if all power supplies were removable, you could fix at least 50 percent of all faults simply by replacing them.

### WHO CARES ABOUT COPYRIGHT ?

Many years ago when I repaired CB radios, I obtained an illegal photocopy of "The CB PLL Data Book" written by Lou Franklin. The photocopied pages were immensely useful but they were unwieldy and heavy in a ring binder. I wrote to Lou and ordered a proper book from him. Since then we have remained good friends and visited each other in our homes in Arizona and England.

**I can't stop you from copying pages from this book** but I would appeal to your conscience: if you DO copy pages, please copy this page as well!
If the information helps you to save money, at least send me a few stamps to show your appreciation of all the hard work I put into this manual over the last six years! Better still, buy the book!

# Repair Section

# Specific Receivers

List of common problems, cures and modifications

The information in this section is intended to supplement – not replace – the information in manufacturers' service manuals. Wherever possible, unless you are simply fitting a kit with instructions supplied, try to obtain the relevant service manual, not simply a circuit diagram.

Without a manual, some of the fault cures listed will not make complete sense. This is especially so where a surface mount component must be replaced, because there is insufficient space in this book to include underside views of circuit boards.

I have tried to list symptoms under sensible headings such as "Power supply Faults" but, where a power supply fault inevitably causes a picture or audio fault, then you may find the symptom listed elsewhere, instead, or as well. All I can suggest is that you take time read the entire book to "get a feel" for the way in which I've presented the facts. It's not a bedtime story but some bits are amusing!
Also look in the fault INDEX which is split into sections, according to model.
Where more than one component is listed as a possible fault cause, I have tried to list them in order of either likelihood or ease of replacement.

In order to help you to diagnose a fault without the need for a lot of equipment, I have tried to indicate where a fault will be seen/heard from different output connections. It is absolutely *essential*, therefore, that you have a television with both easily-tuned RF input *and* a separate video/audio input to allow monitoring of the Scart or Phono outputs of a satellite receiver. Frequently a fault will be listed as (for example) "picture OK from TV Scart but streaky from RF and from VCR Scart."
This information will be totally useless to anyone who can not monitor the Scart outputs. If your TV can't do this, buy a cheap, used set that can!

In addition, I recommend fitting a miniature toggle switch to your Scart plug in order to select either left or right stereo. This is invaluable for tracking down audio problems.

Finally, your test TV set **must not blank the screen** if video level is low!
It's important that you are able to see weak video or "snow" if that's the symptom.

# Amstrad SRX100/200

*No LNB voltage :*
Replace front fuse (630mA).

*LNB voltage low for 17v (13v O.K.). No horizontal channels.*
Replace Q505 (2SA1706) and R532 (15Ω 2Watt).

*LNB voltage too high. No vertical channels.*
Replace Q506 (2SB1143). Also check items above.

I was going to omit the older models from this edition – but I still get lots of questions about them so I decided to leave them

*Channel display flashes briefly at switch-on but front panel otherwise dead or not fully functional. Channel numbers may be all zero or random characters.*
Front switch panel PCB cracked in half or tracks on main board broken. IC101 may be faulty or IC105 (UAA2001). C504 (220µF 10v) may be faulty. In the early stages, C504 may cause "herringbone" pattern on the screen.

*H/V light permanently on, off or dim.*
Replace IC101.

## Useful Voltage measurements

The sketch indicates typical DC voltage measurements. Voltages in brackets () are for Standby mode only. Where only one measurement is shown there is negligible change between Standby and On states. (Some voltages will decrease with LNB connected.)
Later versions of the SRX200 numbered FN------ used a different board assembly.

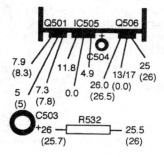

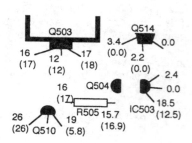

*No tuning, no 18 volt rail:*
Q510 s/c.

*SRX200 used with D2Mac decoder:*
To get sound wire pin 3 to pin 7 on the 15 pin socket.

*AFC pulls channels way off frequency, VR101 has no effect; 12v line is correct:*
Demodulator is not correctly balanced - TC69 requires adjustment to set
pin 11 of SL1455 to 2.5v; effectively setting baseband dc offset to zero as
required for correct operation:-

1) Disconnect the mains; remove tuner can lid.
2) Short pins 18 & 19 of CPU to chassis (AFC defeat).
3) Reconnect mains, power up, select channel.
4) Centralise VR101, check and adjust 12v as necessary. Picture should
be perfect at this stage.
5) Select display counter mode (up/down button)
6) Monitor the voltage on pin 11 of SL1455 (14 pin device, located in
the tuner) with a DVM and very carefully adjust TC69 with a plastic
trimming tool for 2.5v.
7) Watch the display and quickly remove the shorting link - correct any
change of frequency with VR101.

*Two thin horizontal lines across picture.*
Replace Electrolytic capacitor C503 (2200µF 25v)
Check 12v on centre leg of Q503. If high, adjust VR502.

*No sound or picture.*
Check for cracks across the copper tracks, especially adjacent to the
heatsink and across the central screw fixing hole.

If TV shows a snowy screen rather than blank, replace Q510 (2SK301
FET) in front of the smaller heatsink and replace IC503, the AN3146 to
the right of the heatsink (if either fails the other dies, too).

*Display reads "8888":*
Replace MC14499P on the front panel PCB. Other odd numbers in the
display can be caused by crystal X101.

*Only some of the front panel buttons work. Picture & sound may be O.K.*
Check for broken tracks and faulty buttons. Replace IC101.

*Sound but blank screen:*
Check with an oscilloscope that the video going into IC309 on pin 12 is coming out on pin 14. If not, replace IC309.

*Herring Bone pattern on pictures:*
Replace C504 (220μF) next to heatsink.

*Pictures jumping:*
Replace Q713 and Q719 (KTC1815) which go short circuit together.

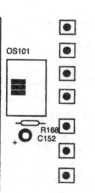

*Black OR white sparklies on most channels:*
The installer has failed to set the LNB OFFSET adjuster which is on the main board. Note that the receiver takes 10 - 20 seconds to react to an adjustment so turn the adjuster very slowly until sparklies disappear.

**Note that there may be more than one fault and the symptoms listed will not correspond to those which you see. Read all of the examples and check for the most likely causes. Measure voltages and look for those which are incorrect.**

## Adding Remote Control Facility

The SRX100 has no handset sensor but can be modified by fitting the parts used on the SRX200 front panel board or just swap the boards.

For Remote handset operation add the Sensor OS101, 47Ω resistor and 100μF capacitor.

Scrape the paint away inside the front panel "window".

Most Amstrad satellite receiver remotes will work, although the button labelling may have to be altered.

### Modifying the audio to suit Eutelsat transmissions

Replace crystal X302 and select Audio 3. You will lose the existing radio channels on Audio 3 and 4. This mod works for the SRD400 as well.

6.65 MHz audio requires a 17.17760 MHz crystal (approx).

There is also a tuneable audio demodulator board available from SatCure. This is low-cost, requires only three wires to be soldered in and may be adjusted from 6.50 to 6.65 MHz. It operates from the TV/SAT button. You don't lose any audio channels by fitting this.

## Adding Extra Channels

Fit microprocessor IC101 from an SRD400

## Circuit Reliability Upgrades

The components most likely to fail through old age and high tempera-ture are the electrolytic capacitors – especially those near to the heat sinks and to the tuner.

We recommend that you replace C504 with a 220µF/10v/105°C type. Also C503 with a 2200µF/25v/105°C electrolytic.

## Connecting your SRX200 to a Videocrypt and a D2Mac decoder

Somebody gave me this sketch. Don't ask me how it works. No idea. Figure it out for yourself.

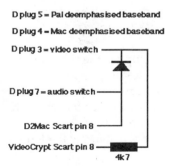

D plug 5 = Pal deemphasised baseband

D plug 4 = Mac deemphasised baseband

D plug 3 = video switch

D plug 7 = audio switch

D2Mac Scart pin 8

VideoCrypt Scart pin 8

4k7

# Amstrad SRD400 Frequently Asked Questions

**Contents**
1. Why do I get no pictures since I changed my LNB for a new one ?
2. My receiver is stuck in standby. Is this Parental Lock Mode ?
3. Some channels are sparkly. How do I tune them in?
4. I can't get 6.60 Audio channels. Is there an upgrade ?
5. Is there a factory reset ?
6. Why do I get poor pictures with wavy lines ?
7. How can l get D2Mac with my SRD400?

**1. Why do I get no pictures since I swapped my LNB for a new one ?**

Perhaps you short-circuited the coaxial cable inner wire to the outer plug. Check the connections very carefully to ensure that strands of wire are not causing a short circuit. Locate the top fuse of three inside the receiver. Replace it with a T1A fuse. Locate a brown disc capacitor labelled CP527 or C527 which usually sits near to the ribbon cable which goes into the main board from the decoder. Sometimes it is soldered across a diode labelled DP506. Sometimes it is beneath the board. Sometimes it is not fitted at all. Remove this capacitor. This is an Amstrad-approved upgrade. If there is still no LNB power supply from the LNB input socket check whether RP506 (6R8, 2W wire-wound) is open circuit. This resistor is located below a little printed circuit board which is fixed to the large, black, finned heatsink.

**2. My receiver is stuck in standby. Is this Parental Lock Mode ?**

Probably; you can check quite easily. Press the front panel button sequence [H/V] [H/V] [Audio]. If four horizontal dashes appear in the display then your receiver is locked. The User Handbook instructs you as follows:

Unplug the receiver from the mains power.
Plug it back in.
Leave it for more than 48 hours to "count down."
Do NOT touch any buttons in the meantime or you'll have to unplug it and start again.
If you can't wait 48 hours, there's a quick method described later.

## 3. Some channels are sparkly. How do I tune them in?

There is a frequency offset adjuster which you can turn by putting a jeweller's screwdriver through a tiny hole in the plastic base of the receiver. However, to avoid damage it is best to adjust this from inside. Set this adjuster to its central position to begin with. Turning it one way will reduce black sparklies and turning it the other way will reduce white sparklies. It reacts very slowly so give it time. It should be set for the best compromise on all channels (usually middle position).

If some channels are still sparkly, proceed as follows:
If black sparklies are present, press [tune up] then immediately press [H/V].
If white sparklies are present, press [tune down] then immediately press [H/V].
Once you have a good picture, press [Preset] twice.

*If you see both black AND white sparklies then tuning will not help as:*
The dish is not aligned or
The cable is kinked, has moisture inside or bad connections or
The LNB is faulty or
The receiver tuner module is faulty.

## 4. I can't get 6.60 Audio channels. Is there an upgrade ?

Yes there is. It's a small circuit board assembly with just three wires to solder in place. You can adjust it to get either 6.50, 6.60 or 6.65 MHz audio channels. However, if you leave it adjusted to 6.60 MHz it will receive the other two with only slight distortion. Get it from SatCure.

## 5. Is there a factory reset ?

No, there's no secret button sequence but you can solder in a new SDA2516 EEprom. This will automatically be reprogrammed to factory defaults on power-up.

## 6. Why do I get poor pictures with wavy lines ?

This is usually caused by electrolytic capacitors overheating. Try replacing all the 100uF and 470uF capacitors around the tuner module.

### 7. How can 1 get D2Mac with my SRD400?

Easy! Connect the decoder to the SRD400 using a modified Scart lead:
Mark one Scart plug cover "Receiver".
Remove the plug cover.
Cut the wire which goes to pin 19 and solder a 200mm wire to it to extend it back out of the plug cover.
Replace the plug cover.
Solder a Phono plug to the wire.
Plug the Phono into "baseband out" at the back of the SRD400.
Plug the "Receiver" Scart plug into the Scart socket on the back of the SRD400.
Plug the other Scart plug into your D2Mac decoder.

Set the decoder menu options as appropriate (D2Mac).
You'll need a smart card.

# Amstrad SRD400

The sketch shows useful points to measure DC voltages in the SRD400 power supply regulator section.

| | Standby | On | No decoder fitted |
|---|---|---|---|
| **TP01** | 7.7v | 7.6 | |
| | 5.0v | 5.0 | |
| | 7.0v | 6.9 | |
| **TP05** | 5.1v | 5.1 | 0.2 |
| | 7.7v | 7.4 | 7.0 |
| | 5.7v | 5.7 | 0.0 |
| **TP03** | 17.3v | 16.6 | |
| | 12.1v | 12.2 | |
| | 16.6v | 15.9 | |
| **TP09** | 0.0v | varies | |
| | 30.5v | 28.9 | |
| | 0.0v | 0.0 | |
| **IP503** | 13.6/17.7 | 13.5/17.6 | |
| | 1.5/5.6 | 1.4/5.5 | |
| | 30.8/30.8 | 28.1/23.7 | |

| | Standby | On |
|---|---|---|
| RP513 | 0.0 | 2.6 |
| | 2.4 | 0.0 |
| TP505 | 0.0 | 0.6 |
| TP504 (2SK301) | 5.88 | 18.55 |
| | 32.0 | 30.0 |
| IP504 | 5.88 | 18.55 |

On: 0.0 11.8 16.7 0.0 5.0 7.8

Standby: 0.0 11.7 17.7 0.0 5.0 8.2

Regulator board — 12v, 5v

The regulators are bolted to a large heatsink which, because of its weight, is itself a source of problems – look for cracks in the board underneath the heatsink and look for broken solder joints on the regulators.

The values indicated are typical and slight variations are to be expected.

Three columns of figures are shown because some voltages vary between Standby and On conditions and one regulator is affected by the absence of the decoder board.

Although you might find DC voltage measurements tedious, they will help to pinpoint many faults which otherwise could take you hours of guesswork. Do, please, make these measurements before blaming the decoder or tuner (or anything else for that matter).

If you need to view the TV picture with the decoder board removed, simply link the two white wires in the white plug connector (1kΩ resistor) after you remove it from the decoder board. The picture will be clear but will flicker because the video signal is now unclamped.

## Parental Lock

*Standby light comes on but receiver won't respond to button pushes:*
Press [H/V] [H/V] [AUDIO] button sequence on the front panel.
If 4 dashes (----) appear in display then parental lock has been set. My
opinion is that it can become set by mains interference, not just by
somebody pushing buttons!

If you read the user handbook you will see that it instructs you simply
to unplug the SRD400 from the mains *then plug it back in again.* Leave it
alone for 48 hours and the internal microprocessor will count down to
zero and reset the parental lock to "off" automatically. Do *not* touch the
receiver or handset buttons for at least 50 hours!

The workshop method takes five minutes:

• Disconnect then <u>reconnect</u> the SRD400 to the mains.
• Connect a 1k resistor to two "Easi-hook" test probes.
• Attach one to the tuner case and the other to the rear end of R106
    (4k7Ω yellow/violet/red) beneath the decoder board (remove
screws and lift out the board.)

• Press STANDBY
(display will show "8").

• Press [H/V] [H/V] [AUDIO] (displays "----") then
[1] [2] [3] [4] from the handset (displays "| | | |").

• Disconnect resistor and press
[AUDIO], [AUDIO], *slowly* and
firmly.
• Repeat the <u>entire</u> sequence if
necessary.

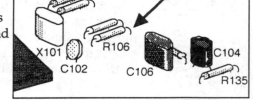

• If all else fails, replace SDA2516 channel memory I.C. with a new one.

*Won't come out of standby or Standby LED flashes (not parental lock):*
Add 100µF across 5v regulated rail on small board which is screwed to
the heatsink. Solder it across wires 4 (-ve) and 5 (+ve) counting from the
front.

## TUNING PROBLEMS

*Sparklies on some or all channels.*
Underneath the receiver, near the front, there is a 3mm hole. Inside the receiver is an adjuster marked "Offset". You can remove the top cover and move the decoder board aside (disconnect the *small* brown connector) to reach this adjuster, or you can put a tiny screwdriver through the hole in the base. Be very careful as the adjuster is fragile. The receiver is very slow to respond to movement of this Offset adjuster. Move it then allow twenty seconds for the receiver to re-tune itself. If the picture becomes worse, turn the adjuster the opposite way and wait again. Replace IC102 (LM324) if offset adjuster has no effect.

*Will not lock on certain channels:*
Failure to lock on a channel is often caused by a faulty SDA2516 which should be replaced. If this fails, try the following:
Inside tuner module solder a 12mm wire to the front end of C20 chip capacitor as shown in the sketch. You can test beforehand to see if this will work simply by touching C20 with a fingertip. (Discharge body static, first!)

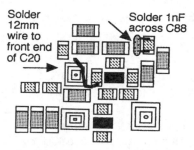

Input section of tuner module

*Tuner tends to drift off frequency or impossible to lock in any channel for more than a few seconds.*
This problem can be caused by a "Screwdriver Expert" attempting to twiddle the two adjustable capacitors, C69 and C70 near the front of the tuner module. Replacement capacitors are available but they are surface mount type and take great skill to solder in place.
Similar fault can be caused by the large 2200µF capacitor.

*Channel select OK but pressing tune button fails to make H/V light alternate on/off for certain frequencies.*
(i.e. normally each press changes the polarity H-V-H-V-H-V etc but instead it may be H-H-V-H-V-H-H etc.) Press Tune twice or press Tune then H/V immediately.
If the setting will not store, change the channel memory I.C. marked SDA2516.

This diagram indicates the voltages and signals you can measure on the tuner connections beneath the main PCB. These pins are also accessible within the tuner.

Beneath tuner module

AGC
5v typical
Baseband
signal
5v    12v
Tuning
voltage VT
12v    13/17v
LNB

The unmarked pins are connected to 0 volts. On later tuners, one of the 0v pins is omitted altogether.

*Won't tune in. Pin 2 of IC105 fixed at 4 volts:*
Some tuning problems are caused by C111 on the main board.

**AUDIO FAULTS**

*No sound on Audio 1:*
Replace IC302 (TBA229-2 made by Siemens).

*No sound on some audio channels.*
Can have many causes but check IC305 first and look for a broken track next to it.

*Hiss or buzz on audio (or without audio) from RF but O.K. from SCART.*
Misadjusted or faulty modulator.

*No sound from RF output but O.K. from SCART.*
Faulty modulator unit or broken track to modulator audio input pin.

*Distortion or crackling on sound from RF output:*
Broken track from modulator to R388 (6k8).

*No left hand channel sound:*
Replace C313 10nf capacitor. (Lots of other causes!)

## LNB VOLTAGE PROBLEMS

*No horizontally polarised channels (usually no vertical channels either) with horizontal sparkly lines across blank screen (may be quite faint). LNB voltage will be too low under load or show oscillation. Whistling noise with Test Bars switched on. Often intermittent or began when the LNB was changed. Very common with a Global Mini Magic™ switch connected or any new LNB which draws a higher current than a 'Blue Cap'. Can often give the symptom "Picture goes blank after warm-up":*

Remove 100nF capacitor CP527 (near to connector CNM4). In earlier versions this capacitor is soldered across the legs of diode DP505.

Some versions have no such capacitor and the remedy is to put a resistor in parallel with RP520 (22k near the front of the main board). Try a 3k9, then a 1k2 if no better.

Taiwan versions already have a 1kΩ resistor and no CP527. Removing CP528 may also help. If RP520 is already 1k, and CP527 and CP528 are not on the board, look underneath.

Receivers of issue J, made in Japan, around serial number FN50012484, had CP527 soldered to the pads of DP505 *beneath* the PCB.

*LNB voltage 17 volts. H/V button and LED work correctly. No vertical channels.*
Replace IP503 on heatsink. This must be an *insulated* 7812 regulator *without* a metal tab.

*LNB voltage 13 volts. H/V button and LED work correctly. No horizontal channels*
Replace 3v9 zener diode close to IP503. Ensure IP503 has *no* metal tab.

*Keeps melting 630mA fuse for no apparent reason. (Lights up but no output. No LNB voltage)*   Replace T630mA with a T1A fuse.

(It is not usually safe to increase the value of a fuse but, in this particular instance, it is permissible to do so).

*LNB voltage too low.*
If no LNB voltage at all then replace top fuse.
Otherwise, check resistor RP506 (6R8) hidden beneath the small 5v/12v regulator board on the heatsink. If still no LNB voltage check TP508 (a 2SB976 PNP) and IP503 (a 7812 insulated type). If LNB voltage present but too low, check the two associated diodes and 3v9 zener.

*LNB voltage stays high in STANDBY:*
Replace TP508 (2SB976 — FXT749 will do).

## PANEL DISPLAY PROBLEMS

*Display reads "1000" or some other number.*
*Buttons may not work.*

Replace IC105 (UAA2001).
Failing that replace crystal X101 and/or IC101 itself.
If display reads "0000" you may need to replace the tuner.
Check IC151 (MC14499) 7 segment LED driver I.C. on front panel by substitution. Check large electrolytics.

*No channel display. LNB voltage O.K.*

*Panel lights and buttons function O.K.*

*Sparkly screen with less sparklies if LNB is disconnected.*

Check 5v on pin 11 of IC105. If higher than 5v replace IC105 (UAA2001)

*Working but no panel display.*
Check IC151 (MC14499) 7 segment LED driver I.C. on front panel by substitution.

*Front panel dead. No supply to 5 volt regulator (small PCB bolted to heatsink).*
Bottom fuse melted or clip bent and not making contact.

*No channel display. No test signal.*

*LNB voltage O.K. Panel lights and buttons function O.K.*
Check middle fuse 2 Amps (sometimes 630mA is fitted by mistake). If 2 Amp fuse continues to blow, check 15 volt zener diode DP12 and PNP transistor TP03 near to the large heatsink.

*No picture, sound or channel display but buttons & LEDs OK.*
Check 12v from 12v/5v regulator board. Check 18v supply to 12v regulator. Check fuse FP30. Look for broken track between bridge rectifier + and connector to 12v/5v board. If input voltage to regulator is correct then output from regulator may be short circuit. Try tracing track back to Tuner; disconnecting links will isolate the fault. Can be caused by a short circuit inside the Tuner unit.

*Standby light remains on. No response to any button press. Pressing H/V H/V AUDIO has no affect (i.e. not parental lock.)*
Measure voltage on IC101 pin 8 which should toggle from 0v to 2.5v as STANDBY button is pressed. If no voltage then replace SDA2516. If still not working, replace IC101 microprocessor.

Note: Fitting IC101 the wrong way round destroys both it and IC151 on the front panel. (Guess how I found out!)

Note: Although we have classified faults under neat little headings you may get a receiver which has more than one fault which combine to give unusual symptoms. If you can't find the solution look under every other heading.

## PICTURE PROBLEMS — FRONT PANEL O.K.

*No colour. Picture rolls intermittently.*
Check electrolytic capacitor C904 which can short to link J94 next to the tuner. Replace all 470µF and 100µF capacitors around tuner.

*No pictures. Lines on the screen:*
*Picture might appear briefly as tune button is pressed.*
*All voltages and waveforms around tuner correct.*
Replace buffer transistor Q711.

*No video from RF socket but OK from SCART.*
Check for broken track below UHF modulator, otherwise replace modulator.

*No video from RF socket or from SCART.*
*Blank screen, no 'snow':*
See "Decoder Problems".
If the symptom remains when the decoder is bypassed and is not caused by any previously mentioned fault, then the problem lies in the video circuitry which requires the use of an oscilloscope to trace.

*Picture "rolls" vertically or "breaks up" (a bit like RTL4).*
Look for broken tracks around Q718 next to rear pillar which supports decoder. Replace all 470µF and 100µF capacitors around tuner.

*Intermittent horizontal lines or severe*
*hum bar instead of picture and severe buzzing on audio (TSG on).*
Check capacitors CP01/CP03 for dry joint. Check DP10 on decoder board (z5v6).

*Blank screen:*
No 12v on pin 10 of decoder connector.
TP04. (see other causes, too).

**No picture or sound** *even from SCART* **or just 2 channels only***:*
Lift lid off tuner and measure voltage on the third pin from the rear. If the tuning voltage "VT" does not alter in steps as the channel frequency is changed check for solder short between tuner pins then check the voltages on TP504 (2SK301), as follows. There should be 30 volts on the leg nearest the heatsink. If not then trace the connection all the way back to the power supply until you find the fault.
There should be 18 volts on the leg furthest from the heatsink ('on' state). If not then replace TP504 *and* shunt regulator IP504. If these are O.K. and "VT" remains high (won't change), try replacing C111, near to IC101, then IC102. Check for dry joint on C701 electrolytic.

If tuner voltages are O.K. or if VT goes only up to about 10 volts maximum as the tune button is pressed repeatedly then replace tuner. VT can also be affected by IC105 (UAA2001) and by track breaks.

*Very low video level and rolling picture:*
Replace electrolytics alongside the tuner. Otherwise suspect decoder.
*Pictures too bright from RF output:*
Broken track from modulator to R759.
*Offset adjuster does not work:*
Replace it! (so far found 4 which had an open-circuit wiper).
at right main board.

## DECODER PROBLEMS

*Blank raster but picture & sound with decoder disconnected and bypassed.*
(Bypass decoder by fitting a 1kΩ resistor between the two white wires in
the small white plug). Usually caused by DP10 short circuit, otherwise:
Check 5v on TP01. If absent or only present with decoder disconnected,
check for a broken track feeding DP28 or the large resistor in series or a
dry joint on TP01. Add 10k between b & c of TP01. If 5v on centre leg of
TP01 but not on decoder board 5v pin, link the two with a wire.

If still no 5 volts then check zener DP28 (5v1) at rear left of main board.
Also check 12 volts on pin 10 of brown connector. If absent, look for dry
joint or broken tracks around TP03. If DP12 is short circuit, replace it
and TP03 (2SB1136).

*Test message appears or decoder will not decode.*
Unplug from the mains then try again.
If this fails, look for current leakage paths between the pins of the card
reader IC on the decoder board, caused by coffee spillage etc.

*"Please Insert Card" message appears with card inserted.*
Heat up cover of card reader and bow inward before re-fitting.

*"Your card is invalid" when the card is known to be  o.k.:*
Check the 5V "VCC Card" test point on the Videocrypt decoder board
before condemning the decoder. The supply should switch on when the
card is inserted and switch off when the card is removed. If the supply is
missing check whether the 5.6V zener  diode DP16 on the main board,
close to regulator TP05, is short-circuit. TP05 is to the left of the decoder
board. If this is not the cause of the   problem, check the rest of the "VCC
Card" supply components -- TP05 (2SD1667), TP6(2SA933), TP07

(2SC1740), DP13 and 14 (both 1SS133) and DP15 (5.6V zener diode).

(The black dot on series 10 Sky Cards may sometimes cause intermittent "Card Invalid" problems. Remove the dot. This mod is NOT approved by SKY.)
*Flashes "P000 T000" briefly when card is inserted:*
This is normal with a series 07 SKY card or later.

*Decodes but poor quality pictures:*
Can be caused by faulty TDA8703.

*Faint horizontal lines across decoded picture; streaky like an oil painting:*
Check for a dry joint on C903 or C904 electrolytics at the front corner of the tuner.

*RL09 1R2 on decoder smokes. TEA2029C too hot:*
Replace both of these.

*Horizontal lines. Pictures jump. Decoder messages distorted or missing:*
Replace CL08 (4µ7 next to TEA2029C).

*Picture rolls vertically:*
Diode DW02 may be short circuit.

*Black horizontal interlace lines:*
IV02 or IV03 faulty (D42101C-3).

*Grey screen with rolling diagonal bands on all channels:*
Suspect IL01 (TEA2029).

*Will not decode. Low contrast video from decoder:*
Check for dry joint on RA22 (10kΩ SMD resistor below the word 'AMSTRAD').

*No messages and will not decode*
Suspect IW03 (TCE 10705400) but there are many other causes as well including TEA2029C, 4µ7F and 503kHz ceramic resonator next to it.

*SRD400 used as a stand-alone decoder:*
You should be able to inject 1 volt video (doesn't need to be clamped,

but should be low-pass filtered to remove sub carriers, etc.) at CA02 on the decoder PCB. Disconnect CA02 negative terminal from RA02 and RA13 and apply video at this point.

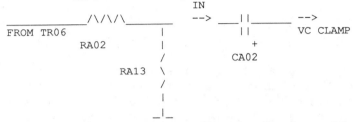

```
                                  IN
_____/\/\/_____   -->  ___| |_____  -->
FROM TR06                      |        | |      VC CLAMP
        RA02                   |        | |
                               /        +
           RA13  \               CA02
                 /
                 |
               _|_
```

Alternatively you could go in unfiltered and unclamped (but de-emphasised) at the interface connector CNM2 (pins 1 & 2), but you would need 2V video with 2V DC bias for TA06 in the decoder. The decoder video output goes out from the scart. (From Giacomo Bozzoni, Milan, ITALY)

### Modifying the audio to suit Eutelsat transmissions

Replace crystal X302 and select Audio 3. You will lose existing radio channels on Audio 3 and 4. 6.65 MHz audio requires 17.1776 MHz Xtal.

There is a tunable audio demodulator board available from SatCure. This is low-cost, requires only three wires to be soldered in and may be adjusted from 6.50 to 6.65 MHz. It operates from the TV/SAT button. You don't lose any audio channels by fitting this.

### Adding Extra Channels (secret handset codes)

Selecting an extra 80 presets is easy. Press PRESET then press either one of TV/SAT or RECALL.
If you pressed TV/SAT your display will now show channel 0 (Zero)!
If you pressed RECALL your display will show a frequency, then the audio mode then 0 (Zero)!
Use the second method if you have an ADX unit connected .
You can only access these extra presets sequentially, by pressing the CHANNEL DOWN key to scroll through them (you can press TUNING UP or TUNING DOWN though).

*Thanks to Mike Ginger for this information.*

## Amstrad SRD400 Channel Expander Control

With the introduction of the Global Communications "ADX-plus" Channel Expander, you can now watch programmes from Astra's fourth satellite, "1D", along with the best. The ADX can shift the entire band of frequencies 500MHz higher. However, the ADX has to be selected manually when you want it to do this — a drawback for "couch potatoes" like I am.

The only switching function which can readily be used on the SRD400 is the TV/SAT button. However, this selection can not be stored on a per-channel basis. The ideal solution would be to allocate a specific number of channels for Astra 1D programmes and to have the ADX switch on automatically when each of these channels is selected.

My initial thought was that it would be a simple matter to select a number-display segment which lit up only for a specific range of channels. The top left segment of display three was chosen as being ideal in that it lights only for channels 40 through 48 (see Fig.1)

The initial enthusiasm was dampened when a glance at the circuit showed that the LED segments are multiplexed. They are actually pulsed by the display driver IC which, in turn, receives serial data, from  the microcontroller, that would be difficult to interpret. In addition, the common cathode of each seven-segment display unit is strobed. There is no steady DC voltage or even usable pulses with respect to the zero volt reference.

Luckily there is a solution. An optocoupler hooked across the relevant LED segment would give a pulse output which could be "smoothed" and used to control the ADX.

The optocoupler LED was connected between pin 16 of the LED driver, IC151 on the front panel, and the centre leg (collector) of the PNP strobe transistor, Q152. With the optocoupler transistor emitter grounded and a 1kΩ resistor between collector and 12 volt supply, the goal was achieved. The pulses from the optocoupler are fed via a 10kΩ resistor to a PNP BC557B (anything will do) and smoothed by a 100µF electrolytic. The BC557B is connected via a 270Ω to the ADX

The few components required cost very little and can easily be assembled onto a piece of "Veroboard"™ or similar. The complete

assemby should be kept small. After attaching wires, insulate it and tuck
it away beneath the decoder board.

The sketch of the SRD400 front panel board shows where to solder
the three wires. Zero volts is point "1", Q152 collector is point "2" and
IC151 pin 16 is point "3".

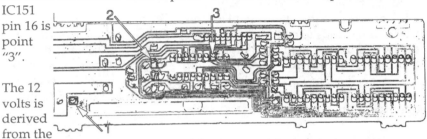

The 12 volts is derived from the small regulator board which is bolted to the heatsink in the SRD400.

A minor drawback of the system is that the chosen segment will
light while you are tuning the receiver. To overcome this nuisance, disconnect the wire and switch the ADX ON while tuning. Once the channels are tuned and stored, switch the ADX OFF, reconnect the control
wire, and it will then be switched on automatically for channels 40 to 48
only.

This system will also work for the Amstrad SRX200, the later version of
which has 48 channels. You will have to hunt for the 12 volt supply (it's
on one of the ICs near the rear of the receiver) but the front panel connections are very similar.

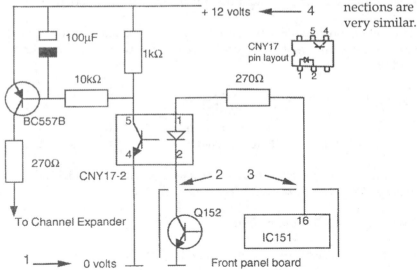

# Amstrad SRD500

*Dead. No voltages from power supply.*
Disconnect from the mains. Replace the 1.25A fuse on the power supply board. If this fails to cure the fault, remove the two securing screws and the two connector plugs and lift out the PSU board. Discharge the large capacitor by short circuiting its pins with a 10Ω resistor. If it discharges with a crack, R2 or R3 (120k) has failed open-circuit. Replace them both with 350 volt rated resistors. Replace C5 with 100µF/35v/105°C and C10 (10µF/50v). Now try the PSU again.

If D8 (1N4148) or R9 (220Ω) fails the output voltages will measure correctly with the output connector unplugged but will fall almost to zero under load. The same symptom is caused by C5 and C10 (above).

If PSU ticks disconnect L707 on main board. If receiver now lights up, replace tuner.

If PSU is dead even with new C5 and C10, replace D1 with a RM11C or 30S4 rectifier and replace R1 with a 10Ω/3W resistor. Solder a 2n2/400v capacitor across D1. If the resistor fails again, replace it together with the power transistor and IC1 and, possibly, the transformer, too.

Many other components have been known to fail: Measure all resistors and diodes — preferably compare the readings against those of a known good unit.

| Typical voltages on the output connector: | a | b | c | d |
|---|---|---|---|---|
| STANDBY | 0 | 12 | 24.2 | 5.03 |
| ON (disconnected) | 0 | 14.4 | 24.6 | 6.3 |
| ON (connected) | 0 | 11.5 | 24.5 | 4.96 |

a b c d

*After warm-up, pressing STANDBY leaves receiver locked in standby. Pressing STANDBY causes LED display to flash "11U"  or similar, momentarily.*
IC1, C5, C10 or D3 could be faulty.

*No vertical channels. LNB voltage less than 5v. Horizontal (17v) O.K.*
Check R512 (11k SMD resistor marked 113) for open circuit or dry joint.

*No horizontal channels.*
Check R517 for o/c or dry joint.

*LNB voltage approx 2 volts even in standby:*
Dry joint on C502 (front Left Hand corner).

*Various picture faults; very poor video; loss of sync:*
C743, C744

*No picture or sound. Panel display OK. May be OK warm:*
C13 (470µF) in PSU causes 23v rail to drop to 15v. (Sometimes just causes some audio channels to disappear or go low in volume. Also replace C14 (2200µF/6v3 or higher).

*No audio from UHF modulator:*
Ensure that R387 (1k) is present and connected to modulator pin 2.

*Decoder messages have "ragged" edges.*
Turn VR1 clockwise to reduce the voltage across D10
(VR1 is on the PSU board and D10 is a 5.6 volt zener on the left edge of the decoder board.) If the voltage is left high for very long D10 and possibly other parts in the decoder will fail.

*Card Invalid" message even with new decoder and card:*
Check Q512 on sub-assembly for short circuit.

*Horizontal lines. Pictures jump. Decoder messages distorted or missing:*
Replace CL08 (4µ7 next to TEA2029C).

*All channels except the top few missing:*
When used with a Universal LNB , the power supply can send 22kHz interference which will switch the LNB to high band. The cause is C514 going low in value. It is a 100µF at the front of the main board. Replace it with a 220µF.
(Maybe someone can use this "fault" to switch a Universal LNB deliberately?)

*Tuning drift:*
Adjust AFT underneath receiver.

*Poor picture/no pictures:*
C730, C745, C754, C760, C171 Also C13 in PSU

Cure most faults by fitting RELKIT 4. Very occasionally you will need SATKIT 4A in addition if the power supply remains dead.

*Blank screen from TV scart + RF:*
Picture gradually fades in as receiver warms up.
C13 (470uF/10v/105'C) front right corner of PSU.
(Included as part of RELKIT 4)

Capacitor negative stripe is indicated by curved line on PCB.

## Circuit Reliability Upgrades

Replace C5 with a 100µF/25v/105°C electrolytic capacitor.
Replace C10 with a 1uF/50v electrolytic capacitor.
Replace C13 with a 470µF/10v/105°C electrolytic capacitor.
Replace C14 with a 1000µF/6v3 (or higher)/105°C.
Replace all 470µF/10v/105°C electrolytic capacitors on the main board.
Replace D1 with a RM11C or 30S4 rectifier.
Replace R1 with a 10Ω/3W upright ceramic resistor.
Solder a 2n2/400v capacitor across D1.
Replace R2 and R3 (120k) with 350 volt rated resistors.

Replace electrolytic capacitors close to the tuner since these are affected by the heat. Use 105°C rated capacitors if available.

These upgrades will help to prevent failure due to overheating caused by incorrect installation.

## A kit is available. Order RELKIT 4.

*The SRD400 tuner replacement supplied by Amstrad does not work:*
The SRD400 tuner fits perfectly in the SRD500 but the three links must be added, as indicated by arrows in the sketch.

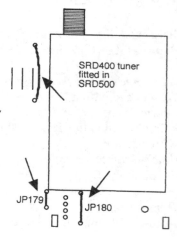

SRD400 tuner fitted in SRD500

JP179

JP180

# Using the SRD500 with a D2Mac decoder

Inside the receiver, connect a wire between pins 3 and 7 on the D socket and also connect it to pin 8 on the Scart socket.

Pins 3 and 7 are int/ext video/audio respectively but there is no automatic switching voltage. By applying the voltage from Scart pin 8 you will be able to press the TV/SAT button to switch the D2Mac decoder in or out.

*Idea supplied by Peter of Aligator Electronics, Gwynedd.*

*For decoder faults not listed here, see the SRD400 section.*

## Secret Handset Codes – None

## Adding Extra Channels – Not possible
Use an ADX

# SRD510 Frequently Asked Questions

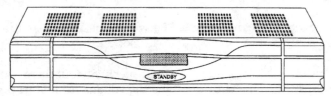

by Leigh Preece at Keele University
http://www.keele.ac.uk/depts/md/sat/
(Most of the questions also apply to the SRD520 which has a channel
number display and to the export model SRX320 which has no internal
decoder. Most of the fault information applies to the SRX320, SRX340,
SRX345, SRX350, SRD540, SRD545 and SRD550.)

Contents:
Q.1) How do I disable the internal decoder ?
Q.2) Can I add channel up and down buttons to the front panel ?
Q.3) What is the SIS feature and what does it give me ?
Q.4) How do I connect an External decoder to the 510 ?
Q.5) My Power-Supply is faulty - what do I need to repair/upgrade it ?
Q.6) Will MAC work with the 510 ?
Q.7) What does that 'C' switch on the bottom of my 510 do ?
Q.8) What are the most common faults and how do I prevent them?
Q.9) Where can I buy any spare parts for my 510 ?
Q.10) How do I receive Astra 1D channels ?
Q.11) Doesn't a Universal LNB also switch to a higher band ?
Q.12) Can I modify my SRD510 to watch digital channels ?
Q.13) Can I have more than 99 channels on my SRD510 ?
Q.14) What do I do if my receiver does not seem to work properly or the
channel frequencies are mixed up?
(Q.15) There is a little circuit connected to the front Standby/ infra-red
sensor board. What does it do?
(Q.16) Can I fit a 22kHz tone generator inside an SRD510?
(Q.17) Can I use my SRD510 with a motorised dish?
(Q.18) Will any other remote control work my SRD510?
(Q.19) Why do I see a flashing LED(s)?
(Q.20) Can I upgrade to a 2 input tuner?
(Q.21) Can I upgrade to an Enhanced LNB?

### Q.1) How do I disable the 510's internal decoder ?

You need to bypass the Videocrypt decoder using this very simple modification that I used mainly for watching VH1 Germany when it
appeared on Astra or for times when Videocrypt info disturbs clear
channels.

Wire a SCART connector with the following pins connected together
within the plug: Video Out (19) to Video In (20). Audio OutL (1) to
Audio InL (2). Audio OutR (3) to Audio InR (6). Attach flying lead out
of plug to pin 8.

Insert this plug into the 510's Decoder port and put the flying lead to Pin
8 on the SCART/Peritel port. When connected to the Pin 8, the internal
Videocrypt decoder is bypassed and the screen will clear. The 12 volts
passed from one port to the other acts to 'enable' or 'disable' the modification. (I have internally wired my receiver, with a small toggle switch
between the 8 pins, so I can 'enable' or 'disable' this, leaving both SCART
sockets clear.) I have been told that this modification works for most
IRDs with external decoders. Some require the 8pin voltage for
enabling/disabling - some don't.

### Q.2) Can I add Up and Down buttons to front panel ?

To add manual channel up down buttons to the 510... Unscrew the small
pcb at the front of the receiver (the board with the red and green LED's
on it) and withdraw it. Turn it solder side up and look for the line of
blobs where the connector to the main PCB is soldered on. Now study
this "diagram" of the PCB:

```
+----------------------+
| oooooooooooo         |
| 1  3                 |
|                      |
+----------------------+
```

The o's represent the soldered connectors... I'm not sure if there are actually 10 points but it doesn't matter...

Now to perform a channel up, ground connector three, and to perform a
channel down, ground connector one. Therefore connect switches
accordingly. It's amazing what you can discover when there's only 25
minutes till the Simpsons and your Remote Control packs up!!! :)
(Compilers note - I found the 0 volts test point on the Videocrypt
decoder to be an ideal ground to use, even though you can probably
find others. Also - Maplin Electronics stock ideal push-buttons for this

modification.)

( PLEASE NOTE: This modification was originally developed by
Mildenhall Satellites - "510s R Us" and a modified panel is sold through
various Satellite magazines. They use the two switches that are normally
operated by the Standby button. Simply cut the track to each switch (one
side of each switch is already connected to 0 volts) and connect wires as
described above. Obviously doing this removes the 'STANDBY' button
though so you need the handset to switch it off.)

### Q. 3) What is SIS feature and what does it give me ?

The upgrade is a very simple one to do and makes your Amstrad 510
think its a Amstrad 520 receiver - giving all of the 520's features if you
also do the Up and Down button upgrade too !

The 'software' for the 510 is upgradeable with a simple piece of wire acting as a link to enable the SIS feature:

Find the largest chip on the main board and connect a wire link between
pins 4 and 20 on the chip (this is the row of pins closest to the rear of the
receiver - count anticlockwise from the corner). When you next power
the receiver up, you will find the SIS Index enabled - showing you the
list of channel names and a marker - move the marker up and down the
list with UP and DOWN on the remote and press EXIT when you reach
a channel you want to view - ideal for when you forget channel numbers.

The 'LNB A / B' switching puts an extra line into the setup screen -
DISH - and when Dish B is selected, Pin 14 of the Decoder SCART has
12 volts put on it, Dish A gives 0 volts. This is selectable on a per channel basis and can be used to enable/disable an ADX converter, etc. or
other decoder..

If you carry out the modification, you will find that the Channel Lock
feature in the Channel Setup menu is also enabled - meaning 'locked'
channels can only be accessed with the remote handset - not the channel
change buttons - a crude way of parental locking (if you hide the remote
that is !). You can tell a locked channel - the screen goes red and the
words 'locked' appear.

### Q.4) How do I connect an external decoder to the 510 ?

This is quite easy to do - mainly involving wiring a SCART Plug up for
the decoder socket and enabling it but does **not** work for decoders that
require a baseband signal input - this includes MAC or some Luxcrypt
decoders. (See further in the FAQ for MAC decoding)

Wire a SCART connector as follows:
510 Video Out (19) to your decoder's Video Input, 510 Audio Out A (1) to your decoder's Audio Input A 510 Audio Out B (3) to your decoder's Audio Input B
Decoder Video Output to the 510's Video Input (20); Decoder Audio Out A to the 510's Audio Input A (2); Decoder Audio Out B to the 510's Audio Input B (6); 510 Video Ground (18) to Decoder Video Ground; 510 Audio Ground (4) to Decoder Audio Ground.
You may also have to enable your decoder - do the following which also switches the Videocrypt off too:
Wire the number 8 pin on the Amstrad's decoder port to the input that 'enables' your decoder (Pin 8 again possibly !) and also attach a flying lead out from the satellite decoder port's pin 8. You may need this flying lead dependent on your decoder type.
Dependent on your decoder type - the number 8 pins enable the decoder to start decoding and also tell the Receiver to accept incoming video and audio from your external decoder instead of the internal decoder.

**Q. 5) My Power-Supply is faulty - what do I need to repair/upgrade it?**
The parts needed are SAFETY CRITICAL PARTS and should be replaced only with parts from an approved kit. This is no joke. It is not a "con" to get you to buy a kit. There is real danger involved!
Check internal mains fuse by measurement, not just by looking! You may need to pull off the glued plastic cover.

(5.1) Power Supply Dead; keeps blowing fuses. No other fault found: 1. Replace T1.25A fuse with the identical type. 2. Change C600 (1uF) to 220nF Mains Voltage rated! (RS part no- 115-203).
This problem can be caused by severe mains interference as a result of faulty mains wiring or a nearby electrical appliance with a large motor (such as a lawn mower, drill or vacuum cleaner). You are advised to find the external cause: check wiring in plugs and sockets. Don't plug heavy duty electrical equipment into the same ring mains supply.

(5.2) Power supply dead. Fuse may be intact:
1. REMOVE MAINS CONNECTION AND DISCHARGE BIG ELEC-TROLYTIC CAPACITOR !
2. Replace the two 47k resistors R602 and R603 with 350 volt types.
3. Replace C612 (220uF/25v/105°C)
These parts are included as part of RELKIT 3

Now plug in and try it. If it works, you've fixed it. If not, carry on:

4. Check D607 for short-circuit. If shorted replace with uprated type BZY95A.

It's important to fit the correct parts for safety.

5. Check, and replace if faulty, ALL the following components, BEFORE switching on again: TR600, R604 (2R2 fusible) and R610 (2R2ohms), R609 (4R7ohms), R608 (220ohms), R611 (1k ohms) and ALL diodes.

RELKIT 3 contains the parts that you'll need if R604 is intact. If R604 is open-circuit, you will also need SATKIT 3.

If ANY of these are faulty then replace IC600. If R608 (220 ohms) apparently gives a very low reading then TR600 is short circuit. If R608 gives too high a reading then the resistor itself is faulty and TR600 may NOT be.

These kits fix the majority of faults that you will come across and include instructions. They will save you time and money, too!

Disconnect power supply board from the main board before measuring D608 to avoid a false reading. If any diode is short circuit, replace the electrolytic capacitor which it feeds since this may have been degraded by excess current through the faulty diode. It's recommended that you replace C615 (1nF polyester/63v), Replace C611 (1uF) with 10uF/50v/105°C type.

NOTE: Failure to replace ALL faulty components in one go may cause the demise of the components you DID replace, at switch-on!

6. When you are sure that all faulty components have been replaced with the equivalent or uprated type, plug in and try again. If it still won't light (maybe pulses or ticks - voltage on D608 cathode goes up and down) then the transformer T600 is probably faulty.
If Opto-coupler IC601 has failed (rarely does), this will cause all DC voltages to be too high. Be sure to measure them.

(5.3) ALSO do the following modification while doing ANY repairs to the power supply:
Solder a wire from the little metal box (front of power supply board) to the test pin marked "0v" on the card-reader board. Connect a voltmeter with negative probe stuck through the tuner earth braid and positive probe touching the power supply connector on the main board - third pin from the front. Connect the LNB and switch the receiver on. IMME-DIATELY adjust RV600 on the power supply board until the voltmeter

shows 4.95 volts. This modification prevents all sorts of intermittent faults such as remote control not responding, squealing noise, red & green LEDs flashing when receiver is warm, going into standby on its own, etc.

### Q.6) Will MAC work with the 510 ?

The SRD510 will work with most D2Mac decoders as follows: Use a very short SCART to SCART lead, preferably with only 9 wires, not 21. Label one plug "Receiver end" and remove its cover. Pull out pin 12 and discard it (cut it off). (The pins have a tiny securing tag which needs to be pushed aside with a sharp point). Pull out pin 19 and push it back into position 12. (The Mac de-emphasised signal comes out of number 12 on the decoder socket). Replace the SCART plug cover. DO NOT select "Mac" in the menu! This will cause loss of sound on ALL channels the next time you switch the receiver on from standby. The audio is automatically routed in from the D2Mac decoder with "PAL" selected as normal. However your D2Mac decoder should have "Mac" selected in its menu (if this option exists).

Note: Pin 10 on the decoder Scart socket gives FLAT baseband so use this instead of pin 12 if your decoder needs it.

Amstrad 510 to D2MAC (a Philips CTU900 in this example!):
Take a fully wired 21 pin SCART to SCART lead and label one end 'Decoder' and the other 'Receiver'.
At the 'Receiver end', remove the cover and pull out pin 12. (The pins have a tiny securing tag which needs to be pushed aside with a sharp point). Pull out pin 19 and push it back into position 12.
This takes the baseband from the receiver to the decoder rather than video. The Audio does not need to be modified, but leave the menu set to PAL and not MAC or you'll get no audio whatsoever.
Insert the plugs into the relevant sockets and - you'll find nothing works until you do the following:
Switching between Videocrypt and External Decoders:
Take two pieces of wire and a small toggle switch - Maplin do a good range of square push-switchs that match the 510 quite nicely. (Why not get two push-to-make buttons while you are there and do the up and down conversion while you have the lid off too !) Connect one of the wires internally to pin 8 on the TV SCART socket and the other onto pin 8 of the DECODER SCART socket. Fit the push-switch to the front panel

of the 510 - right hand side is best - and solder both wires to the switch. Enabling and disabling the switch will then toggle between the 510's internal VideoCrypt decoder or whatever is coming back in from the DECODER SCART socket. Simple as that. (Basically the DECODER socket needs 12 volts onto pin 8, which is constantly being fed from pin 8 of the TV SCART socket.

This setup works well for me with a CTU900, Converted BSB and a Churchill D2MAC decoder and could also be used for any external decoder requiring baseband.

I do have a similar switching arrangement in operation with an SRD545 but use the INSTALLATION MENU to do the TV/AUTO switching to provide the 12 volts rather than using a manual switch.

**Q.7) What does the C-Band switch underneath my 510 do ?**
It inverts the video signal to make it compatible with C-Band LNB signals. This switch could be useful if you have C-Band receiving LNBs fitted to your system - (looks like Amstrad had other uses for the 510 besides Astra/Eutelset...etc. and also can improve/worsen undecoded Luxcrypt pictures. Unfortunately, it also causes "blank screen" faults so it's best to desolder it and fit a wire link between the two tracks!

**Q.8) What are the most common faults and how do I prevent them?**
There are a few faults that 'crop-up' on the 510. They are listed (in no particular order) below:

(8.1) The most common fault is power supply failure. Fit RELKIT 3 to prevent such problems.

(8.2) The next most common fault is loss of picture or very weak picture caused by failure of C54 on the main board next to the power supply connector. Replace it with a 100nF supplied in RELKIT 3.

(8.3) No audio, just hissing noise. Usually caused by a bad soldered connection on the surface mount chip beneath the main board. Leave this to the experts! (No audio and no hissing is often caused by your selection of MAC instead of PAL in the menu. Don't!)

(8.4) Intermittent blank screen. Picture comes and goes if unit is tapped. Bad solder joint on C55 next to the upright "daughter" board or faulty C-Band switch.

(8.5) No decoder messages. Picture remains scrambled. Try unplugging from the mains for a minute. If this doesn't cure it then the fault may be inside the decoder box or the daughter board.

(8.6) Sparkly pictures. Lots of causes! If your dish, cable and LNB are OK, make sure that you have video deviation set to "Narrow" not "Wide" in the menu. If sparklies are only black or only white (not both) then your tuning may be incorrect.

(8.7) Red and green lights flashing on and off simultaneously: indicates a short-circuit cable or no LNB voltage. If it only happens when warm, add the wire as described previously. If it stops when the LNB cable is disconnected, the cable, connector or LNB has a short-circuit.

(8.8) Red and Green lights flash alternately: indicates Standby button is held in when mains is applied. Sometimes carbonised glue on the Standby button solder joints will cause this. Sometimes standby button is jammed.

(8.9) Pictures only black and white bands swirling about. Make sure that C-Band switch underneath is in the "normal" position.

(8.10) Receiver goes to Standby all by itself when warm. Black, carbonised glue on Standby button solder joints. Scrape it away. Another cause is loose connections in the power plug!

(8.11) "Your Card is Invalid" message with no card in the slot. Faulty switch contacts in the back of the card reader. Lift out the card reader board, remove the two tiny screws which hold the card reader to the board and prise off the top moulding, carefully. Clean the switch contacts with WD-40 and make sure that all the card contacts are clean and in line with each other.

(8.12) "Your Card is Invalid" message only with card in the slot. Test the card in another receiver. Make sure it's the right way up/round. Spray the card contacts with WD-40 and push it in and out of the slot a few times. If fault remains, replace all 8 1N4148 diodes on the right hand side of the card reader board (two rows of four). If fault remains, replace card reader board completely. If fault remains, replace decoder box.

**Q.9) Where can I buy any spare parts for my 510 ?**
You can order them from SatCure, PO Box 12 Sandbach, CW11 1XA
England. See the SatCure Internet Web Site.

**Q.10) How do I receive Astra 1D channels ?**
You need a frequency shifter called an "ADX". The standard type moves
EVERY channel higher by a count of 500MHz. However, this presuppos-
es that your standard LNB will receive the Astra 1D frequencies (often it
will not - or not very well). A better way is to fit a new "Universal" LNB
on your dish and use an "ADX PLUS". This works like an ADX but also
has an internal switch to make it shift all channels DOWN by 500MHz if
you wish. Now a Universal LNB moves the channels UP by 250 and the
ADX PLUS moves them DOWN by 500 so the result is to move them all
down by 250! Confused? Well, the result is that you have to retune your
receiver for every channel. With the ADX PLUS switched OFF the
Universal LNB will send the Astra 1D channels up by 250 so that's
where you tune them. With the ADX PLUS switched ON, the rest of the
channels will be 250 lower than the magazine listing. Most suppliers of
ADX PLUS's supply tuning details - usually they are correct and contain
a Channel Guide with what to expect and where ! You can switch the
ADX automatically by fitting an "AutoSelect" unit inside. This produces
the "dish A/dish B" option in the menu but also provides enough current to drive the ADX switch via the decoder SCART. (Sometimes if you
simply add the wire to the microprocessor as described previously, the
current drain of the ADX might be too high for it to operate reliably).
There is just enough room to fit an ADX inside the 510 - you need to
drill two holes in the rear of the plastic case and fasten the ADX using its
F-socket nuts. If your ADX has a plastic body, remove this to leave a tin
box with the two F-sockets and switch and LED exposed. Do not take
the tin box apart - all components are fragile, surface mounted and non-
repairable. All wiring (except for a small coax link from the ADX to your
original LNB input) can then be done inside your receiver to leave a neat
job. This conversion has been advertised by "510s R Us" (Mildenhall
Satellite 01638 712345) for more than a year and a half. They will do it
for you if you wish. Also, see "TELEVISION" magazine page 280 of the
February 1996 edition where the complete modification is described.
You can also use an "Enhanced" 9.75 GHz LNB directly. (See Q.13) To do
this you must replace the micro with a 199 channel version. The memory
chip must also be replaced with a 24C16. Most tuners will then go as
high as 11.600. The tuner can be modified to reach 11.700.

**Q.11) Doesn't a Universal LNB also switch to a higher band ?**
Yes. If you feed a 22kHz tone to it, it will shift to a higher band so (in theory) you can watch other channels. On Astra most of these channels are planned to broadcast using digital compression. On other satellites you might see clear pictures.

**Q.12) Can I modify my SRD510 to watch digital channels ?**
No. You need a separate digital receiver.

**Q.13) Can I have more than 99 channels on my SRD510 ?**
Yes, you can fit a later SRD540 microprocessor to give 199 channels. However, it does not have the "dish A/dish B" option. You must also fit the later channel memory IC to match. There is also another micro available which gives 199 channels, extends the tuning range so you can use an Enhanced LNB and gives an additional switching function (per channel) which you might use for a 22kHz tone switch!

**Q.14) What do I do if my receiver does not seem to work properly or the channel frequencies are mixed up ?**
Sometimes a "factory reset" will solve your problem if it's caused by something you've set wrongly in the menu or if the memory chip has been corrupted by interference. Try pressing "Standby" so the red light comes on. Then press "OK","SETUP" and "STATUS" - hold "STATUS" until the red and green lights flash. Your receiver is now reset as it left the factory.
(Don't be tempted to try this to see if it works - it does and I spent 2 hours retuning and finding all those radio stations I spent 1 hour tuning - Leigh)

**(Q.15) There is a little circuit connected to the front Standby/ infra-red sensor board. What does it do?**
This was Amstrad's attempt to cure the "won't respond to handset" fault. It is supposed to square the IR sensor output pulses so the microprocessor will recognise them. However the REAL fault is caused by a bad 0 volt connection to the power supply. Adding the wire described above will usually cure the problem. You can remove the "bodge" circuit and thereby increase the handset range from 4m to 6m.

**(Q.16) Can I fit a 22kHz tone generator inside an SRD510?**
Yes, in theory. Martin has designed one and fitted it inside a PRD900 so

it should be possible to do the same in an SRD510. Unfortunately, the only software switch available is the dish A/ dish B menu selection unless you fit the 199 channel special upgrade micro. A better option would be the twin input tuner conversion which will give you everything the SRD550 has! However, the SRD550 tuner is very exopensive.

**(Q.17) Can I use my SRD510 with a motorised dish?**
There is no reason why not but remember that you have no way to adjust polarisation skew. You must use a standard 13/17v switching LNB in order to get both polarisations and the position of the LNB will be a compromise. It will give best results if the dish arc is limited to move between, say, Astra at 19.2'E and Eutelsat at 7'E. You will need a positioner unit to drive the actuator which moves the dish. You can build one by using a transformer which supplies 24 volts at 2 Amps through a bridge rectifier. A two-pole two-way switch (with centre-off position) is needed to reverse the polarity to drive the dish both east and west. Telepart can supply a suitable low cost mini positioner.

**(Q.18) Will any other remote control work my SRD510?**
Yes. Any earlier Amstrad satellite handset will work, although the button labels are different. You should be able to get an SRX200 or SRD400 handset very cheaply.

**(Q.19) Why do I see a flashing LED(s) ?**
If both LEDs flash see 8.7 and 8.8. If only one LED flashes, a timer event is set. Read your user manual to find out how to set and alter timer events.

**(Q.20) Can I upgrade to a 2 input tuner ?**
Yes. An SRD550 tuner will fit but you will also need the matching micro and 24C16 EEprom. You will have most of the options of an SRD550, including 22kHz tone-switching. The tuner has to be mounted upside down and connected to the PCB with wires. It is expensive!

**(Q.21) Can I upgrade to an Enhanced LNB?**
Yes. An Enhanced LNB will work with your SRD510 but all frequencies must be tuned 250 higher. You will not receive frequencies above 11.690 GHz. The higher channels will be missing. You can fix this by fitting the 199 channel kit and also a modified tuner.

# Amstrad SRD510/520 (SRX320 no decoder)

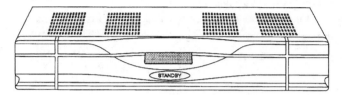

### Gaining Access

• Disconnect the mains power supply by unplugging.
• Remove the seven screws – two at each side and four countersunk at the rear. Lift off the metal cover. Lift out the mains cable plastic clamp.
• Lift out the mains cable and grommet.
• Remove the two screws from the power supply board.
• Remove the single screw which holds the card-reader board and prise off any glue with a knife.
• Use a magnetised screwdriver to remove the screw which holds the decoder box (through the hole in its lid).
• Remove the two or three screws which secure the main board.
• Lift the power supply board out of the receiver.
• Tilt the decoder box and move it forwards away from the main board.
• Push the card reader board back then lift it forward as far as it will go.
• Release the plastic clips at front left and right while lifting the main board forwards and upwards.

### Amstrad SRD510/520, SRX320

*In every model, you should first solder a wire from the corner of the little metal screening box at the front of the power supply to the pin marked "0v" to the right of the card holder. Turn RV600 adjustment to give exactly 5 volts on the power supply connector (third pin from front on main board). You MUST measure this with a meter. This is a standard upgrade.*

**Order SATKIT 3 for a kit of power supply repair components**

### Power Supply Faults

*Power supply dead; keeps blowing fuse.:*
Replace T1.25A fuse with the identical type. Plug in to mains.

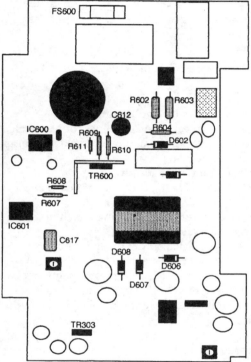

If the new fuse melts immediately, replace the rectifier bridge D600 and check the large capacitor C609 for s/c. The white ceramic 10Ω resistor will probably have failed, too. Luckily, this fault is quite rare.

However, if the receiver works just with a new fuse, the fault was caused by a mains surge. Check the mains plug for loose connections. If it's OK, advise the customer that the problem was caused either by faulty house wiring, or by the use of a lawn mower or similar plugged into a nearby socket, or by a mains spike. Change C600 (1µF) to 220nF/400v ac, which will make the fuse less prone to melting, and supply a mains spike suppressor to the customer. (This type of fault is not covered by warranty).

*Power supply dead. Fuse intact:*

**Remove mains connection and discharge the big electrolytic capacitor!**
Replace the two 47k resistors R602 and R603 with 350 volt types.
Replace C612 (220µF/25v/105°C). Plug in to mains.
If this does not cure the problem, do the following:
Measure all diodes for short circuits.

Disconnect the power supply board from the main board before measuring D608 to avoid a false reading. If any diode is short circuit, replace the electrolytic capacitor which it feeds since this may have been degraded by excess current through the faulty diode.

Replace all of the following suspect components (obtainable as a kit):
Replace D607 and D606 with uprated type BZV95B.
Replace TR600, R604 (fusible) and R610 (2R2Ω), R609 (4R7Ω), R608 (220Ω), R611 (1kΩ). If *any* of these is faulty, replace IC600. Replace C615 (1nF polyester). Replace C611 (1µF) with 10µF/50v/105°C type.

Failure to replace all faulty components in one go may cause the demise of the components you did replace, at switch-on!
We have seen a few instances where the Opto-coupler IC601 failed, but this is unusual. If faulty, it will often cause DC voltages to be too high.

**The following assumes that you have fitted RELKIT3 and SATKIT3.**

*Transformer buzzes or PSU ticks:*
C609 (68µF/400v) look for brown ring beneath. D603. Transformer. C611 (1uF, 50V).

*Screeching noise from P.S.U. (R + G lights may flash as well).*
Fit a wire as described above. If that does not help, replace C617, D603.

*Receiver won't respond to the handset: (check the batteries!)*
Fit a wire as described above. If that does not help, replace the front panel sensor. Ensure that its centre leg is soldered to its screening can.

*Blank screen with Graphics rolling vertically:*
(No 12 volt supply. No LNB voltage. Possibly TR304 overheating.)
Replace TR304, TR12 and TR17.

*Capacitors explode. 12v and LNB supplies go to 60 volts:*
Explanation: Feedback from the 5 volt output determines the other outputs. If the 5 volt output is low, the power supply will increase ALL outputs in its attempt to reach 5 volts.
The fault is caused by one or more of the following:
C622 (2200uF) open-circuit; D608 open-circuit or dry joint. Optocoupler faulty. Broken copper tracks taking 5 volts to Optocoupler.

## Front Panel Symptoms

*Red LED flashes by itself:*
A timer event has been set for some time in the future.

*Green LED flashes by itself:*
A timed event is in progress.

*Red and Green LEDs come on or flash together (flashing display on SRD520):*
The LEDs flash simultaneously if a mains interruption has occurred while a timed event was in progress. In this case, pressing Standby will cancel the warning. Make sure there is no short in the LNB cable connections. The LEDs flash together if micro pin 5 detects low LNB voltage. You can disable the warning by disconnecting D4 in front of the daughter board. If the LEDs still flash then the micro may be faulty or the 10kΩ pull-up resistor to D4 may be o/c or there may be a bad connection around the micro. If the LEDs stop flashing with D4 disconnected, check TR303 inside the metal can. Check R609 (4R7) and R610 (2R2) on the PSU board.
If the LNB voltage is OK and everything else checks out, disconnect SDA (Serial DAta) track to pin on tuner. If LEDs now work normally with standby button there may be an EEprom or tuner fault. Check R24 (4k7) next to EEprom; it feeds serial data to the EEprom.

*Both LEDs flash alternately:*
Receiver is waiting for computer data transfer, initialised by holding standby button while turning on the mains. Ensure standby button is not jammed. Disconnect from mains power, reconnect and try again. Look for carbonised glue on the front panel PCB which can short out the standby switches.

Pins 10 & 12 of the TV scart socket are serial data connections. Some TVs put a voltage on these pins (eg Beko) and damage the EEprom, microcontroller or tuner

*LED display shows "0011" or similar on SRD520:*
Carry out factory reset sequence (see handset codes). Note: SCART pin 12 is a data input line which may pick up interference. Disconnecting this pin if a SCART connector is used may eliminate problems.

*"88" displayed continuously on SRD520:*
Check C87 for dry joint (next to end of the large microprocessor I.C.)
Fit a 0v wire as described previously. Could be a serial data bus fault.

*Receiver goes to standby intermittently:*
Ths may occur every few minutes, days or weeks. Without any buttons being pressed, the green LED goes out and the red one comes on.
Make sure that the 0v wire has been added and voltage adjusted.
Look for carbonised glue on the front panel PCB and for faulty standby buttons. Look for a bad connection on the mains side of the power supply. Note that *any* interruption in the mains supply, however brief, will cause this effect. Check the mains lead and plug for loose connection and loose fuse. Check the mains socket where the unit is plugged in. Finally, plug the unit into a different mains supply and leave it on test. If that is OK then the original mains supply must be faulty.

Tests: when the fault occurs, press standby to bring it back on. If it has reverted to channel 8 instead of the channel you were watching then mains failure is to most likely blame.

You can also set a very long duration timed event which will leave the green LED flashing. If mains failure occurs then both red and green LEDs will flash simultaneously. You can cancel this warning by pressing Standby. (If pressing standby does not cancel it then mains failure was not the cause). If the receiver goes into standby during a timed event and the LEDs do *not* flash then mains failure was *not* the cause.
Another possibility is that the microcontroller IC is in a socket which has bad contacts.

### LNB Supply Problems

*LNB voltage more than 20 volts. No vertical channels:*
Replace TR303 (2SB1143 or equivalent) and 100µF capacitors in metal can at front of PSU board. If this fails, replace IC601 Opto-isolator.
RV1 may need to be adjusted to give the correct LNB voltages (13/17v).

*LNB voltage will not change (either no vertical or no horizontal channels).*
MICRO pin 17 switches between 0v and 3v to control TR41 (next to PSU connector) via R164 (1k). You should measure PSU plug pin 6 (2nd from front) switching 0v/12v as you change polarisation. If not, replace TR41, R164 or MICRO (whichever is at fault). If you can measure 0v/12v on the connector, suspect TR303 on PSU board.

*LNB voltage 18/24v not 13/17v. All PSU voltages too high.*
*No horizontal channels.* Replace IC601 Opto-isolator.

*No LNB voltage. No 12 volt supply. TR304 overheating.*
Replace TR304 on the PSU and TR12, TR17 and C54 on the main board.

*LNB voltage changes only 2 volts between H & V.*
Replace R314 which should be 43k. Adjust RV1 to give 13 and 17 volts.
Make sure nobody replaced IC300 with a 3842 instead of an LM392N !!

### Picture Faults
*Replace C54 (green 100nF near PSU connector on main board). This is a*
*standard upgrade which cures many picture problems. You should also replace*
*R80 (10k near C54) and R9 (470Ω between TR6 and TR7).*

*Picture appears to be painted on a 'venetian blind':*
(Horizontal lines every 15mm, approx). TEA2029 on
Daughter board which is mounted vertically on the
main board or electrolytic capacitor C287 next to it
(wires shorted together). To remove hot melt
adhesive either freeze it and crack it away or apply
heat from a hair dryer to soften it. To remove brown
adhesive scrape with a sharp instrument.

This section lists
possible causes
of picture faults
but this is no
substitute for
proper fault-
finding with an
oscilloscope! Fit
RELKIT3 before
bothering to trace
faults. It saves
time and money.

*Horizontal lines every 2mm approx:*
TR303 may be faulty. Check electrolytics nearby.
Tuner faulty (rare).

*Almost vertical lines sweeping from L to R (even from decoder scart):*
C46 470uF/10v next to tuner.

*Tunes only to Sky Movies and N3:*
Replace tuner. Adjust RV2 to give 9.0v on TR9 right hand leg.

*"Wavy" pictures on all channels (inverted video looks like RTL4):*
Check C Band video invert switch beneath the receiver and replace C54.

*Grey picture rolls and pulls. Sound OK.*
Replace C54 on the left of the main board (green 100nF capacitor) & R9.

*Very weak video on all channels. Pictures breaking up. Perhaps almost blank screen. Often intermittent or changes when tapped. OK from Decoder SCART.*
Check C-Band switch. Replace C54. check R9, check C55 connections next to TEA2029C daughter board. Replace decoder module (secured by screw, visible through hole in metal lid). If decoder is at fault, replace SM transistor nearest 4 pin connector with BC856B (PNP).

*Slow to show pic on channel change. No pic in tuning menu:*
Video bandwidth set to "wide" in menu. Otherwise, replace C54, R9, R80 (10k/1% often in parallel with 470k underneath the board - throw this away - and scrape away any glue). If no horiz sync pulses on IC5 Micro pin5 check TR14, R154 (4k7), track o/c or s/c. R74 (6k8) or TR16 or associated components. Check R67 (750Ω).

*Low video with wiggly graphics*
R80 (10k 1% near C54) or R9 (470R near little decoder plug).

*Low video level:*
R16 2k7, C6 10uF and glue beneath it. R9 470R. C81. See decoder faults.

*"Wiggly" menu graphics and picture interference:*
Reduce value of R319 (4k7 front right corner of PSU. Add 47k in parallel). TR304 regulates the 13v supply to 12v. If the 12v is adjusted too high, TR304 has insufficient "head room" in which to function - it can not regulate properly. By reducing its output to 12v or less, we provide greater head room.

*Blank screen when board is flexed. Baseband into graphics IC (on R60) decreases. 10v DC appears on C55 +ve:*
Look for link J64 next to C55 touching adjacent track.

*Blank screen*
C54, C55, R9, C6. Tuner 9v supply too low. Check TR9 right hand leg for 9v. Replace TR9. No 12 volt supply. Replace D607 and TR304 at the front right corner of the PSU board. Check C BAND switch is not central (or open circuit). Replace TEA2029C daughter board (dry joints or dead capacitors). Replace R9 (470ohm).

*Blank screen but audio OK. No signal after TR2:*
Measure junction of R4, R5. Should be 2 volts. If 0v, replace R5 (12k).

*Blank screen - Graphics and audio but no video:*
TR1 bias too high. R1 (1k next to TR2) o/c.

*Blank screen after 10 mins. OK from decoder SCART:*
IC10 (SRD520)

*Diagonal, dashed lines swirling across picture:*
Replace C32.

*Sound affects picture:*
Remove IC10 (74HC4053). If sound still creates lines on the blank screen, there is a short circuit from an audio track to the track to pin 4 of IC10. Otherwise replace IC10. If fault persists, repeat this analysis with IC9 (SRD520 only).

*Picture goes off after 2–3 minutes:*
Freeze IC9 or IC10 and replace it if the picture reappears.

*Picture unstable - jumps or rolls vertically:*
Replace TEA2029 on daughter board. Check for broken tracks around PL303 at front of PCB. Check for dry joints on daughter board – especially on 0v pin. Replace all electrolytics on this board.
Check PL400 on card reader board, PL302 on main board.

*Cogging or jumping picture:*
Blank screen from TV SCART -OK from Decoder SCART. TEA2029C daughter board. Picture jumping and bent verticals; video signal is corrupted, check TR19 base voltage: it should be about 2.0 volts. If not then R80 10k ohm 1% resistor is open circuit. (Sometimes there's a 470k resistor in parallel with it. This is mounted beneath the board and covered with glue that carbonises when hot! Discard both resistors and fit 10k 1%.) Also C54 100n and C11 100n both polyester capacitors can cause this symptom. Check PL400 on card reader board, PL302 on main board.

*Picture OK from Decoder scart but weak/black raster with lines from TV Scart.*
Check decoder by substitution. Replace C54, C55. Glue on the components and tracks may cause this problem. Clean it all away.

*Streaky pictures/ wavy pictures:*
Check R80 (10k 1%).

*Faint horizontal lines closely spaced (as if no interlace) plus some diagonal lines moving about. Or heavy horizontal lines full width of screen:*
C86 (100µF behind TR9 regulator).

*Horizontal streaking most noticeable on decoded channels:*
C621 (470µF/35v near front of PSU).

*Poor pictures. Maybe blank screen. Low video level going into decoder.*
C6 10µF, non-polarised or R5 (12k) behind micro.

*Low video level, blank screen on channel change, no picture behind menu, poor H syncs on micro pin 5:*
PNP output transistor inside decoder. Use BC856 [3B] PNP SMD.

*Horizontal streaks, especially on decoded pictures, perhaps not affecting left 2cm of picture:*
C6 10µF, non-polarised.

*"00000000" on screen instead of channel name:*
Symptom cured by disconnecting IC2 SDA pin beneath the board. IC2 is faulty.

### Audio Faults

*Hiss but no audio (or only 1 audio):*
Bad solder joint IC2
Make sure that 5 volts is reaching IC2; we have found a number of dry joints on legs of components in this area.
Faulty IC2 (TDA6160)
Faulty IC3 (LM1894N)
s/c or o/c L10 (1u8H)
Broken track to:
IC2 pin 1 (0.5v p-p 4.0MHz from TR40 emitter)
IC2 pin 27  (SCL via tuner) check tracks around tuner lugs.
IC2 pin 28 (SDA via tuner) check tracks around tuner lugs.
IC2 pin 26 (5v from 78L05)
IC2 pin 4 (5v via L10 + VCO oscillation)

*No audio and no hiss.*
Can be caused by selection of "MAC" in the menu (global setting).

Select "PAL" or carry out factory reset sequence (see Handset Codes).
If no better, try replacing IC2 and IC3. Check for dry joint on the wire
which fits in hole marked C50 near front edge of board. Check for other
dry joints in this area. Check for broken tracks as listed above.

*Video buzz on audio.*
Could be C771 shorting on adjacent track.

*Loud motor boat noise on L & R audio*
C32 (10μF/16v non-polarised)

### Decoder Faults

*Card Invalid" message with no card:*
Clean contacts and switch contacts inside card-holder slot.
If this does not cure fault, replace card-holder. If fault persists, replace
decoder module with a known good one.

*"Card Invalid". Decoder OK:*
If a new card-holder board works OK then test the old one: Check two
rows of 1N4148 diodes D401 - D408 on card-holder board for reverse
leakage (desolder each one to measure). If a new board does not work
then the decoder is faulty. (Except SRD540/545 - check R205 10R next to
card reader 4-pin socket, front left corner of main board.)

*Very low video output from decoder:*
(OK on 7802 but low on CP101).
Replace CP101 10μF inside decoder module.

*Very weak video signal after new decoder fitted.*
Check the small socket in front of IC10. The decoder plug should have
one of the white wires on the left hand side when inserted in the socket.
If not, desolder the socket from the main PCB and solder it back,
reversed. You should always make this check when fitting a different
decoder. Fitting it the wrong way round will damage the decoder. You
will have to replace the PNP transistor, TR103 (PNP SMD, marked "3B"),
nearest the 4 pin connector inside the decoder with a BC856B . TR102
occasionally goes faulty (BC846B).

*Intermittent decoder.*
Check 28MHz crystal/solder joints inside decoder module. Check C403, disc ceramic capacitor mounted near the screw of the card reader board.

*No "Please insert-card" message on the screen:*
IC6 (TEA2029C), which is on the daughter board, or decoder faulty. Usually a bent pin on the TCE10705400, faulty IC or faulty PTV-2 IC. This decoder module also suffers from dry joints on the surface mount ICs.

## On Screen Graphics Faults

*No overlay text on channel change (i.e. blank screen for 4 seconds)*
*No overlay of text onto incoming signal. No pic in tuning menu:*
Video bandwidth set to "wide" in menu. Otherwise, replace C54, R9, R80 (10k/1% often in parallel with 470k underneath the board - throw this away - and scrape away any glue). If no horiz sync pulses on IC5 Micro pin5 check TR14, R154 (4k7), track o/c or s/c. R74 (6k8) or TR16 or associated components. Check R67 (750Ω).

*Grey video background (characters OK but no colour background)*
C91 incorrectly adjusted.

*Rolling text on incoming video*
Check TR36/37 circuit.

*No menu:*
Dry joints on IC10 or a fault on the sync lines to U10 or a fault in the tracks connecting to graphics I.C. Try resoldering all the pads around, this I.C.

*Poor on-screen graphics and/or slow to change channel:*
Adjust RV1 for the best compromise. If contrast is low, replace decoder.

*On-screen graphics wiggle and picture may be poor:*
Change menu option video bandwidth from wide to narrow or do factory reset. Check C54, R80.

## Secret Handset Codes

Only one – factory reset puts all channel settings back as new.
All of your customised settings will be lost!

In Standby press—
OK
SETUP
STATUS    (hold this button until both red and green LEDs flash)
          (or 88 appears in display)

### SRD510/520 recommended upgrades:
Power supply
C622 2200μF/6v3 or higher
C621 470μF/16v or higher
C620 470μF/35v or higher
C305 470μF/16v or higher
C611 10μF/35v or higher
C612 220μF/25v
R602, R603 47k/350v

Main Board
C54 100nF polyester
C11 100nF polyester
C46 470μF/10v or higher (next to tuner)
C6 10μF non-polarised (further left of tuner)
C86 100μF behind (TR9 regulator)
R80 10k/1%
R9 470R
R74 6k8
R5 12k

## Miscellaneous Faults

*Timer gains several minutes per week:*
Add 15pF across 4.00MHz crystal

*Tuning stuck on a very low channel frequency:*
Should be 23v on R22 100R feeding tuner. If not, look for cracked track on the inside corner of the board next to the PSU. Alternatively this track may be cracked or corroded elsewhere. Connect a wire between R22 and 23v pin on connector from PSU.

# Amstrad Handsets, all models

*I/R output but wrong codes:*
Remove/resolder R4/R5

*Continuous code (not pulsing) when used:*
Remove/resolder C1 /C2

*No output:*
Dl o/c or dry jointed/TRl dry jointed

(Thanks to Kevin Halsey of Protel for this and other information)

*Amstrad SRD510/520*

# Amstrad SRD540/545/550

## *See SRD510/520 section for all faults.*

### Secret Handset Codes

Only one – factory reset puts all channel settings back as new.
All of your customised settings will be lost!

STANDBY
OK
SETUP
STATUS    (hold this button until both red and green LEDs flash)

**Please see the previous section for a full list of faults.**
The design of these models is similar to that of the SRD510/520.

*Poor audio or hissing*
Remove the main board and resolder all the legs of the surface mount IC
underneath with a 1mm tip iron. (You need to be skilled in the use of a
soldering iron to do this – it is easy to destroy the IC and copper tracks
so that nobody can repair it!)

*Hum bars travel up or down the picture:*
This is generally NOT caused by the 68uF capacitor. It is caused by fit-
ting a power supply unit or a transformer from an SRD510.
Transformers for SRD540/545/550 are numbered 006 or 007.
Transformers for SRD510/520 are numbered 001 to 004.

*Stuck in AV (channel zero):*
You can get various intermittent problems because of trouble with the
socket for the large chip in the middle of the main panel. If cleaning the
socket doesn't cure the problem, try removing it and soldering the chip
directly to the panel. This will ensure that there are no further connector
problems.

*R+G LEDs flash when warm. Adding 0v wire does not cure it:*
Replace IC300 at front of PSU.

**The power supplies of SRD510/520 and SRD540/545/550 are similar but NOT interchangeable!**

The transformer output voltages and current are different:
LLP004AR provides 23 volts for the tuner of the SRD510/520.
LLP006AR and LLP007AR are both identical and provide 28 volts with a higher current output for the 13/18v LNB supply.

### SRD550 only
*Will not work reliably with Juno LNB or Mini Magic:*
Solder a 2Ω2 resistor in parallel with R308 (0Ω91) or replace R308 with 0Ω68/0.5W. This is the LNB current-sensing resistor.

*LNB input switching does not work properly:*
(Short Circuit indication or input "A" may remain powered when "B" is selected.)
There are four discrete SR60 transistors in the tuner.
Remove these and replace them with four FXT749. The lead configuration is identical.

*IF 13/18 volt switching differential is too low (eg. only 13/16):*
Measure R314 left of RV1. Should be 43k (47k + 150k).

*Very poor video; loss of sync; sound ok from scart:*
C81 (10uF)

*Will not select card B:*
Red wire from micro not connected to card reader board.

*SRD550 PSU faulty:*
D609 can go s/c. Not needed in cct. Just protects transistor.

### Upgrades
*Same as SRD510/520 but some have already been done by the manufacturer.*

*In every model, you should first solder a wire from the corner of the little metal screening box at the front of the power supply to the pin marked "0v" to the right of the card holder. Turn RV600 adjustment to give exactly 5 volts on the power supply connector (third pin from front on main board). You MUST measure this with a meter. This is a standard upgrade.*

# Amstrad SRD600

*Display shows* PIN?
Disconnect mains power. Press reset switch with a match stick and hold. Restore mains power. After 5 seconds, release switch. (Reset switch is accessible via a 3mm hole in the lower front panel, when the hinged cover is open). Also handy for various strange problems.

*Blank screen on D2Mac channels:*
Ensure that the Brightness, Contrast and Colour settings are fairly high for these channels. Use the Special Features button on the handset to select each of these features in turn. Increase them by pressing the "up" button and store by pressing the "Preset" button on the receiver.

*D2MAC channels will not decode.*
Replace IC1 (DMA2286) or the DMA2281. A special tool is required or, alternatively, use strong glue to fix a steel wire loop to the IC and pull!

*Picture and sound may vanish if channel is changed .*
(LNB voltage drops to 3 volts on changing from horizontal to vertical) Replace C31 (2μ2F/50v) in the power supply (rear, right) with a 10μF/16v.
(The LNB short-circuit detection circuit occasionally reacts too quickly).

*Audio modes can't be changed:*
Look for broken tracks on top of PCB around tuner.

*Receiver dead:*
Power supply fault caused by C13 or alternatively CCU3000 faulty.

**Secret Handset Codes**
Press service button inside near the power supply and simultaneously press TV/SAT on the front panel. This puts the receiver in Service Mode. *Don't* use this unless you understand what you are doing! TV/SAT to exit

The Service Mode aids debug and allows various setups to be made. The mode is entered by pressing simultaneously the [Service Key] on the main board inside and the [TV/SAT] key.
You should first select a Mac channel and the mode will be displayed on screen.

**The following list shows Service mode functions and their effect:**
[Service]+[TV/SAT] Enters service mode. Displays software version if MAC.
[Search Up/Dn]      VCO value (synchronisation time of Mac-adjust for match).
[Red][Reveal]       Red Cutoff (RGB and RGB/PAL amplitude/black level).
[Green][Hold]       Green Cutoff (RGB and RGB/PAL amplitude/black level).
[Blue][Update]      Blue Cutoff (RGB and RGB/PAL amplitude/black level).
[8][Status]         Red White drive (RGB and RGB/PAL amplitude/white level).
[9][Func.Sel]       Green White drive (RGB and RGB/PAL amplitude/white level).
[Audio][Fn. Up]     Blue White drive (RGB and RGB/PAL amplitude/white level).
[Yellow]            Toggles between 1Vp-p and 2Vp-p MAC inputs.
[Select]            Start displaying Black/White levels (AGC/clamp confidence).
[TV Programme Up/Dn]  Displays NVM data (aids debug).
[Up] [Down]         Changes NVM data at address selected by [TV Prog] keys.
[Sat Programme Up/Dn] Selects Card Reader modes for Vpp, Vcc setup and debug.
NOTE:               Do not change these with a card inserted!
[Store]             Stores changes during Service mode.
[TV/SAT]            Stops Black white level display if enabled.
                    Otherwise exits Service mode.

Please note that the ex-factory settings have been very carefully chosen to produce the best picture. Also note that pressing RESET rewrites all information except VCO adjustment which should never change after having been adjusted during production. Service mode should be used only to check VCO, to set Vpp and to check RGB settings.

The [Service Key] can also be used to execute the special single commands by pressing certain keys with it:

[Polarisation]   IM Bus Off. (Used to drive the Mac chips from a PC for development/debug)
[Standby (IR)]   IM Bus On.
[Text On/Off]    Manually selects E7 de-emphasis.
[Full/Mix]       Toggles AFT.

**Upgrades**
A 27C1001 Eprom upgrade gives an extended tuning range in SRD600E.

**SRD600 as a decoder.**

Modify your Amstrad SRD600E to act as a D2MAC decoder.

Open up the Amstrad. Inside you will see that there are two PCBs on the right in piggy back configuration and a single PCB on the left. The PCBs on the right are the tuner, videocrypt and card interface. The PCB on the left is the D2MAC decoder. Locate the white PCB header in the middle of the three which connect the D2MAC card to the tuner card.

You will need to cut the second connection down from the top – marked BB (for baseband) – and to solder the centre core from a BNC plug to the left side of the connection. The outer shield of the BNC plug must be soldered to the pin at the top of the connector block (a GND rail) – do not cut this pin.

The cable complete with the BNC plug can be fed through a small hole at the back of the case and the SRD600 reassembled.

Connect the BNC input to the decoder output of the other receiver and tune the Amstrad to any channel except 0 (0 - is the auxiliary and will blank out the picture).

The decoded output is now available at the right hand SCART socket on the Amstrad.

# Amstrad SRD650 (D2Mac)

*"Check the Card" when card is OK:*
Replace open-circuit 10R resistor which you will find next to TR19 at the front left corner of the main board. This resistor fuses if a faulty or incorrect card is inserted.

*PSU hissing:*
Transformer T600 faulty. (A PSU repair kit SATKIT 21 is available).

*Horizontal lines across picture - fixed and sharp, not moving:*
C46 100uF next to tuner.

# Amstrad VS1000/1140

*Blank screen or wavy grey rolling pictures:*
CV42 (47uF/16v) on decoder board. Also check R537 (680R) and 33uF
capacitor next to TO220 transistor - capacitor shorts to transistor.

*Poor video/no videocrypt messages
(sync truncated):*
CA02 (470uF/lOV) on decoder board.

*White horizontal streaks on pic. Decoder mes-
sages unstable. "Wrong card inserted" message. Poor pictures (bent, with bars moving
vertically down the screen) when the signals
are in the clear. Scrambled signals are not
decoded:*
CA05 (100µF/35v) on decoder board.

*Picture jumps or lines:*
CL08 (4µ7/50v)

*Other possible causes:*
CV31 (10µF/35v)
C513 (33µF/25v) use 47µF*
R530 (560Ω)
CA07 (100µF/25v)
CV09 (100µF/25v)

*note: board polarity marking incorrect.
Replace ALL these to save time

*No LNB voltage:*
R515 (3R3) at front of tuner board.

*LNB voltage drops under load:*
C502 at front of tuner board.

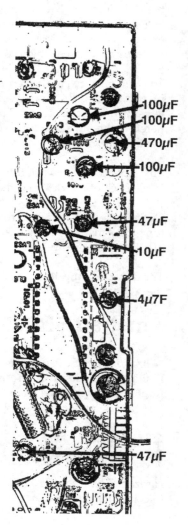

# Amstrad
# SR950/SRD700/SR950+/SRX301

*No Decoder messages. Will not decode:*
Press "SETUP" on handset.
Ensure video bandwidth is NOT set to "Wide".

*Auto tune:*
Press SETUP [>] [>] [>] SETUP [speaker]
Auto tune will record all odd number channels (17 volts) then all even
number channels (13 volts).

*Factory Reset:*
There is NO factory reset. Once you have retuned channels there is no
turning back!

**Note:** There is NO way to select a 10.0GHz LNB for the SR950.

*Picture scrambles briefly when bright picture occurs:*
If receiver suffers with momentary scrambling with a valid card and a good signal
coinciding with high contrast changes or flicker/shimmer and/or jitter at bright
white parts of the picture etc..

a) Solder a 33K 1% resistor between test pin TP900 (0v) and link LK901

b) Solder a 22K 1% resistor between link LK901 and link LK905

c) Cut link LK902 and solder a 10uF 16V non-polarised capacitor across the
    cut link (or 2x 22uF with -ve together).
    d) Check and adjust RV901/RVl if necessary.

Adjust the clamp voltage (RV901 wiper 1.45V) and video level (RVl on tuner board
to give 1.85V at CVin on decoder board).

*Power supply failure:*
A kit is available and this includes the TOP202, the high voltage
avalanche diode and other parts. DO NOT replace only the fuse!

*Crackling or interference on stereo audio:*
TDA6130 on tuner assembly.

*Noise only on audio, will not tune in any mode:*
Check R3 on main board for continuity (27k).

*Missing video, audio OK, or low video level, loss of synchronisation:*
Replace the 10uF electrolytic located near to the corner of the screening can. Use a tantalum type as replacement.

*One minute after switch-on, the receiver won't respond to any button:*
*Blank screen with audio:*
Remove micro and wash flux out of I.C. socket.

*Blank screen for 5 seconds on channel change.*
*Terribly "sparkly" pictures with patterning as if dish moved:*
C41 10uF inside tuner

*Streaky pictures on decoded channels (White horizontal lines in centre 2/3 of screen) or OSD jumps vertically on screen. Receiver slow to respond on channel change:*
C68 10uF inside tuner. Use a tantalum bead 10uF/6.3V as replacement.
Replacing C66 (near to the screening can corner) with a tantalum bead 22uF/6.3V is also recommended.

You need another tuner in your hand so you can see the position of each capacitor. Then you can solder new ones in parallel on the topside of the tuner board. Only a 5 minute job done this way!

*No decoder messages unless RV901 turned fully clockwise:*
C69 10uF inside tuner

*"Red flashing light":*
AMS42577, the chip on the PSU board that generates the LNB supply.

*Stuck in standby. LNB voltage tripping:*
EEprom faulty. *

*Autotune works but no channels stored:*
EEprom faulty. *

* The EEprom can be damaged by voltages applied to the TV scart socket by certain models of TV. To prevent reoccurrence disconnect R95, R96.

**SRD700/SR950
TUNER**

The picture shows the
underside view.

Capacitor negative
(stripe) end is indicated
by a black spot.

**SR950+ Decoder socket upgrade**

You will need the following parts:

| | |
|---|---|
| C20, 26, 27, 29, 41 | 10uF |
| R38 | 100k |
| R55 | 10k |
| R53, 34 | 470R |
| R51 | 22k |
| R49, 50 | 270R |
| R52 | 15k |
| R46, 47 | 75R |
| R54 | 1k |
| L6, 7 | wire link |
| IC4 | MC14053 |
| TR5, 15 | 2SC1740 |
| TR6 | 2SA933 |
| Clip-in Scart socket | |

You will also need the following
if not already fitted:

| | |
|---|---|
| C28, 24, 25 | 10uF |
| R37, 39, 42, 43 | 270R |
| R36, 44, 45 | 10k |
| R40, 41 | 1k |
| TR2, 3 | 2SC1740 |

For stereo audio output you will
need:

Twin phono socket assembly

| | |
|---|---|
| C21, 22 | 10uF |

**SRX501**

This is a continental model. Uses same main board as SRD540/550 but a different micro (AMS42803-600) and the new TOPswitch power supply. Displays clock on front panel in standby mode.

The receiver needs a preprogrammed EEPROM to function properly. The (usual) factory reset sequence or fitting a blank EEPROM lead to spurious OSD messages (languages mixed up) and loss of reception (bad frequency entries). I assume the micro "thinks" it is a decoder version because some "CARTE A" messages appear along with channel names.

# PACE 3xxx and 6xxx

<u>SS3000</u>
Ferguson SRA1

<u>SS6000</u>
Ferguson SRA1S
Ferguson XSRA1-S
Ferguson ESRA1-S
Network SS6000
Bush SR3200
Philips STU800/01R
Allsat SR2001S
Teleciel S6000
Saba SSR 1 TC
Telefunken
Normende
Thomson

---

### Removing the main PCB assembly

Remove all fixing screws and tuner nut. The SCART sockets and the circuit board are held by plastic rivets. Release the plastic rivets by prising the heads up with sharp cutters then pull out the complete rivet. Lift the board out, gently.

---

<u>SS6001 with mag polariser</u>
Ferguson SRA1-S
Bush SR3200
Dansat

<u>SS6002 with timer</u>
Granada M92GR3
Hinari SR3500
Bush SR3500

<u>SS6032 with clock/inst. timer</u>
Teleciel SS6032

<u>SS6061 60 ch. with mag polariser</u>

<u>SS6060 60 channel</u>
Bishopsgate SS6060
Ferguson XSRA1-S 60
Allsat SR2001S
Seemanns 7000XT
Schwaiger SS6060

Network SS6060
Teledirekt SEA 1000
Teleciel SS6060
Saba SSR - TC60
Thomson SRS2-60

# Pace SS3000/SS6000/SS6060

*SRA1 Handset not working.*

This handset has a paper-phenolic printed circuit board which soaks up moisture like a sponge. It can be dried out simply by re-soldering every joint. In a very bad case you might find one or more copper tracks have corroded away beneath the green resin coating. Scrape away coating which looks black and tin the copper to bridge any open circuits.

The SRA1 and SRA1-S handsets are identical apart from the printing which effectively changes the function of each button. The printed covers can be swapped to change one type to the other. If you have the wrong version available
you can still use it provided that you note the different button designations.

## Faults common to both models

| | | |
|---|---|---|
| 1 | 2 | 3 |
| 4 | 5 | 6 |
| 7 | 8 | 9 |
| 0 | V | Λ |
| 1* | 2* | 3* |
| STATUS | H/V | MODE |
| STORE | SETUP | MUTE |
| STORE | NORM | STNDBY |

SRA1-S

| | | |
|---|---|---|
| 1* | 2* | 3* |
| STNDBY | STATUS | MODE |
| 1 | 2 | 3 |
| 4 | 5 | 6 |
| 7 | 8 | 9 |
| 0 | V | Λ |
| STORE | SETUP | NORM |
| STORE | H/V | MUTE |

SRA1

*Horizontal bar moves slowly up or down the picture.*
Replace large bridge rectifiers.

*Receiver dead*
Check 3A fuse link R148 and large bridge rectifier. In bad cases, the transformer may also be damaged. Also check R145 and R146. If 2200µF electrolytic capacitors are discoloured by heat, replace them also. Look

for broken tracks and broken solder joints on early models which have the mains transformer mounted on the board.

*LNB voltage zero (no voltage to regulator on side of chassis).*
Replace bridge rectifier BR3 and fusible resistor R145 (1Ω superseded by disc).

*LNB voltage high and not switching.*
Replace the regulator which is mounted on the left side panel. It may be a 7815 or an LM317. Also check transformer solder joints on early models and R145 (1Ω).

*Will not come out of Standby. Ignores handset.*
Ensure that handset is working. If the right hand panel LED does not flash in response to pressing handset buttons, ensure that front panel and top cover are fitted. If necessary, tape a cardboard shield around the sensor which is very susceptible to interference from light sources. Some early versions had no "bars" across the detector shield "window". Wires must be soldered across this aperture to improve the screening.
Replace all large electrolytics in the power supply section.
Replace relay RL1.
If the fault still remains, replace the microprocessor.

## Connecting a Videocrypt Decoder

Connect the decoder by means of a SCART to SCART lead.
If this does not descramble the pictures, do the following:

Where there is an on/off switch on the rear of the receiver, remove the cover screws (mains unplugged!) and change over the "VIDEO LINK" near the centre of the board to its rearmost position (marked L.T.)
Replace the cover with screws and plug back in to the mains.

Where there is no on/off switch at the rear, press [SETUP] [1] [4] [7].
Select AV MODE and press both [STORE] buttons together.
There is no internal link to change.

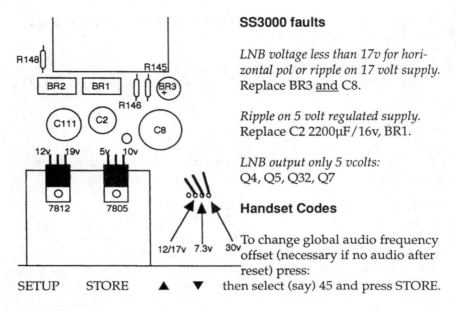

## SS3000 faults

*LNB voltage less than 17v for horizontal pol or ripple on 17 volt supply.* Replace BR3 <u>and</u> C8.

*Ripple on 5 volt regulated supply.* Replace C2 2200µF/16v, BR1.

*LNB output only 5 vcolts:* Q4, Q5, Q32, Q7

## Handset Codes

To change global audio frequency offset (necessary if no audio after reset) press:

SETUP     STORE     ▲     ▼     then select (say) 45 and press STORE.

## SS6000 faults

*LNB output only 5 vcolts:* Q27 on heatsink TIP32A (PNP).

*Locks up at switch-on.* To prevent unwanted lock-up on EARLY 6000/6060 models and Bush, remove LK5 near U4. Add a link between LK5 hole nearest U4 and the hole for pin 4 of U19. If this modification results in no picture then the receiver is a LATER model.

*Interference on picture - Horizontal channels only (17v to LNB)* If oscillation on collector of Q4 (centre leg), replace C69 (10µF/16v). It is also advisable to replace C75 (10µF/25v) and C100 (10µF/16v) and to replace C8 and BR3 since all of these components are likely to have been degraded by heat.

*Tearing of picture, all channels. Possibly severe picture distortion/interference. Sparkly pictures as though the tuner were dying:* Replace C139 (100µF/16v near Decoder Scart socket).

*Receiver dead. No 5 volts. No LEDs lit:*
(Touching Q28 with wet finger makes the receiver light up)
Change C176 from 1uF to 4.7uF.

The sketch shows AC RMS voltages from the transformer as measured at the PCB connector.

### Handset Codes

To Lock/Unlock
Press SETUP    9    8    7

Reset to factory settings —
(Sixteen Astra 1a channels with
the rest untuned!)
Press the sequence:
SETUP    1*    2*    3*
STORE    ▲    ▼

For on-screen menu press
SETUP    1    4    7
To adjust frequency press
SETUP    2    5    8
To scan all frequencies press
SETUP    3    6    9

(Since the circuitry of the
**SS3000/SS6000 is similar to that of the SS9000/9200, many faults common to all models have not been duplicated here but will be found in the next section.)**

### Circuit Upgrades

Replace all electrolytic capacitors in the power supply section and bridge rectifier BR3 (W005 from Farnell).

This upgrade will help to minimise problems caused by overheating due to incorrect installation.

# PACE SS9xxx

### SS9000IRD
Ferguson SRV1
Grundig GIRD2000
Philips STU801/05R
Network 9000IRD
Bush IRD150

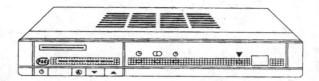

### SS9001IRD Magnetic polariser/Polarotor
Maspro SRE 350S

### SS9010 Dual input tuner
Saba SSR2TC
Telefunken SR3100
Maspro SRE350S
Normende STS2100
Thomson SRS3
Teleciel 9010
Pace 9010 'C' band

### SS9011 Dual input tuner/Mag polariser
Philips STU801/01R
Philips STU801/02R
Philips STU801/19R
Portenseigne STU800/19R
Saba SSR850
Telefunken SR1000Z

### SS9200IRD
Nokia SAT1500
Bush IRD151
Grundig GIRD3000
Maspro SRE350S
BAe 9200IRD
BAe SPORTSCAST
Network 9200IRD
Philips STU801/05R

### SS9210IRD
Maspro SRE-350S*and others*

### MRD920 with D2Mac/Eurocrypt decoder
Finlux SR5700
Wisi MRD920
Ecosphere MRD920
Alba SAT6600
Maspro SRE450S
Thomson SRS4
Tantec S/LNB
Above also available with dual input tuner.
### MRD920 with Mag polariser/Polarotor

### MRD920 with polariser and dual input tuner
Tantec TT5001

# Frequently Asked Questions - Pace SS9000/9200

CONTENTS
1. Why did my power supply fail?
2. How do I repair the power supply?
3. Can I get extra channels?
4. Can I use an "Enhanced" LNB?
5. Can I upgrade to "Enhanced" menu software?
6. Can I upgrade my SS9200 to a twin input SS9200?
7. Are there any "secret" handset codes?
8. I get only "snow". What has happened?
9. Can I use a "Universal" LNB?
10. How can I tell how old my receiver is?
11. How can I download the memory?
12. Why do I get no decoder messages on screen?
13. Why do I get intermittent "Card Invalid" message?
14. Why do I get lines on the picture?
15. Why has the picture quality become poor?
16. Why doesn't my receiver work with pirate card/PC software?
17. Why can't I name channels 33 onwards?

**1. Why did my power supply fail?**

C9 (1uF) dries out and often causes failure.
The transformer T2 can go short circuit.
These are the main causes, apart from mains surge.

**2. How do I repair the power supply?**

If the fuse has NOT melted, the cause is probably a broken track. All other causes make the fuse melt. If you replace the fuse without first repairing the PSU you will cause more damage.
The copper tracks and pads are very fragile. Use fine "solder wick" – DO NOT use a pump-action desolder tool! Ensure normal safety precautions.
If the fuse HAS melted, you will need the complete kit of parts.
Remember, these are classed as "Safety Critical" components. You MUST use the Pace-approved parts. If you don't you risk damage and fire hazard.

### 3. Can I get extra channels?

The SS9000 has 60 channels and can be upgraded to 90.
A new microcontroller and EEprom are needed, so it's not cheap.
The SS9200 has 90 channels and can not (so far) be upgraded.
(I did look at a method of toggling between two EEproms but gave up!)
You can also fit an AutoSelect inside which will allow you to control an
ADX automatically by selecting it in/out for each channel in the menu.
See http://www.netcentral.co.uk/~davsat/ for more details.

### 4. Can I use an "Enhanced" LNB?

All SS9200 receivers will tune up to 12.100GHz in the menu. About 80%
have tuners which will go that high. So, if you fit an "Enhanced" LNB
and tune each channel 250MHz higher than the magazine listed frequency, you should receive all or most of Astra 1A-1D programmes.
The SS9000 menu will *not* allow you to tune high enough. You will miss
out on the top channels. You can either upgrade to the 90 channel micro
and EEprom or use an ADX.

### 5. Can I upgrade to "Enhanced" menu software?

No, it doesn't exist but, if you upgrade to the 90 channel software and
tune each channel 250 higher, you can use an Enhanced (9.75) LNB.

### 6. Can I upgrade my SS9200 to a twin input SS9200?

Yes, it's possible, but the twin input tuner is expensive and you would
have to drill an extra hole in the rear panel and file out the existing one.
There are other changes to make, too. Not really worthwhile unless you
have the twin-input tuner already.

### 7. Are there any "secret" handset codes?

Yes. The "factory reset" will set the first 32 channels to Astra 1A and 1B
channels. It will then repeat these channels up to the limit of 60 or 90. If
you are happy to lose your customised settings, press:
Menu, P, 2, 3, Store, Right arrow, Left arrow.

BEWARE! on early SS9000 receivers with a microcontroller number end-

ing in "25", or "26" you will find that channels 25 to 31 have their polarisation reversed. You will need to change each one from H - V or vice-
versa.

The 60 channel version has another secret code:
If you take your receiver abroad, you will need to change the RF modulator output from "PAL I" to "PAL G". This is simply achieved by pressing SETUP, MUTE, NORM, STORE, [up arrow], STORE (and the same to
reset it back to PAL G).

On the 90 channel version the microprocessor output which controlled
this PAL selection is, instead, used to select the internal decoder automatically via the rear pin of the 10 pin connector.

To reset the PIN to 1234 on early SS9000:
In standby, press STANDBY then STORE and hold STORE for twenty
seconds. During this time the channel ident should remain in the top
right corner of the screen, otherwise press NORM and try again.

To reset the PIN to 1234 on later SS9000 and all SS9200:
Remove power from unit.
Hold STANDBY, UP and DOWN buttons on the front panel, simultane-
ously, and restore mains power. Release the buttons.

To reset PIN to 1234 on MRD920 D2Mac versions:
Remove mains power from unit.
Hold STANDBY button and restore power.
Release STANDBY button after 3 seconds.

## 8. I get only "snow". What has happened?

Presumably there is no signal. Is there any LNB voltage?
The most obvious cause is that your LNB is not connected.
Sometimes LK210 near the front (0.47 Ohm or 18uH inductor only in
later SS9200) has burned out because you short-circuited the input.
There are many more faults which will cause this symptom. Later
SS9200s with a Sharp tuner sometimes do this because a resistor was
omitted. Unplug the receiver from the mains and plug it back in. If the
pictures return, you need to fit a 27k resistor from C134 + leg to LK202.

### 9. Can I use a "Universal" LNB?

A "Universal" LNB will work exactly the same as an "Enhanced" LNB unless your receiver incorporates 22kHz tone switching to access "High Band" frequencies. The 22kHz tone switches the LNB internal oscillator from 9.75 GHz to 10.6 GHz. SS9xxx receivers do not incorporate this feature but it CAN be added. A kit is not available but you can build it yourself on stripboard. But first consider why you want to use a Universal LNB. What do you expect to receive on High Band? Or do you want the tone switch in order to utilise an external switcher box?

### 10. How can I tell how old my receiver is?

The date of manufacture is incorporated in the serial number.
For example:  RAE03456/2245
The "2" indicates 1992
The "24" indicates week 24 counting from first week in January.
The "5" indicates Friday.

### 11. How can I download the memory?

There is no facility for doing this. However, it is possible to copy the EEprom and to fit the copy into another receiver, provided that it has an identical microcontroller (if it hasn't, it will automatically reprogram your EEprom to factory defaults!)

### 12. Why do I get no decoder messages on screen?

In the 60 channel version you have to select "AV INT" and "DECODER INT" in the menu for each scrambled channel. Pressing the factory reset sequence will change most channels back to "AUTO" which is fine for the SS9200 but not for the SS9000.

### 13. Why do I get intermittent "Card Invalid" message?

The series 10 SKY card seems prone to this on certain receivers.
Make sure that the card contacts are clean and the card slot spring contacts are clean and not bent or twisted.
If this doesn't help, provided that you occasionally get a picture when you insert the card (even if momentarily), then try scraping the black

spot off the card. This works 100% for me.
THIS MOD IS NOT APPROVED BY SKY OR BY PACE

## 14. Why do I get lines on the picture?

If these are dashed lines swirling across the picture, more evident on
decoded channels, then the cause is C29 (right hand edge of main
board). It must be replaced with a 100uF (or higher) 35v (or higher)
105°C low ESR capacitor.

If the lines are NOT present on the picture from the Decoder Scart then
there is a problem around the TEA2029C chip. Possibly the chip itself or
the 4u7F capacitor next to it or a dry joint underneath.

If the lines totally obscure the picture on ALL outputs (check!) when the
receiver is warm (maybe looks like a scrambled picture) then the culprit
is the tiny 2u2F electrolytic inside the tuner module. Desolder the tuner
and prise the side covers off (you can discard these to keep it cooler).
VERY carefully, remove the tiny cylindrical capacitor C416 and replace it
with a 2u2F tantalum bead type of 6v3 rating (or higher). Observe polarity ("+" leg furthest from the metal side). Use VERY fine solder and solder tip to do this. Be extremely careful because it is easy to destroy 40
quids worth of tuner!

## 15. Why has the picture quality become poor?

Replace the parts mentioned in 14.
If the picture is streaky, you need to replace several electrolytic capacitors. These MUST be low ESR, high temperature 105°C type or you'll
make it worse!

Start with the large capacitors at the front of the power supply.
C21 and C25 are prime suspects. After that, replace ALL the electrolytics
at the front of the PSU. Then replace the 1uF and 10uF capacitors near
the tuner (these get hot) working outwards in a circle. (The darkened
ones near the Scart connectors carry mostly audio so ignore them).
Also, spray the decoder connector with WD-40 and work it up and
down a few times to clean it. You might find that the decoder messages
are now darker when you power it up. A reliability upgrade kit is available. Also a power supply repair kit.

### 16. Why can't I name channels 33 onwards?

The facility to name channels on the SS9200 is available only for the first 32 channels. Unfortunately, the amount of memory can not be expanded for the remaining channels.

### 17. How do I use a separate decoder?
Whereas videocrypt decoders will accept baseband input, some decoders require plain video. (The early "RAI" decoder from Premier Video Products accepted baseband but the SATVIEW one needs video.)

The Pace requires a simple modification to send the decoded video to the UHF modulator.

This mod is *not* required if the TV is connected to the TV Peritel socket but note the following setup:
Connect the RAI decoder to the VCR Scart socket on the SS9200.
Connect the TV via the UHF modulator or the TV Peritel socket. Set a channel to the appropriate frequency but leave "source" and "decoder" set to AUTO in the on-screen menu. Loop in the decoder by pressing the TV/SAT button.

*Description of modification:*
Disconnect receiver from the mains.
Locate C163 electrolytic capacitor (centre rear, near VCR socket).
Cut + leg of C163 and link it to pin 19 of the TV Peritel socket.
Pin 19 is on the bottom row nearest to the P.C. board and is the 2nd from the right — just accessible below the edge of the decoder board.
The UHF modulator now receives its video signal internally direct, or externally from pin 20 of the VCR socket when the TV/SAT button is pressed. The external decoder receives its signal from pin 19 and sends it back into pin 20 of the VCR socket.
A partially wired Scart lead is adequate.

# Pace SS9XXX and MRD920

**Removing the main PCB assembly:** If the board is bowed or twisted the surface mount components beneath can be invisibly damaged. Remove all fixing screws and tuner nuts. Black painted units have a screw in the PCB. Release the black rivets by prising the heads up with sharp cutters then lift out the complete rivet. Use fine-nosed pliers to squeeze in the locking tab in the decoder support pillars and lift the decoder board out. Use fine-nosed pliers to squeeze together fully the split ends of the two white support pillars for the main board. Lift the board off, gently.

### Power Supply Faults

If the power supply has failed or gives no output then *all* the components marked by this arrow should be suspected. R12 (4k7) and R13 (0R22) are fusible resistors and must be replaced *only* with identical devices supplied by the manufacturer. Use of other components may cause an electrical safety hazard. The black arrows indicate convenient points to measure the power supply output DC voltages. Actual measurements may be slightly higher than the nominal values shown.

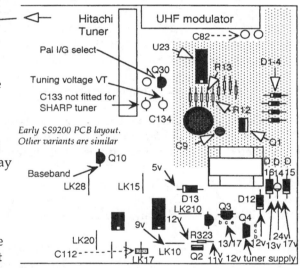

*Early SS9200 PCB layout. Other variants are similar*

⚠ **WARNING**

⚠ On no account measure any voltages within the area shown shaded. All components within this area are at **mains potential**. Great care must be taken when working on any such unit where **live parts** are exposed. Ensure any components replaced have leads cropped short beneath the PCB because a serious **shock hazard** could result if the leads come near to the metal chassis.

**page 73**

*Power supply dead.*
**(Disconnect the mains! Discharge C7 - 350 volts** – by shorting its pins together with a 10Ω resistor.**)**

Measure the fuse for continuity. *If it has melted, do **not** apply mains power with a new fuse fitted until the repair has been completed:-*
Measure the voltage drop across each of the four 1N4007 diodes with a diode tester. They should read approximately 0.6 volts in one direction and infinity in the other. If one or more of the diodes is short-circuit, replace it.
If they read approximately 0.6 volts in *both* directions then remove Q1.
If the diode readings are now correct, Q1 was faulty: renew it.
If the diode readings are still 0.6 volts in *both* directions, remove C7.
If the diode readings are now correct, C7 is faulty: renew it. (If there is a brown ring beneath C7 or it bulges at the top, renew it anyway.)
If the diode readings are still 0.6 volts in both directions, renew the transformer, T2. If it has been stressed by the power surge, an old transformer may fail at switch-on, even if it seems to be all right now.

**Use desoldering braid to remove solder, NOT a suction action pump!**

Measure the mains filter choke (the second largest component in the PSU) for continuity of both windings. The winding wire can snap where it is soldered to each pin. This fault is often caused by drop damage.

Measure R12 (4k7) and R13 (0R22). R13 must be very accurate and will prevent operation if its value is only slightly wrong (LEDs flash) so replace it if in doubt. R12 and R13 are fusible resistors.

Always replace C9 which dries out with heat and causes PSU failure.
Measure R1 for open circuit. Failure of R1 often means that Q1 is dead and that T2 may also be short circuit or D1 - D4 may be short circuit.
Measure diodes D12 to D16. Failure of a diode will cause excessive current demand and the PSU will not start up.

Failure of U23 can not easily be detected. However, it will not usually cause repeated failure; the power supply will simply not work or may whistle. Replace zener D11 with a 470Ω resistor to give 9 volts on LK10.
Check for cracked tracks near holes and dry solder joints — especially the transformer.

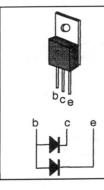

The sketch shows that Q1 can be measured as if it consists of two diodes. Most digital multimeters have a range for checking diodes. The reading in one direction should be around 600 (600mV = 0.6 volts) and, with the opposite connections, the reading should be infinity or maximum on the meter scale. If either 'diode' fails to give the proper readings then the transistor is dead. Normally your multimeter red probe will apply a positive voltage which will give a reading of infinity when it is attached to the cathode (bar) end of a diode.

*Now* apply mains voltage, taking normal precautions against shock etc.
*Power supply whistles or hisses.*
Replace C11 (1µF/25v) and check solder joints on C8 (680pF/2000v). Measure D5. This fault has also been caused by U23, surface mount capacitor C12 (33nF) missing, C18 (100nF) or C16 (820pF). Look for cracked tracks leading to U23 and, if all else fails, replace transformer T2. C7 can cause a buzz or hiss.

*R5 100Ω resistor beneath PCB overheats (early SS9000 only)*
Remove C10. To restore the correct output voltages, change Surface Mount resistor R256 (000) to 270Ω (271).

*Faint diagonal white dashed lines across decoded picture.*
Replace C29 (100µF/35v/105°C) at front right corner. (Early production units sometimes suffered physical damage during assembly). Capacitor must be a low ESR type.

*Low humming sound on audio. Ripple on picture.*
Replace C7.

*Only one polarity. LNB voltage 17v only or 13v only.*
Replace Q3 (FXT749) with the same part. Do not use an "equivalent".

*No LNB voltage at all.* (Later models with Sharp tuner):
Check LK210 (0R47Ω) which carries the LNB current from Q3 and can melt if the LNB input is shorted. Latest variant used a 12µH inductor which prevents power supply interference from reaching the tuner and may be fitted instead of 0R47Ω.

*LEDs flash, dimly, in sequence ("tripping" PSU):*
Measure D9, D6, 100Ω SMD resistor underneath (the one which gets hot). Measure exact value of R13 (0Ω22) and R11 (4R7Ω). Broken track to C11. Transformer T2 (very rare). C17 (470µF/16v) very rare. R7 1k SMD high in value (very rare).

*LEDs flash briefly then die :*
R13 resistance (0Ω22) is too high; replace it with an identical fusible one. Otherwise, replace R3 (large 100kΩ resistor). Tuner lugs not soldered.

*Standby LED lights dimly but receiver does not respond to button presses:*
The lugs of the tuner nearest to C7 have fractured their pads and earth continuity has been lost. Scrape the green coating away from the pads beneath the board and re-solder.

*Stuck in standby (also see "miscellaneous faults"):*
Replace large electrolytics at front of power supply (RELKIT 2)

*LNB voltages too high:*
SMD R257 = 6k8. Try 10k or 15k.

*Does strange things when hot - lights flashing or goes off completely. Sometimes reverts to factory default settings:*
Dry joints on T2. Also, replace C9 and C11.

*Standby LED lights brightly but will not come out of standby:*
Measure 5v rail on LK12. If low, replace C25 and C21.

*Slight mains hum running down the picture, noticeable on certain scenes only:*
Replace C7 47µf.

*Powers down after five minutes. U4 gets very hot:*
Replace U4.

*With horizontal polarisation selected the Universal LNB switches to high band:*
Replace C33 (1000uF/25v). If vertical affected replace C37.

## TUNERS

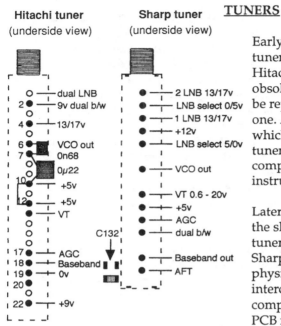

**Hitachi tuner**
(underside view)

**Sharp tuner**
(underside view)

Early Pace variants used tuners manufactured by Hitachi. This tuner is obsolete and, if it fails, must be replaced with a different one. A tuner kit is available which contains a tiny Sharp tuner, surface-mount components and fitting instructions.

Later SS9200 variants use the slightly shorter B75G25 tuner manufactured by Sharp. The two are physically **not** interchangeable and various component changes and PCB modifications were made in order to accommodate the later tuner (e.g. C133 is *not* fitted). The Sharp tuner requires a maximum tuning voltage of just 20 volts (measure on C134).

A fault exists whereby the Sharp tuner can lock up if the tuning voltage exceeds 20 volts. This "lock-up" can occur when mains voltage is applied (more common when already hot but sometimes when cold) or when the frequency is scanned to the maximum.

*The symptoms of lock-up are:* there is no audio — other than hiss — and no picture — other than "snow".The graphics menus operate normally and the *displayed* frequency can be changed. The only way to remove the fault is to unplug the receiver from the mains, until it is cool, then re-apply mains power.

A permanent modification exists whereby a 220kΩ resistor is soldered to position C132 underneath the tuner. This modification was introduced from about week number RA-----------/2202 (**except** where a B7Z̲G25 (2GHz) tuner was fitted).

An easier solution is to solder a 22kΩ resistor between LK202 and the + leg of capacitor C134 which is to the right of the tuner, as shown in the following sketch.

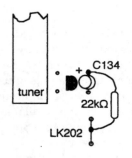

**Before** adding a resistor you **must** ensure that there is definitely no 220k fitted beneath the board. To do this, apply mains power to the receiver (**care!**) with top cover removed and <u>no</u> LNB connected. Press [SETUP] [3] to scan up in frequency and fit resistor only if the voltage between C134+ and LK202 exceeds 22 volts during the scan. Use a meter to measure it. **DO NOT MODIFY** if a B7<u>Z</u>G25 (2GHz) tuner is fitted otherwise the full tuning range will not be achieved.

⚠ **WARNING** *The resistor must be positioned well away from the shaded area of the board which carries mains voltage.*

*Note:*
Symptoms of a dying BF9 Hitachi tuner include: inability to tune out sparklies – goes from white to black sparklies with no clear picture in between; high contrast picture with tearing and long sparkly bits on edges of bright colours. Replace tuner because the (unobtainable) I.C. is dead.

## Picture faults

*No picture (blank raster but graphics visible):*
Connect a TV to the DECODER SCART. (With an oscilloscope you can also view the baseband output from the tuner on LK20 or Q10 emitter). Lack of baseband signal (blank TV screen) indicates a faulty tuner, if supply voltages are OK, however this symptom is also produced if the thicker of the two tracks is broken between the front two fixing lugs of the Hitachi tuner. Where a Sharp tuner is fitted, check continuity of the short track which carries baseband signal from the 2nd pin from the front of the tuner to an adjacent pad.

If a Hitachi tuner has shorted out the 9 volt supply, the tuner is almost certainly beyond repair. R323 will have burnt out but replace the tuner as well. Use Sharp tuner upgrade kit (Pace 266-9537525).

*Sound with test bars but no picture except from Decoder SCART.*
Replace Q26 if faulty. If not, check the power dispersal section around Q26 for a broken track or other faulty component.

*Blank screen except from decoder SCART. No graphics. Q27 hot:*
On early SS9000, diode D44 beneath the PCB can short to an adjacent pad. The fault will also occur if any of the resistors which affect the voltage on Q23 emitter is faulty. Check R342 (680Ω, 510Ω or 220Ω) and R206 (2kΩ) in particular.

*Blank screen on encoded channels (maybe only when warm):*
Check decoder by substitution. If O.K. replace U7.

*Blank screen or low video from RF & VCR Scart. OK from TV Scart:*
Q29 (BC547).

*Blank screen or low video from TV Scart. OK from RF and VCR Scart:*
Q24 (BC547) or decoder board shorting to top of C210 below.

*Blank screen when cold:*
Picture gradually appears but with horizontal lines like tuner capacitor fault.
C21.

*White or black lines across picture. Maybe only when warm or cold.*
If picture from decoder SCART has no lines, see next paragraph instead. Usually a tuner fault, perhaps due to overheating. Replace tuner and eliminate cause of overheating (sometimes customer's installation position). Check power supply for signs of overheating. C9 is often discoloured and *must* be replaced. If the tuner *is* faulty you can often repair it by replacing the tiny electrolytic capacitor, C416 inside the tuner, marked 2.2µF/50v. Replace it with a tantalum bead 2.2µF/35v capacitor; make sure the leg marked "+" is furthest from the side of the metal can. If the tuner voltage supply on LK10 is higher than 9.0 volts, replace zener D11 with a 470Ω resistor.

*Horizontal lines across picture (similar to tuner fault):*
Can be distinguished from tuner fault since picture from Decoder SCART is O.K. Replace C176 (4µ7F/16v near U6). Replace any other overheated components. If the picture looks as if it is printed across a venetian blind, look for an open circuit track near Q23. Measure tracks with a meter.

*Horizontal lines on picture like 4µ7F fault but also from Decoder Scart:*
Broken tracks between Q11, Q12 next to tuner.

*Horizontal lines across picture (similar to tuner fault):*
Lines much closer together than tuner fault and picture still clear. Looks as if interlace is off — even from decoder SCART. Replace capacitor C21 (2200µF/25v). Check for a dry joint on SM capacitor beneath U6.

Many picture faults can be fixed by using RELKIT 2. Saves time in trying to trace a fault which is already well known!

*Picture flickers:*
Suspect X9, U6 or cracked track adjacent. If flickers occur only at the top of the screen, look for a dry joint on C177 under U6.

*Snowy screen but no picture or sound. LNB voltage O.K.*
Ensure that the tuning voltage (VT) on C134 +ve varies as frequency is changed (push channel up/down buttons while meter is connected).
If it doesn't then replace U20 (LM7001 Pace part 109-0700101).
Broken tracks near U20 or tuner can also cause this symptom.
On Hitachi tuner models, if no 9v supply on LK10, replace Q4.
If still no 9v supply on LK10 check R323 (4R7Ω fusible resistor).

Q2 (NPN) can also fail and reduce the 9 volt supply. (D11 zener should be replaced by a 470Ω resistor.) If everything else is all right, check diode D27 and transistor Q28 by substitution. Otherwise suspect faulty tuner.

*Horizontal streaks on picture:*
C21 (2200/25v), C125 (use 1000µF/16v) or other electrolytics nearby. This problem often shows up after a replacement (Sharp) tuner kit is fitted. Replace LK205 near tuner with a 100µH inductor. If streaks persist, replace C168, C183 (100µF below decoder) with 1000µF/16v (bent over).
*Lines on picture:*
Replace C134 (if not other causes).

*Picture disappears leaving only "snow" after 1 hour warm-up.*
Check U20 by applying freezer spray. If picture returns then replace U20 (LM7001). A similar fault occurs with some Sharp tuners.
Check transformer T2 pins for dry joints.

## Audio faults

*No audio at all — no hiss or hum even from SCART:*
U1 (U2829B Pace number 109-0282901).

*Hissing, popping, or crackling on audio (which might be low-level background noise or so high that it obliterates the audio — often only after a warm-up period)*
Check Q8, Q9 (BC547) and U1. Check for cracked tracks around U1. If fault remains, replace C112, a surface mount 47nF capacitor on the underside of the board. Located beneath LK17, this capacitor is near the front edge of the board. It sits next to a 103 (10kΩ) SMD resistor and may be replaced with a conventional leaded multilayer ceramic capacitor.

*Hiss only:*
SS9000 may have PAL G set instead of PAL I. See Handset Codes. X7.

*One audio channel missing, faint or noisy.*
Replace U1 (U2829B).
Replace U15, U14, U13, U12, U11, (LM324 Pace number 100-0032400) testing after each one to see if a cure has been effected.
Replace *all* 47nF capacitors beneath U1 *and* C112 (Pace 951-4735601).

The associated ceramic resonators, inductors or U1 itself might also cause the fault. If audio is drowned by a hiss replace U1, Q8, Q9. If no <u>mono</u> audio — replace C104 beneath U1.

*No audio but loud hiss or hum which alters as picture changes.*
Replace X7, U17, Q8 and Q9, testing after each one.

*No sound on a D2MAC channel but picture OK:*
Select EXT AV in decoder menu.

## Miscellaneous faults

*Picture or graphics remain on screen in STANDBY mode but LEDs & buttons work OK. Perhaps also not decoding*
Q4 or D18 faulty.

*Stuck in standby. Standby and Timer LEDs come on. No functions.*
Replace C21 and C25 (2200µF). Look for track breaks, especially around the PCB support pillar in the power supply area. Check U3 socket if fitted. Replace both U3 and the microprocessor. Replace U4 if timer LED stays on for just one minute. Ensure that the correct U3 is fitted. NUM3060 and 93C66 are *not* interchangeable.

*Stereo and Timer LEDs come on. No functions.*
Replace U20, U17, U4.

*No menu appears on screen when SELECT 1, 2 or 3 is pressed.*
*Other screen graphics are normal.* This "fault" occurs because channel "0" has been locked (Menu lock facility — see user guide). Unlock channel "0" or enter factory reset code and try again. If there are *also* no channel idents replace U9.

*After warm-up, graphics "roll" vertically.*
Check U6 (TEA2029C) with freezer aerosol. If replacement does not cure it, replace electrolytic capacitors nearby.

*When warm, the picture jumps occasionally:*
Remove C27. Solder an 82µH inductor from Q23 base to Q32 emitter.

*Wrong frequency displayed in the tuning menu:*
Receiver is set to the wrong frequency band, i.e. DBS or telecom instead of FSS. The FSS band is required for current Astra programmes.

## Decoder faults

*SS9200IRD scrambles clear channels occasionally:*
Press SETUP 1 and, in the menu select INT for AV SOURCE. On the next menu line select NONE for DECODER instead of AUTO. Press [STORE], twice.

*Not decoding. No decoder messages.*
**To decode Sky Sports & Comedy channel etc. on SS9000 IRD / SRV1 etc.**
With the appropriate channel frequency selected and stored, press SETUP 1 4 7 and, in the menu select INT for AV SOURCE. On the next menu line select INT for DECODER instead of NONE. Press store, twice. The full button sequence is:
SETUP 1 4 7 SETUP SETUP SETUP ▼ SETUP ▼ STORE STORE

Ensure decoder board is pressed down onto its connector. Check for dry joints on connector or corrosion. Spray connector with switch-cleaner and move the board up & down. If this helps the decoder board connector needs to be replaced. (Pace recommend replacing the male connector on the main board, too). Check decoder board by substitution.

*After warm-up of 30 minutes or more the decoded picture becomes increasingly sparkly (black) until colour inversion occurs.*
Apply freezer spray to U1 (TDA8703). If this cures it then U1 is at fault. Most videocrypt type decoder boards use this I.C. (not PRD---).

*After warm-up of 30 minutes or more the quality of the decoded picture becomes increasingly poor:*
U4 (74ALS541N) on the decoder board may be at fault.

*White dots on Sky channels, only with card inserted:*
Select Decoder NONE in the menu. If this cures the problem then the decoder board requires modification in that a 100pF capacitor must be added between pins 6 and 8 on U1 (TDA8703). If the capacitor is already there, then U1 may be faulty.

*Flashes "P000 T000" briefly when card is inserted:*
This is normal with a series 07 SKY card or later.

*Flashes "Please Wait" intermittently but does not decode.*
May also say "Please insert card" or give no messages at all. May decode intermittently. Try increasing the contrast to "High" in menu 2 ([SETUP] [2] [4] [7]). If this improves decoder operation then do the mod for "Faint decoder messages", below. Also, replace C21 (2200μF/25v).
If all else fails, try putting 100Ω resistor in parallel with R131 (surface mount 150Ω beneath board near VCR SCART) to increase video level. The fault may be caused by a failing tuner module.

*Faint decoder messages, grey instead of black*
• Replace R13 (0R22).
Change R92 on decoder board to 43kΩ <u>and</u> change R342 SMD beneath C171 on the main PCB to 680Ω.

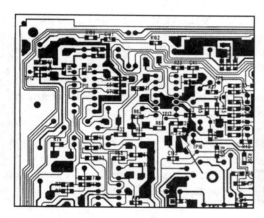

Ensure 5 volt to Micro is 5.25 volts and ripple-free on LK12. Otherwise, replace C25 2200μF/16v.

Ensure 12 volts is 12.25 v and ripple-free on LK5. (C21 2200μF/25v). On early receivers a surface mount capacitor beneath the PSU was removed. This lowers the PSU output voltages. Increase them by replacing the 0 Ohm surface mount link with 270 Ohm. (Compare the PCB with another).

*Streaky pictures:*
Replace connector on decoder board. Replace C21. Fit 1000µF for C125.
Replace all electrolytics near C21.

*No decoder messages and channel idents roll up/down the screen:*
Replace C115, C116, C120 (10µF/16v near tuner) then TEA2029C.
Otherwise check sync pulses at decoder connector, pins 6 & 7.

*Streaky decoded pictures only:*
It's caused by the gradually demise of ALL decoupling capacitors on the 12 volt rail. Upgrade C128 to
100uF. C125 to 1000uF/16v. Replace LK125 with
100uH inductor. Replace C21 (2200µF/25v low ESR).
Replace C168 and C183 (100uF beneath decoder
board) with 1000uF/16v. You have to lie them flat or
they short on the decoder board. (Order RELKIT 2).

Many picture faults
can be fixed by
using RELKIT 2.
Saves time in try-
ing to trace a fault
which is already
well known!

*"Snow" and "channels missing" with Universal LNB:*
Caused by the death of the LNB supply electrolytics. They let the PSU
oscillation go up to the LNB which switches to high band!

*Moving horizontal bands with Sharp tuner or upgraded with Sharp tuner kit:*
The speed of movement varies from almost stationary to an invisible
flutter -dependent on tuner temperature. The flutter is most noticeable
on decoder messages. Replace C120 10uF next to tuner.

*"Card Invalid" message, intermittently, when card is in for a short time:*
Scrape black spot off series 10 card (not recommended by Sky or Pace).
Also cut centre leg of Q16 (BD139) near front of decoder board. This
transistor used to be used to zap the card with 15 volts.

*Intermittent loss of sync, restored by flexing the board:*
1.5nF surface-mounted capacitor C180 cracked beneath TEA2029C.

*"No Programs Remaining" or "Card Invalid" when card is inserted:*
D11 5v6 zener. Also Q8 (BD139 NPN - base to left = 5v6, emitter near
edge of board = 5v). Also 10 way connector bad contact or 10705400 IC.

### Automatic turn-on

It is occasionally desirable, in hotel installations for
example, to have the receiver turn on by itself after
mains failure. A simple modification will do the
trick. Simply solder in the transistor and two resistors as indicated in the sketch. The transistor may be
any general purpose silicon NPN type. Its collector
is soldered to link LK49 next to the microprocessor
I.C. Its emitter goes to LK62 and its base goes via a
4k7Ω resistor to LK50 near the front edge of the
board. Finally, a 4k7Ω pull-down resistor connects
the base to 0 volts on LK62.

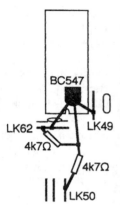

*The front panel buttons and handset no longer function* and, when the mains
is connected, the receiver selects channel 1 (which you tune to any
desired station *before* modification) and turns on.

### WARNING!
Before carrying out an installation with a receiver modified in this way,
please consider the fact that the receiver will tend to run hotter if the
mains is never turned off and care must be taken to provide adequate
ventilation and to guard against fire hazard.

## Upgrading the PACE SS9000/SS9200

The BF9 Hitachi tuner voltage measured on LK10 should be slightly less
than 9 volts. Remove zener diode D11 near the front of the board and fit
a 470Ω resistor.

The BF9 Hitachi tuner becomes very hot and degrades the electrolytic
capacitors inside. The tiny 2μ2 capacitor near one corner inside the tuner
should be replaced with a 2μ2F tantalum bead rated at 35v. Observe
polarity. The negative lead is nearest the side of the tuner. Failure of this
capacitor can cause horizontal lines across the picture.

When you replace the tuner, bare as much copper as possible on the two
pads for the tuner lugs nearest the centre of the board. Be generous with
the solder since the lugs provide continuity for the 0 volt track from the
power supply. A bad connection, here, results in the standby LED

glowing dimly and no response to button presses.

The ten pin socket on the decoder board is prone to bad connections after aging and should always be replaced with the new type which is brilliant white in colour. The reddish-brown type suffers from corrosion and deflection of contacts when hot. The early white type may suffer from flux ingress which can be seen as a yellow stain. Cleaning affords only a temporary cure if corrosion is present.

C9 (1μF) in the power supply may be dried out by the heat of R3. Replace C9 and twist R3 (large 100kΩ resistor) away from it. Failure of C9 causes several power supply components to fail.

Replace C11 (1μF) if discoloured.

Bend all other electrolytic capacitors away from hot components — especially those close to the tuner. The capacitors near the SCART sockets can become very discoloured but seldom cause a fault.
If the power supply whistles or hisses there is a faulty component which *must* be replaced before failure occurs. Several components can cause this fault, including U23, C11, D5, and the surface mount capacitors C12 (33nF) and C18 (100nF).
Whistling can also be caused by a broken copper track.
C29 should be replaced with a 100μF/35v/105°C electrolytic capacitor 148-851 from Farnell, since it tends to fail with age and will cause faint, dashed, diagonal lines to appear, especially on decoded channels.

C200 can cause lines on the picture and should be replaced with the same type as above.

C7 can deteriorate and cause a faint buzzing noise — louder when not in standby. No need to replace unless faulty.

C21 and C25 should be replaced with 2200μF/105°C electrolytic capacitors. These cause various faults.

**Many picture faults can be fixed by using RELKIT 2.**
**Saves time in trying to trace a fault which is already well known!**

# Microcontroller line-up

| Model | Micro | OSD | Notes |
|---|---|---|---|
| 9000 | 809-8621527 | NEC | NVM3060 EEPROM |
| 9000 | 809-8621529 | NEC | 93C66 EEPROM |
| STU801 60 CHANNEL | 809-8621530 | | PHILIPS GERMAN |
| STU801 60 CHANNEL | 809-8621531 | | PHILIPS UK |
| 9200 | 809-8621533 | PACE | REPLACES 809-8621532 |
| 9200 | 809-8621534 | NEC | |
| STU801 90 CHANNEL | 809-8621535 | | PHILIPS UK |
| STU801 90 CHANNEL | 809-8621536 | | PHILIPS GERMAN |

## Secret Handset Codes for Pace SS- derivatives

*To change PAL I to PAL G and vice-versa, on SS9000 only, press:*

SETUP
MUTE
NORM
STORE

STORE

This software function is *not* available on SS9200 series.

PARENTAL LOCK PIN NUMBER LOST?

*To reset PIN on 9200 and some 9000 models to 1234.*
Remove power from unit.
Hold STANDBY ▲ ▼ keys simultaneously on the front panel and
restore power.

*To reset PIN on 9000 models to 1234.*
Go into standby. Press STANDBY then STORE and hold STORE for 20
seconds. During this time the channel ident should remain in the top
RHS of the screen.

## LOST SOME CHANNELS OR SETTINGS?

### *To set factory default on all SS9xxx models.*

Press the sequence   SETUP   P   2   3   STORE   ▲   ▼
quickly but smoothly. It is a good idea first to change the frequency of
the current channel so you can observe the reset as it happens (up to
twenty seconds after the button sequence is entered).

WARNING — factory defaults on early SS9000, SRV1 etc. were incorrect
for channels 25 to 32. Be sure to change each of these channel polarities
individually.
From microprocessor ---527 onwards, the settings were correct.
Note, however, that *no* Pace receivers up to April 1994  included Astra
1C or 1D in the factory programming. Only Astra 1A and 1B are there.

### *To set factory default on Ferguson SRV1.*

Press SETUP   PROG   2   3   STORE   ▲   ▼

(The standard SS9200 or SS9000 handset may be used with the SRV1)

### Philips STU801

Based on the Pace SS9000 but has a modified microprocessor which
accepts the codes from Philips own handset. A German language microprocessor was also produced for some export units.

### *To set factory default on Philips STU801.*

Press  MENU 9   6   3   0   1   2

(If you are successful the menu will be replaced by the program picture.
If not then press [NORMAL] and enter the sequence again. You may
have to practice this several times before the procedure will work).

# Pace VC100 Videocrypt Decoder

As with all decoders, if a
fault should occur,
your first action
must be to unplug
it from the mains
power for a few minutes
then re-apply power.

Never stack a decoder and receiver on top of each other. Always separate them by a shelf which is open front and back or put them in a cabinet which has a fan. Overheating is a major cause of failure.

*Intermittent decoding on warm-up. Failure when hot. Will not decode:*
Replace C2 at the rear of the lower board. Original board marking is
incorrect and the + leg should be at the left when viewed from the front
panel. This modification was introduced into production units with
board number ending in 104. Also suspect C3, C4 (100µF).

*No messages. Pin 8 on SCART low all the time:*
If voltage on Q15 is low or 0v then replace U1.

*Horizontal & diagonal banding on normal channels and vertical rolling on
encrypted channels:*
Replace Q503. Look for track break between pins 12 and 14 of T501.

*After warm-up the decoded picture becomes increasingly grainy until decoder
no longer works:*
Upgrade R523 (8k2) to 6k2Ω to reduce the 5 volt rail voltage.
Note: R58 (4k3Ω) should be upgraded to 4k7Ω.

*To reset VCO when unit is warmed up:*
Press [MENU] , [TEXT], [TEXT] then hold both [MENU] and [TEXT]
until the Service Menu appears on screen. Press [+] or [-] until the
scrambled picture is almost stationary (not moving left or right).
Hold [MENU] to store the new setting.

*Dead:*   See SS9200 PSU faults. Check C527.

# MRD920

*To reset PIN on MRD920 to 1234.*
Remove power from unit.
Hold STANDBY key and restore power.

*To set factory default on MRD920.*
Press MENU P STORE > <

*MRD920 will not lock on to Mac channels:*
Replace U8 (SP4633) *not easy!!*
R257 missing
Many other causes...

MRD920 no audio:
U12D

*MRD920 gives no card messages. Will not decode and, when warm, gives blank screen on Mac channels:*
Replace U8 and U9 on decoder board. Press MENU 3 2 7 6 5 then
❭ and ❬ until scrambled picture stops moving. Press STORE.

*MRD920 radio channels missing or slow to react to buttons.*
Fit later decoder software version. Compatible microprocessor may be needed, too.

*Polariser current changes from negative to positive with no adjustment between:* Replace U3 (TLC272) on polariser board.

MRD920 with Eprom version 807-2201004 (latest)*To set VCO Press:*

Menu
3 (Install)
2 (Mac Install)
7
6
5
Then press left or right buttons until picture is almost stationary.
Press Store

*Blank screen through decoder*
U8D, U13, Tuner

*Vertical coloured lines across D2MAC picture*
U19 (HEF4066BT) and U14 (Sony RGB encoder CXA1145M) Pace part number 109-0114501.

*No D2MAC Audio*
U12D

*Message says "Please Insert Card":*
With the card inserted, the audio appears, but the picture remains scrambled, after 4-6 seconds the message "Check the Card" appears. Sound goes muted.
CCU3000 or NVRAM NUM3060

*Various symptoms can be cured by fitting **RELKIT 5***
which includes the following parts (and others):

| | |
|---|---|
| C29, C200, | 100μF/35v |
| C21 | 2200μF/25v |
| C25 | 2200μF/16v |
| C33 | 1000μF/25v |
| C37 | 1000μF/16v |
| C176 | 4μ7F/50v |
| C183 | 1000μF/16v |
| C168 | 1000μF/16v |
| C125 | 1000μF/16v |
| C128 | 100μF/35v |
| C120, C115, C116 | 10μF/35v |

Decoder Board

| | |
|---|---|
| C25,27,52 | 22μF/35v |
| C30 | 10μF/35v |
| C42,58,65 | 100μF/25v |

# MRD95O

*The following modification enables J17 de-emphasis to operate:*
(1) Remove link 89 on the main PCB.
(2) Fit a wire link (100 x 0.5mm insulated) from the solder pad for link 89 farthest from the edge of the main PCB to pin 3 of PL1 on the underside of the MAC PCB. Secure the wire link with a spot of silicone adhesive at each end.
(3) Change U4 on the Z8 microcontroller board to version 2, part no. 805-0950101.

*Poor MAC audio when warm*
U8D

*Poor Mac picture quality*
Capacitor on MAC board no. C72 was low in value. Also replace capacitors in power supply.

# MRD960

*Audio slow to come on and bit error rate too high:*
Replace two 22μF electrolytics on the Mac board and all power supply electrolytics.

*"Check Card" with card in*
Q58D missing

Various symptoms can be cured by fitting **RELKIT 7**.

# MSP Positioner

*To set factory default on MSP990 positioner.*
Press     NORMAL   P   STORE   STATUS
NOTE: All positions and limit settings will be lost!

*Latest microcontroller part numbers:*

MSP990   809-8621701
MSP991   809-8621706
MSP995   809-8621707

## Positioner Problems

*When PRD goes into standby the positioner goes to P1:*
Fit later revision Eprom U4 to positioner, part number 805-00105 or later.

*MSP990 loses memory intermittently:*
Fit 33R/5W between links LK24 + LK25.
Use only proper motorised ribbon cable and connect screens to 0v only at the receiver end (not at the dish).

*MSP991/995 errors in dish position due to mains interference:*
*Also intermittent, random movement of actuator:*
Remove links LK21 and LK36. In place of LK36 fit 330pF/100v/10% ceramic capacitor (150-3317651). In place of LK21 fit an inductor 100uH/10%/1R8 dc resistance (130-1000611). In place of R1 (10k) fit 100k/0.25W/5% carbon film resistor. Across R1 solder a 1N4148 diode with its cathode band furthest from SK1. Fit a 4n7F, 10 per cent, 100V 5mm ceramic capacitor (150-4727651) between pins 5 & 11 of U1.

MSP995:-The software has been upgraded to Provide compatibility with photo-interrupter type actuators that produce fourteen pulses per rotation. To carry out the modification replace processor U1 8621 with the later version part no. 809-8621707.

*Satellite position number doubles:*
A compatibility problem may occur occasionally between Enhanced PRD **receivers** with boards marked 182-0190203 and dish positioners.

The D.C. level on the data line (pin 12 of decoder Scart) **in the receiver** may need to be increased by adding a 2k2 resistor from the inductor, L14, to D98 cathode.

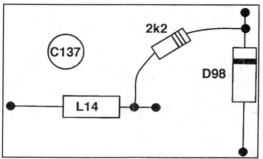

Note that count problems can also occur if the cable is not screened or if the screening is not correctly grounded. The screen around the motor pair should be connected to the ground terminal at the positioner (but not connected at the dish end). The screen around the pulse pair should also be grounded at the positioner but not at the dish.

*MSP995 err when E or W pressed:*
D3, D4 protection diodes.

If a Pace MSP995 positioner is reported to suffer the problem of constantly lit segments on the LCD, then replace U3 (74HC244) on the main board

# PACE 800/900

PRD800IRD
Maspro SRE250S/1
Philips STU802/05M
Philips STU812/05M
Ferguson SRD5
Goodmans ST700
Granada M/N92MR1/A
Mitsubishi ST-PB10
Hitachi SR1050D
Thorn SAT99

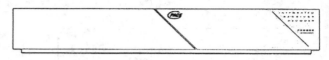

PRD900IRD
Nokia SAT1600
Grundig STR1 IRD
Maspro SRE350S/1
Philips STU-824
Ferguson SRD16
Panasonic TU-SD200
Panasonic TU-SD250 (=PRD900 plus)

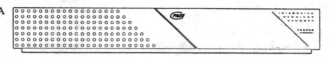

PSR800
Manhattan 850

In the **part code**, the third digit 7=1.75GHz and 8=2GHz.
The last digit 0=standard and 1=Enhanced software.

PSR900
Manhattan 950

DATE CODES

Look at the first four numbers after the Manufacturer's letter code in the **serial number** which is printed twice on the label underneath the receiver.

The first number represents the last digit of the year of manufacture.
The second and third represent the week of manufacture starting from January.
The fourth number represents the day of the week.

RAAYAI3245000123

1993    week 24
(mid June)

# Frequently Asked Questions - Pace PRD800/900

1. Why did my power supply fail?
2. How do I repair the power supply?
3. Why is the audio distorted on foreign stations?
4. Can I get extra channels?
5. Can I use an "Enhanced" LNB?
6. Can I upgrade to "Enhanced" menu software?
7. Can I upgrade my PRD800 to a twin input PRD900?
8. Are there any "secret" handset codes?
9. I get only a blue screen. What has happened?
10. Can I use a "Universal" LNB?
11. How can I tell how old my receiver is?
12. How can I download the memory?
13. Why do I get no decoder messages on screen?
14. Why do I get intermittent "Card Invalid" message?
15. Why does my receiver turn itself ON when I plug it in?
16. Why won't my receiver go to a single-digit channel?
17. Why does the display show an upside-down "F"?

## 1. Why did my power supply fail?

In very early versions R8 was 0.75 Ohm and sometimes caused failure at plug-in. It was upgraded to 1 Ohm fusible.
In some early versions, the mains input socket was often under stress and would pull its pins out of the solder pads, causing arcing.
The capacitors C5, C7 and C8 were prone to failure when the receiver became too hot.

## 2. How do I repair the power supply?

If the fuse has NOT melted, try replacing C5 (22µF), C7, C8 (10µF) with 105°C low ESR electrolytics. Observe polarity and be extremely careful when soldering/desoldering. The copper tracks and pads are very fragile. Use fine "solder wick" – DO NOT use a pump-action desolder tool! Ensure normal safety precautions.
If the fuse *has* melted, you will need the complete kit of parts.

Remember, these are classed as "Safety Critical" components. You MUST use the Pace-approved parts.

### 3. Why is the audio distorted on foreign stations?

The PRD receivers have narrow audio bandwidth for Astra channels. Only the later PRD-plus versions have wideband and J17 audio choices. The early one CAN be upgraded but it's a workshop job since over a dozen surface mount components must be added, as well as conventional components. A kit with instructions is available from SatCure, however, if you really want to do it yourself.

### 4. Can I get extra channels?

The PRD800 has 120 channels and can easily be upgraded to 199. Just one I.C. and one resistor are needed. The following functions are also activated:

1. Favourite channels
2. Colour choice selection
3. Radio blanking option

Kit with instructions is available from SatCure. Both PRD800 and PRD900 can be upgraded to 250 channels but this is a workshop job.

### 5. Can I use an "Enhanced" LNB?

Yes, usually. The early PRD receivers had a "75G" tuner but most of these will work almost to 2GHz. Remove the "224" surface mount resistor next to the tuner solder lugs and replace it with a "474" (470k) resistor. The later receivers were fitted with a "77G" tuner which is designed to work up to 2GHz. These receivers have "2GHz" printed on the serial number label, underneath. Some receivers do not have this 2GHz label but they DO have a "77G" tuner. Make sure that a "684" (680k) resistor is fitted if it won't tune up.

You will need to tune EVERY channel frequency higher by 250 in order to receive the signals from an "Enhanced" LNB unless you have Enhanced software.

## 6. Can I upgrade to "Enhanced" menu software?

Yes. A kit is available from SatCure and includes a new microcontroller with instructions. However, if you have a very early receiver with an Eprom board fitted upside down on plastic pillars, the Eprom can be changed for one with the "Enhanced" software. The "Enhanced" menu gives you a choice of LNB frequencies so you can choose "Standard", "Enhanced" or "Telecom". There are also other features such as different colour backgrounds. Enhanced Eprom is available.

## 7. Can I upgrade my PRD800 to a twin input PRD900?

Yes, it's possible, but most PRD800 receivers will need to have at least 30 surface mount components fitted, as well as conventional components (Q60, Q61 etc.) and an expensive two-input tuner. A few PRD800 receivers already had all the surface mount components fitted but the only way to find out is to look under the board; and you still need an expensive tuner.
Unless you have a dead PRD900 to rob parts from, it's not feasible.

## 8. Are there any "secret" handset codes?

Yes. The "factory reset" will set the first 32 channels to Astra 1A and 1B channels. Early micros will then repeat these channels up to the limit of 120 or 199. If you are happy to lose your customised settings, press:
Menu, P, Store, Right arrow, Left arrow.
You will see "-E2" in the display for a few seconds.
If the reset does not work, you probably have a faulty EEprom.
On the later PRD-Plus versions the "P" key has no function so press:
Menu, 0, Store, Right arrow, Left arrow.
BEWARE! on "PLUS" receivers with a microcontroller number ending with "027" this will reset your receiver to just 99 channels! You will then have to order a new, preprogrammed EEprom or a later microcontroller in order to correct it, or use the "PaceLink" computer system (read on).

## 9. I get only a blue screen. What has happened?

The blue screen appears if there is no signal.
The most obvious cause is that your LNB is not connected or, on a twin-input receiver, is connected to the wrong input.

Sometimes R543 near the tuner (1 Ohm in twin input receivers) has burned out because you short-circuited the input. There are many more faults which will cause this symptom. Make sure LNB power is ON in the installation menu. If you get power when input 2 is selected but not input 1 then Q61 (FXT749) may be o/c. To remove the blue screen while looking at weak signals press "F" then "Store". Press the same sequence to reinstate the blue screen. For low threshold models press the button marked with a rectangle and a "+".

**10. Can I use a "Universal" LNB?**

A "Universal" LNB will work exactly the same as an "Enhanced" LNB unless your receiver incorporates 22kHz tone switching to access "High Band" frequencies. The 22kHz tone switches the LNB internal oscillator from 9.75 GHz to 10.6 GHz. PRD receivers do not incorporate this feature but it CAN be added. A kit is available from SatCure. But first consider why you want to use a Universal LNB. What do you expect to receive on High Band? Or do you want the tone switch in order to utilise an external switcher box?

**11. How can I tell how old my receiver is?**

The date of manufacture is incorporated in the serial number.
For example:  RAAYAH3245xxxxx
The "3" indicates 1993
The "24" indicates week 24 counting from first week in January.
The "5" indicates Friday.

**12. How can I download the memory?**

You connect a fully wired Scart to Scart cable between the Decoder sockets of identical PRD receivers then follow the on-screen instructions from the Installation menu. You can not download successfully from dissimilar receivers and, to be certain, you should use this transfer facility only between receivers which have identical microcontroller ICs (U2). If you are going to program a large number of receivers, try Kesh Electrics in County Fermanagh (013656 31449). They have designed a PC Windows program and interface to do this. It costs about 200 pounds. Unfortunately they have not designed a Macintosh version.

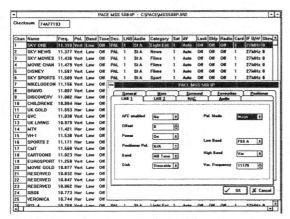

The PaceLink customisation screen.

You can upload and download PRD and MSS receiver memory settings, storing the file on disc and using the PaceLink program to manipulate the channel settings until you get them exactly as you require.

### 13. Why do I get no decoder messages on screen?

Try setting the contrast higher in the Installation menu.
If this doesn't work, and you have checked the tuning, you probably have a fault in the decoder section.

### 14. Why do I get intermittent "Card Invalid" message?

The series 10 SKY card seems prone to this on certain receivers.
Make sure that the card contacts are clean and the card slot spring contacts are clean and not bent or twisted.

### 15. Why does my receiver turn itself ON when I plug it in?

This is a feature provided for use with systems in hotels and similar establishments. If power fails the receiver always awakes on a specific channel when power returns. To turn the feature on or off, press:

[F] then [Recall] then [P] then the channel number and [Store].

### 16. Why won't my receiver go to a single digit channel?

The incorrect "P" mode has been stored. If you want the receiver to require a double-digit channel number ("01", "02", "46" etc.) then press the "P" key until you see two dashes in the display and press [store]. If you want it to respond to single digits press "P" until you see just one dash in the display and press [store].
Note: "Plus" versions do not use the "P" button but rely on a delay instead.

### 18. Why does the display show an upside-down "F"?

Your receiver is set for a timed event. To cancel press [F] then [standby].

# Pace PRD800/PRD900

**Power Supply Problems**

To reduce the possibility of power supply failure, caused by overheating when the receiver is installed with inadequate regard to cooling, the following modifications should be made:

Replace C5 (22µF), C7 and C8 (10µF/50v/105°C radial electrolytic capacitors). Ensure that these capacitors are away from Q1 before soldering in position. Observe correct polarity. Ensure that Q1 is upright.
Later units used a fast-blow fuse and different resistors. It is advisable to upgrade any power supply, received for repair, as follows:
Replace FS1 with a F1A fuse. Put a label "F1A" over the rating "T1A".
Replace R1 with a non-spiral 10Ω/2W. (Pace 143-1007621)
Replace R8 with a non-spiral 1Ω/1W. (Pace 143-0106521) or 1Ω fusible.

Pace recommend:
After failure of the power supply, the value of C2 should be checked. The simplest method of determining whether it should be replaced is to check the rectified mains voltage across it. This should be in excess of 330V D.C. (N.B. this is dependent on the mains input voltage). If it is less, the capacitor should be changed. A safer way is to measure the ESR of C2 which should be 3Ω or less. The integrity of C3 and C4 should be checked also. A reliability kit RELKIT 1 is available from SatCure.

The long-term reliability can be improved by changing the following resistors to increase the base drive to the power switching transistor, if it is a BUL 54 AR, since this transistor has a wide gain spread.
R6 from 15R to 8.2R, 0.25W     (Pace part number 140-0822501)
R15 from 68R to 33R, 0.25W     (Pace part number 140-3302501)

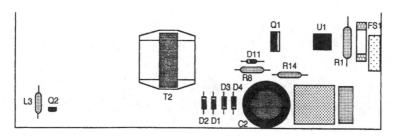

*Receiver dead. No display or function whatsoever:*
Ensure that mains socket pins are soldered beneath the PCB.
Replace C5, C7 and C8 then apply mains ONLY if the fuse is intact.
If the fuse has melted, replace it and fit the capacitors then:-
Measure R8 and R14 and replace if open-circuit.
Measure D1 - D4. If any is short circuit, replace it and measure again.
If D1 now measures low in both directions, replace Q1.
Measure D11. If it is short circuit replace both it and D10.
Measure D10. If its forward voltage is less than 0.5 volts replace U1 then
measure D10 again. Finally, check R17 (4R7), the 220Ω SMD and C2.

If power supply is working except that the 5 volt secondary supply is
low, check C15 (2200µF/25v) for open circuit connection.
Too high—replace C5 and C4 (1n2 SMD). If still too high, reduce the
value of the resistor which is in parallel with the 2k0 surface mount
resistor. Normally, this "trimming" resistor is 22k but it may need to be
15k or 10k to compensate for poor tolerance of the 2k0 resistor. You may
then need replace D17 with a wire link to increase the LNB supply voltage to 13v for vertical polarisation.

*Power supply clicks and LED flashes.*
There may be a short circuit on LNB cable. If 5v is swinging to 7 volts,
replace C4 (1n2 SMD near U1). Otherwise, R129 SMD 220Ω o/c. R15
(68R) o/c. C87 next to tuner shorting to 0v; s/c on 5v rail; Broken track
L57 - R534. Q11 =BFR193 SMD transistor under RF modulator screen.

*PSU fails after 1/2 hour and Q1 gets very hot:*
Replace C4 SMD 1n2. Replace C2. Also, low gain Q1 can cause this.
Also o/c R129 SMD 220Ω across Q1.

*Power supply whistles.*
Faulty U1, D10, D9, D8, C5, C7, or C8 and check R2 and D13 for dry
joint.

*PSU hisses/buzzes:*
C2 (47µF)

*Switches to standby after a few minutes:*
C5 (22µF) transposed with C7 or C8 (10µF) or o/c R129 SMD 220Ω.

PRD800/900+
*Power supply blows up:*
If not any of the above, replace C2 (47µF/400v capacitor "LCC" type).

PRD800/900+
*Whistles but will not light up:*
Red wire beneath board not soldered.

PRD800/900+
*PSU will not start up or slow to start up:*
Ensure R2 is 47k in series with another 47k.

*PSU blows up R14 etc. after fitting kit:*
Ensure that R2 is 100kΩ NOT 10Ω. Check D10, D11 orientation and measure them. Replace C2 (47µF/400v). Measure R17 4R7. Look for broken tracks, especially to 10µF capacitors.

**Picture Problems - Interference.**

Pace instituted a number of upgrades on later models. I've translated these into practical solutions which may usefully be implemented on all models in order to reduce interference on pictures:
C87    left of tuner. Increase to 1000µF/16v
C110   front left of tuner. Increase to 1000µF/16v
C23    front right corner. Increase to 2200µF/25v
C11    in front of transformer. Increase to 220µF (can cause lines on RF - not Scart - or lines may disappear when Sky card is removed).
C16    left of transformer. Increase to 100µF/35v
C324 (not fitted to later models) left of transformer. Increase to 100µF/35v
L3     front right corner. Increase to 100µH DC res < 0.48 Ohms
L31    front of tuner. Increase to 100µH DC res < 0.48 Ohms
In addition replace:
C278   2200µF/16v
C15    2200µF/25v
C21    2200µF/25v (dashed lines on all UHF channels & pic only from decoder scart)
All capacitors should be rated at 105'C
A kit is available from SatCure (RELKIT 1).

*Soft edged white horizontal lines 1cm apart (varies). Will not decode. Picture sometimes loses lock and looks like Nagravision scrambling:*
(No lines on picture from decoder scart. Sometimes happens only when hot). Replace C207, U18, U25. Possible faulty tuner. On revision A3 and A5 boards, C207 (near U18) should be fitted the "wrong" way round. Symptom also caused by L56 short-circuit (near U18).

*Horizontal streaks follow highlights in picture (RF only - Scart OK):*
C540 1µF/50v inside RF mod can.

*Picture problems with Sony TV or VCR:*
At the PRD end of the VCR Scart lead, add a 180R resistor in the wire from pin 19. At the TV end of the TV Scart lead cut the wire from pin 19.
*Interference on Tatung TV connected via SCART:*
Cut wire to pin 19 inside SCART plug at TV end.
Be sure to label the plugs accordingly.

*Interference on recorded pics with Sony SLV-373 VCR:*
Replace R431 [270] SM resistor near VCR SCART with 47R. Cut track between this resistor and Scart pin 20. Bridge cut track with 27R.

*Diagonal, dashed lines swirling across picture:*
Replace C15, C21 (2200µF/25v), C13, and C23 (1000µF/25v) in the psu. Inductor L3 may be s/c. Test by shorting it out. If no change, it is s/c.

*Severe streaks on Sky pictures:*
C99 10µF next to U9 "Nicky" I.C. or U22 (rare).

*Sparkle patterning on bright colours, especially cartoons:*
Replace U20 (SP973T8 eight bit A-D convertor).

Tracing "streaky picture" faults can be time-consuming. Save time by fitting RELKIT 1 which contains all the electrolytics you are likely to need.

*Weak picture with patterning and dark diagonal lines:*
(Picture OK from SCART socket). Look for a component lead bent and shorting to a track beneath modulator. Possibly Q105 on version xxx4.

*Shadowy horizontal bars move up picture:*
(PSU voltages may also be too high) Replace C5.

*Picture appears on "venetian blind" type horizontal bars.*
Problem usually appears at switch-on and disappears if the receiver is

unplugged from, then reconnected to, the mains.
Early receivers (1992), fit an 82µH axial leaded choke in parallel with R306, beneath the board. Solder one end of the inductor to the X7 resonator pin nearest the edge of the board and the other end of the inductor to pin 19 of U23 which is 0 volts. Later variants include this choke.

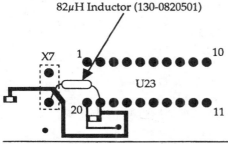

Front edge of PCB

*Interference on picture from UHF modulator, especially on TV chan. 25.*
Disconnect track beneath the PCB from the earth screw point on early receivers. Replace all RF leads with double-screened leads and plugs. Patterning on some terrestrial TV channels can be caused by harmonics radiated by the 14Mhz Videocrypt clock. Fitting good-quality r.f. leads should cure this. If necessary the following modifications can be carried out:
Fit a Gold air-wound 200mH coil in place of the wire link at L52.
Fit a Gold air-wound 200mH coil in place of the 100 ohm resistor at L53.
Remove C250 (surface-mounted type). Change C340 to 27pF (surface mounted). Fit a 27pF surface-mounted capacitor in position C341.
A further reduction in the level of interference can be achieved by earthing the u.h.f. modulator's can to the receiver's chassis. This can be done by soldering braid to the can and trapping it between the can and the rear metal-work - with some receivers it may be necessary to scrape paint from the inside of the back panel to achieve good electrical connection. Later versions have a screw.

*Low video level. Maybe no contrast menu visible. No decoder messages:*
Replace C99. Q100 FET. Other causes, too.

*Rows of strange characters or dots flashing on the picture in a rectangle:*
Replace graphics I.C. U10 (M50555).

*Satellite picture rolls.*
Renew C207 and, on revision A3 and A5 boards, fit it the opposite way round to combat reverse biassing.

*White, dashed lines swirling around picture on horiz chans only:*
L3 short circuit (front RH corner). Test by shorting it out.

*"Wavy pictures":*
Rear tuner lugs not soldered.

*Interference on picture Eurosport and German channels:*
(disappears if audio mode 50μS selected)
Add 2k2 resistor in series with C55 rear left corner of board.

*Tuner drifts off frequency. Pressing buttons may produce picture:*
Tuner. (Factory reset may cure symptom temporarily).

*Sparklies on all channels:*
Tuner (assuming LNB, dish etc. are OK).

*Vertical bar scans from right to left:*
Especially noticeable on blank radio screen. Replace C96 next to tuner with 1μF low-leakage multilayer ceramic capacitor. 157-1055751. (With receiver tuned to 10.950, C96 can be reverse biassed). Another possible cause is the FET, Q15.

Replacing C96 can often destroy Q15 because of static electricity or from voltage remaining in the circuit. Be prepared for "no pictures" after replacing C96. You may have to replace Q15 as well!

*Dark Vertical band moving from L to R across screen ( like a hum bar but flowing horizontally ) Picture is fine but graphics when superimposed on picture are distorted, when superimposed on blue screen are o.k.:*
Replace the FET Q15

*Pics OK from Scart but UHF output can't be tuned in:*
Nicky chip

*UHF output stuck on channel 20 and the tuning stuck at lowest frequency:*
Look for supply track broken next to C11.

**Picture Problems - Blank Screen, Blue Screen.**

*Blank screen and no LNB voltage:*
REG1 or no connection from D14 to REG1.

*Blank screen from RF output. Audio OK. Picture OK from Scart:*
L7 or broken 5 volt track to modulator. Q105 BC546B. (many other causes, too).
After date XXXXXX345100000 (board revision ends in 4 and underside has component designations in white):
Remove R559 [331] emitter resistor and replace Q105 (BC546B).

*No picture from RF socket or no input from TV aerial:*
The sockets can become bent or damaged by rough handling. Lift the top of the modulator screen and secure the 4 socket lugs by soldering.
Push the centre connector of the TV aerial socket into place then quickly run solder down the *outside* of the centre connector to secure it. Later sockets are modified to eliminate this problem. Also check for cracked 5v track next to PCB support pillar and near D78 in front of modulator.

*No pictures. Tuning Voltage, VT, stuck at minimum on C96 + leg:*
Reg1 or Q15 s/c or C97.

*No pictures or only one channel. VT stuck at maximum:*
Q15 o/c or broken tracks to Q15 or C97.

*Picture disappears when warm: (sound may be OK).*
REG1, U9 or tuner or any 10µF capacitor shorting to copper near U9.

*Intermittent blank screen.*
Replace Q49. Q105 (affects RF only) can also cause intermittent lines.

*Blue screen after warm-up on **all** channels".*
Capacitors C98, C99, C109, C544 near to tuner may have bent legs which touch the copper on top of the P.C.B. in early versions (1992).
Desolder each capacitor and twist away the copper with a drill bit.
Q96 can cause loss of video & audio. Q98 does not cause loss of audio.
Also look for dry joints on tuner pins. Check REG1

*Blue screen after warm-up on **some** channels.*
Suspect tuner fault, U9 ("Nicky I.C.") or channel tuning incorrect.
Also check value of R543 (1Ω near tuner). If the LNB or cable suffers a partial short circuit, this resistor can go high resistance (maybe as much as 50Ω) and the effect is to reduce the LNB supply voltage so some channels go very sparkly or disappear. You may even lose all Horizontal channels. Always check installation before re-fitting receiver if R543 is damaged.

*Blue screen all the time.*
Same causes as above but may also be Q100 surface mount transistor or U2 pin 31 to SK5 pin 8 short circuit.

**Menu Problems**

*Menu is not displayed. No channel identification.*
Check for dry joint on U2 (usually pin 40). Check for broken track between X2 and U10. Try pressing [F] [STORE].

*Wrong frequency displayed in the tuning menu:*
Receiver is set to the wrong frequency band, i.e. DBS or telecom instead of FSS A or FSS B. The FSS band is required for current Astra programmes.

*Interference on picture when "MENU" selected:*
Replace X2 (17.73447 MHz crystal) with the later type and change the two SMD capacitors C126 and C127, connected to X2, from 56pF to 12pF. Replace C196 100µF with 1000µF near the rear of the board. Note: with this fault, selection of the tuning menu (e.g. MENU 4 1) is still possible and individual channel identification graphics remain unaffected.

*Menus displayed displaced about 25mm to the left with a black bar to the right:*
(Scoping comp sync in on p30 to the graphics chip ch 1 and pin 12 vid out ch2 when menus selected shows that the graphics sync is running free). Replace U10, M50555 graphics generator.

## LNB Voltage Problems

### No horizontal channels
*No 17 volts only 13 volts:*
Broken track to U3 pin 16. Check Q2 (FXT749) at front right corner of PCB. Alternatively, R543 (1Ω near tuner) has gone high resistance because of momentary short circuit of LNB or cable.
Or dry joint C23

### No vertical channels
*No 13 volts:*
D16, Q2. Check Q2 (FXT749) at front right corner of PCB.

*Blue screen. LNB voltage only 5 volts:*
C21 2200µF/25v; R543 high resistance.

*Only one polarisation:*
Dry joint R28; R543 high resistance.
If the receiver will not switch polarity and has a number immediately preceding the H or V symbol while trying to alter the polarity using the right and left arrow keys in the programme set-up menu - for example "1V", you should check for dry joints on the IR receiver can, and that pin 20 of U2 is held low by R52 (47K) to ground and is not floating. After checking and repairing, it will be necessary to carry out a factory reset with the remote control. If this fails, replace the EEprom.

*"Blue screen" . No LNB voltage:*
On a <u>dual input</u> receiver: Ensure LNB is connected to the correct input. Also, select LNB1 for POWER ON in installation menu screen.
Check Q60 and Q61. If this does not cure the fault, or if only single LNB input, check carefully for cracked tracks at – and around – tuner securing lugs. Check Q2, L3 (18µH near Q2), R543 (1Ω near tuner) and replace if open circuit. Check 1k5Ω resistor fitted in C28 position.

*No H or V switching. Numbers appear next to "H" or "V":*
EEprom memory corrupted. Try factory reset or. Replace EEprom if reset unsuccessful. Check Infrared sensor pins for bad solder joint.

*LNB voltage out of tolerance:*
Replace R12 (9k1Ω 5%) with 9k1Ω 1% resistor.

## Front Panel Problems and odd effects

*Some segments of display not lighting:*
Resolder joints on LED display. Replace display. Check for track breaks where the µP board pins are soldered to the main board. Check orientation of option diodes on *early* µP daughter board. Replace U2 micro. Replace U4. Dry joints on U4, U5, U2 or broken tracks to U4 or to micro.

*"-E2" permanently on LED display:*
Micro U2

*"888" in display when hot:*
Micro U2

Many strange effects can be caused by memory corruption. Try factory reset. Replace U4 (EEprom). Check infrared sensor for bad solder joints. Check power supply output voltages are free from ripple (replace low ESR capacitors if high frequency ripple is present).

*PRD "Plus" has only 99 channels after factory reset:*
Download from an identical receiver or replace 809-8661027 microprocessor with 809-8661029 or use "PaceLink" system to reprogram.

*Will not respond to remote when warm:*
Check IR sensor for dry joints. Replace X1 4.00MHz crystal

*Responds incorrectly to handset buttons (handset checked O.K.)*
Resolder joints on I.R. sensor. Replace U2 and U4.

*Will not respond to handset correctly - needs double digits:*
press "P" until a single dash appears then STORE

*Will not respond to front panel buttons. Picture from Decoder Scart only.*
*Incorrect response to handset buttons. No 5v to L24:*
Look for broken track. U2 and C2 may cause similar fault.

*Erratic behaviour on start-up. Maybe stuck in standby or wrong options such as no LED display or PRD800 thinks it is a PRD900.*
Replace U2 microprocessor. Fit latest type (refer to end of chapter notes).

*Erratic behaviour when warm.*
(For example: virtually no audio; will not respond to button press; no LED display. Very early receivers with pre- 809-8661004 micro can suffer from loss of channel or tuning memory). Replace U2 microprocessor. X1 crystal can also cause problems. EEprom U4.

**If PRD800 EEprom is faulty, why not take the opportunity to upgrade to 199 channels and get coloured menu background, favourite channels, on-screen channel names, 8 timer events?**

PSR800 (& derivatives)
*After a couple of minutes the picture quality degrades badly.*
*The unit stops responding to the remote control.*
*The +5V rail slowly drops to 3.5V.*
*The diode (D13 in PSR!) goes VERY hot.*
Small SMD capacitor fitted in parallel to the diode is missing/broken.

*Rapid channel change causes receiver to switch off momentarily:*
Check 220Ω surface mount resistor across Q1 in the power supply.

*PRDxxx+ channel order wrong + AFC very slow:*
Tuner + upgrade U2

*Models with later Pace tuner do not display tuning menu if there's no signal:*
This is normal. Press the [+] button to give a blue background.

*Menu and channel names distorted when warm:*    U20

**Tuning Problems**

*Will not tune below 950MHz:*
Although the 020 micro displays a wide tuning range, the Sharp tuner may not tune lower than 950MHz. This is normal.

*Some channels can not reliably be tuned:*
Faulty tuner, Nicky chip or associated component.

*Tuning drifts but hovers near lowest frequency:*
Look for cracked 30v track feeding R130.

*Will not tune as high as it should:*
Faulty Nicky chip, 75G tuner or incorrect tuning limit resistor.

*Channels missing. Remaining channels 850MHz too low:*
Power supply capacitors - PSU interference switches LNB to Hi band.

## Audio Problems

*Whining noise. Possible rumbling in blank screen mode:*
Replace C278 (2200µF/16v/105°C). Solder a 4Ω7 resistor in series with
L29 in the power supply section (stand them on end). If noise persists,
add the surface mount resistor as shown in the sketch.

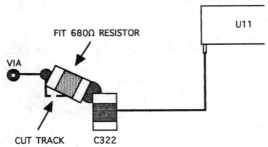

*Distorted audio on Telecom channels, Italian and Greek channels.*
The PRD800 and 900 can be upgraded to include the hardware for
menu-selectable wideband audio and J17 or 50µS de-emphasis.

*High pitch (12.5kHz) whistle from left or right channel:*
Replace U11 and U5.

*Loud background hiss on non-Astra channels:*
Channels on Eutelsat, Intelsat, etc. are usually mono. Select MONO
instead of STEREO in the audio menu and tune the audio frequency as
appropriate.

*Low audio on PSR... mono1/J17/50µS:*
Change SM resistors R256 from 4k7 to 2k7 and R442 from 10k to 18k.

*No audio from RF connector when used with European televisions.*
The PRDxxx can be converted to PAL G audio. Simply lift the screening
can off the UHF modulator section and turn the only adjuster clockwise.
Later screening cans have a hole provided. Alternatively, connect the
receiver directly to the television via the TV SCART socket. To convert
the PSR export version from PAL G to PAL I it is necessary to unscrew
the adjuster. There is often not sufficient adjustment and an audible
buzz remains even with the adjuster removed. In this case, insert a tiny
bead of aluminium foil and wax in position or change the value of the
coil padder capacitor beneath the board from 180pF to 150pF.

*"Hissing" or distorted audio, esp. on German channels:*
U11 can cause this fault and check for a broken track to X5. If faulty from new, cut track to pin 20 of VCR Scart and add 27k across cut. Change R431 (75Ω) to 47Ω. Add R426 and R423.

*Distortion of audio peaks on some channels:*
Replace R185, R186 (zero ohm links in series with ceramic filters) with 330R resistors. If no better, replace all ceramic filters (matched set).

*Distorted audio:*
D40, X1, U11

*No audio at all from RF output (O.K. from Scart):*
Check track which connects U15 pin 1 to C541 +ve. This track runs round the outside of the board, beneath the Scart sockets, and close to the corner of the UHF modulator screen. It may be shorted to the screen or may be open-circuit.

*No audio just noise:*
Broken track X5 - U11 or modulator core adjustment (check SCART audio).

**Decoder Problems**

*Not decoding. No decoder messages:*
Check contrast level in Installation menu. Set to 4.
Ground test pin TST2 at the centre of the board. This forces video to go through the decoder. If the picture disappears, check that the 5 volt supply is reaching U28 pin 4 via L24. If not, link RH end of L20 (5v) to rear end of L24. Check solder joints of inductor L20 near the front of the board and look for track breaks there. If all dc voltages are correct, check for horizontal sync pulses which should come from Q103 collector (conventional leaded transistor near card reader) and feed to U25 pin 7 and to U27 pin 10. If sync pulses are present and of the correct shape and amplitude then U20 or U29 may be faulty.
If none of the above then:
U19 pin 9 should be at 12v for picture to route through decoder. If it remains low, replace Q30. If you then get a blank screen through decoder, replace Q99 (BC546B) and U20 if necessary.
Look for a broken track between U27 and U25.

U20 and/or U21 may be faulty. D70 or D76 may be faulty.
Check Q3 for dry joint. U8, U25, U22 may be faulty.
(Heck, these decoder faults are tricky!)

*No picture through decoder (Picture appears during channel change):*
U25

*Blank screen on encrypted channels OR inverted colours and colour distortion:*
(Putting 820R across D76 improves the picture)
Line memory chip faulty - U22 or U23.

*Decoded picture gradually scrambles from bottom to top of screen:*
5 volts too low. Replace C25

*Intermittent "Card Invalid" message:*
Dry joint Q42, D55, D54, D53, D52 or leaky diodes. Dry joint on SMD ICs
near card slot. Dirty card slot contacts. Power supply voltages incorrect.
If an older series card (good but expired) also gives "Card Invalid" message then the card holder or decoder circuit is faulty.
(Historical information: The Early series 10 card had a tiny black square
on one contact. This is a 2k (approx) resistor. Determine which card-
holder spring contact mates with the black square on the card. Turn the
PRD main board upside down; locate the solder pad for this contact and
cut the track adjacent to it. Solder a 2k2 resistor across the cut using the
unused solder pad which the track runs through. You may need to
reverse this modification, removing the 2k2 and bridging the cut track).

*Displays "Card Invalid" message after card is inserted:*
See above.  Otherwise, try replacing D63, D52, D53, D54, D55, D64, D65.

*Displays "Card Invalid" message before card is inserted:*
Check card reader contacts.

*Black sparklies on encrypted channels only:*
Suspect U25 in the decoder section.

*Displays "No Programmes Remaining":*
Check for 5v on Q43 when card is inserted.
If no 5v, replace Q45 (BC846B).
(Many other causes!)

*Kills Sky cards (really):*
Remove Q42* and replace 5v6 zeners D52,53,54,55 as a precaution.
Check power supply 5 volt rail; should not exceed 5.28 volts at U2.
(*Not authorised by Sky or by Pace. Note that this modification will *not* prevent a Sky card from being invalidated legitimately by Sky).

*Speckles on decoded pictures:*
This effect may be most noticeable on "QVC". It can also cause the pictures to scramble intermittently - more so as the receiver warms up.
Freezing U18 might give a temporary "cure."
Links J1 - J4 may need to be changed to suit Videocrypt® chip set.

*Black speckles on flesh tones of decoded channels:*
Replace U20.
Dry joint on C257.
Add a 22pF capacitor between pins 5 and 14 of U20.
If the fault occurs only after warm-up then test U25 with freezer spray.
Also J1 - J4.

*Weak signal from decoder scart socket (external decoder gives a blank screen):*
C197 faulty.

*No decoder messages; flickering pictures or double image on German channels:*
If U18 not generating sync pulses. Replace X7, U18, C210 (10µF) & other electrolytics. Check for dry joints, broken tracks around U18. Finally, replace every IC which receives sync pulses from U18 since one of these could be short -circuiting the sync pulse line.
Similar fault caused by C36.

*Split picture or "ghosting":*
U28 (many other causes - usually horizontal sync pulses are distorted).

*Silver sparkly pattern on very bright yellows on encrypted channels only:*
Suspect A-D convertor I.C. U20 in the decoder section.

*Mottled pictures through decoder:*
74LS554 or U20 or U24.

*Flashes "P000 T000" briefly when card is inserted:*
This is normal with a series 07 SKY card or later.

*In the decoder menu, the AUTO option message is gibberish:*
Suspect U28 in the decoder section.

*If picture flickers when warm, also, — like 'loss of vertical hold' — suspect*
D69 & U18.

*After warm-up the decoded picture loses colour and becomes very speckly:*
Suspect U20 (SP973T8C).

*Decoded pics distorted:*
U22, U23 or U20.

*Decoded pics judder:*
U22, U23, U21

*Intermittent scrambling:*
U25 (Many other causes including faulty Sky card).

*Rippling effect on high colour saturation decoded chans, esp. UK Gold:*
Add 10k between U24 pins 3 and 20.

*Videocrypt graphics jitter:*
Change C215 from 10µF to 100µF 16v and change C121 from 220nF SMD
to 4µ7F 16v radial electrolytic. Add L57 18µH.

*Very grainy pictures through decoder - German channels OK:*
Incorrect Line memory I.C.s fitted (type 1 instead of type 2).

*Distorted channel numbers on changing channel:*
Broken track to D44 near U20.

*Decoder works but grey message bar remains on the screen:*
Replace U28.

*Not decoding. Flickering pictures - one a few cm above the other on the TV*
*screen:*
Replace C207. Looks like there is an echo of the frame sync pulse:
Possible fault in one VC chip causing excessive loading on H sync pulse
track. H sync may be missing altogether.

*No decoder messages:*
Ensure contrast is set at "4".
Ground TST2 to force the video through the decoder. If you get only a flashing "Please Wait" message and hair dryer has no effect...
Replace the PTV-2 if no other fault found.
If grounding TST2 creates a blank screen, check 5v and 12v supplies to all decoder ICs. Track breaks around L20 are common. Use a 'scope to check U20 data output pins. If no data, replace U20.

*Hitachi badged PRD900 with dual card reader will not decode:*
Look for a hairline crack in the clock line next to the second card holder's right hand support pillar on the main board.

## TV picture problems

*TV picture very poor (No UHF loop-through):*
Check for dry joint on aerial socket centre pin or cracked track nearby. On early versions, if picture is simply a little noisy, remove resistors R92 and R93 (22Ω SMD) and add short-circuit links in their places. Check Q10, Q11, Q105, Q2,Q1 (surface mount), U17. Check for a cracked or corroded track running along the side of the metal frame (beneath tape in early versions – often occurs if water runs down the TV cable).

*Interference on TV picture when receiver is on:*
All RF leads should be double screened cable with the plugs soldered. The centre core should be short and the braid *soldered* in the TV aerial wall socket. Fit a masthead amplifier on the TV mast itself.

*TV picture very grainy through modulator:*
Surface mount resistors R92 and R93 (22Ω) should be replaced with zero Ohm links in early versions.

*After a power supply rebuild it can't be tuned in anywhere in the u.h.f. spectrum and it won't enter the modulator tuning mode (F 5 on the handset):*
By wiring via a scart lead and entering the main menu, unlock the menus, using code 0000.

*UHF output stuck on channel 20 and the tuning stuck at the bottom of the Astra 1D band:*
Look for supply track broken next to C11.

## Timer Problems

*Timer loses up to 45 seconds each week:*
Change surface mount capacitor C32 from 33pF to 47pF 5%, part number 950-4705501. C33 next to it should be 22pF.

**Notes:**
On board revisions A3 and A5, Capacitors C166, C182, C207 and C276 are fitted the opposite way round to that which is indicated on the PCB. Revision B1 board and later are correct. R583 (68$\Omega$ 2W) tended to run too hot and may be replaced with an 82$\Omega$ 3W metal film resistor, part number 142-8207511.

Some videocrypt pictures show sparklies. The fix requires several components to be changed, with due relation to previous change implementations, and is, therefore, best left for the manufacturer to correct. Those early units which may need to be upgraded may be identified by L52 and L53 which were ferrite beads.
On revision B1 boards, Capacitor C100 should be reversed and R265 should be a 10k resistor.

A 33pF capacitor was fitted across the tuner output to cure a noise problem. Early versions used a leaded capacitor and later versions have a surface mount device.

Early PRD900 was fitted with a small sub assembly board above the 809-8661004 microprocessor. If the micro fails, remove the sub assembly and transfer IC4 to the main board. Replace the micro with the later version 809-8661006. If X1 is on the sub assembly, transfer it to the main board, together with the surface mount capacitors connected to it. Discard the sub assembly board. Failure of the micro often causes loss of LED display; no response to buttons. The fault may occur after warm-up and the receiver might continue to give a picture.

Customers wishing to use their NICAM VCR to provide terrestrial stereo via the VCR scart on the PRD receiver will find that the receiver will not allow AV loop through whilst in standby mode unless the VCR is in play mode (i.e. pin 8 is high). This may be enabled with the following modification:

Connect a 10k 0.25W resistor between the cathode (band) end of D67 and pin 16 of U35. Connect a 4k7 0,25W resistor between pin 6 of U3 and pin 8 of U20. This modification was implemented in production from board numbers ending in 203 (due to customer requests).

## Microcontroller line-up

| | | | |
|---|---|---|---|
| PRD sub assy. Eprom | 805-0800102 | | |
| PRD sub assy. Eprom | 805-0800131 | | PRD PLUS english only |
| PRD sub assy. Eprom | 805-0800132 | B3 | ASTRA lD upgrade |
| PRD sub assy. Eprom | 805-0900021 | | Grundig STRl |
| PRD masked Micro | 809-8661002 | | Grundig STRl |
| PRD masked Micro | 809-8661006 | | issue 3 |
| PRD masked Micro | 809-8661008 | | Philips |
| PRD masked Micro | 809-8661019 | | Philips STU824 |
| PSR sub assy. Eprom | 805-0800110 | | |
| PRD enhanced micro | 809-8661020 | | |
| PSR sub assy. Eprom | 805-0800124 | | Philips French |
| PRD900+ micro | 809-8661029 | replaces 8661027 | |
| PRD micro (kit) | 808-8663032 | | Enhanced upgrade |

## Secret button codes

*To remove parental lock:*
Hold the [STANDBY] button on the front panel and switch mains on.

*To set factory default on PRD800/900*
Press  MENU P   STORE  >  <

*To set factory default on PRD800/900 Plus and MSS models*
Press  MENU 0   STORE  >  <

The LED display will instantly show "-E2" and this plus the blue menu screen will disappear after a few seconds to be replaced by the channel number and the picture on screen. If "-E2" does not appear then press NORMAL and try the sequence again. The buttons must be pressed quickly and smoothly.

*To turn blue background on/off on PRD800 etc.*
Press  F   STORE

**Replacement Tuners**

The following tuners are no longer available:

221-2077391 BSFC77G39 S/LNB Sharp
221-2177391 BSFG77G39 D/LNB Sharp

They are now replaced with kits as follows:

221-2077391 for PRD800 use 265-6288001
221-2077391 for PSR800 use 265-6388001
221-2177391 for PRD900 use 265-6289002
221-2177391 for PSR900 use 265-6389002

Notes from Pace:

In order to improve the long term reliability of the video driver transistor Q105(SMD BC846B), its power dissipation must be reduced. This has been achieved by increasing its emitter load resistance by the removal of parallel resistor R559 in the emitter circuit. It is recommended that this resistor is removed during routine servicing or repair as a preventative maintenance measure. Only PCBs with a part number ending 204, 214, 224 (Printed on top side of PCB next to card reader) are affected.

DOWNLOADING (all models)
We have had several queries from people attempting to download channel and set-up data from one model of receiver to another. Downloading is only possible between receivers of the same model number and specification.

Other notes

**Manhattan SR950 and all Pace models with Pace tuner**
It is a feature of these models that you must press the status [+] button in order to generate OSD when no signal is present. This is because the No-Signal noise from the new tuner is so low that the Graphics chip can't detect it and does not generate the OSD automatically. Press the status button to see the menu/tuning display and press it again to see the picture.

**Will not work reliably with D2MAC**
Remove 4k7 R602
Replace R586 with 120R or lower if necessary.

# Front panel repairs

The plastic tags at each side of the moulded front panel can snap off if they become brittle with age or heat. I've seen ingenious solutions to this problem. One customer even used tiny screws to fix half a watch strap to the panel!

As with most things, there is a simple answer and I just happened to be the one who thought of it (and I'm very modest, too).

Simply take a standard size paperclip (33mm long) and use your soldering iron to melt it into what remains of the front panel tag while holding the panel in position against the steel base.

The large loop of the paperclip hooks around the metal tag on the side panel and the inner loop nicely encircles the threaded screw hole. It couldn't be neater!

## Converting PRD800 to 199 Channels

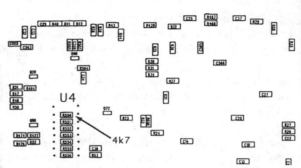

## Instructions

*This modification is NOT approved by Pace*

• First test the receiver.
• Disconnect mains power.
• Remove the cover screws and the cover.
• Remove all screws at the rear.
• Using a pair of side cutters, gently lift each plastic rivet head from the PCB and remove the two-part rivets.
• Using a pair of fine-nose pliers, squeeze together the tips of the two white plastic support pillars and lift the PCB up and forwards.
• Take great care not to bend the PCB since this will crack components underneath!

### On the underside of the PCB, solder the following SM components:

• 4k7 [472] next to pin 7 of U4.

### On the top side of board fit:

• U6 a blank 24C16 EEprom I.C.
Be sure to insert it with the notch or dot next to the notch indicated on the PCB.


• Reassemble the receiver and connect mains power.
You will see "-E2" in the display (if it has a display).
Wait about 20 seconds.
The receiver will now operate normally but with 199 channels.
(All original customised settings will be lost)

### The following functions are also activated:

1. Favourite channels
2. Colour choice selection
3. Radio blanking option

## Adding an LED number display to Ferguson SRD5 and similar

• Remove the push buttons and resolder them in positions SW4, 7, 6 and 5 to match the new PRD front panel which will be required.
• Cut link J12 near the SW1 button position. Add link wire J13.
• Remove the card reader from its daughter board. Discard the board and pillars.
• Resolder the card reader to the main board in the rearmost position.
• Remove the three 560 Ohm resistors with insulated wires which are soldered near the board front edge.
• Solder the new LED display in position LED9 so that the wires protrude about 4mm through the board. Crop the wires shorter.
• Remove all "472" surface mount resistors beneath U4.
• Add resistors to suit replacement microprocessor.

*This modification is NOT approved by Pace or Ferguson.*

## Fitting a new microprocessor to gain the "Enhanced" features.

SatCure supply a complete kit with instructions.
The part number is 808-8663032.

## Difference between early and later microprocessors.

Microprocessors from 809-8661020 onwards have a slightly different pin function from earlier versions. A modification is required to ensure that the data line for external positioner operation is connected.

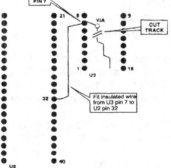

On boards which have already been modified you will see a red insulated wire alongside the microprocessor.

This red wire is added between pin 35 of U2 and pin 7 of U3. The track is cut as shown.

Later boards include the modification in the form of surface mount links R100 and R101. One or other should be fitted, dependent on which microprocessor is fitted.

Note also that microprocessor version 809-8661004 had a different pin configuration from all others and a diode board was used in conjunction with it. If any other microprocessor is to be fitted, this diode board should be discarded and the small ULN2003 IC should be transferred to the main board.

## Converting PRD800/900 to include J17 Wideband Audio in Menu

• First test the receiver to ensure that it is working.
• Disconnect mains power.
• Remove the cover screws and the cover.
• Remove all screws at the rear.
• Using a pair of side cutters, gently lift each plastic rivet head from the PCB and remove the two-part rivets.
• Using a pair of fine-nose pliers, squeeze together the tips of the two white plastic support pillars and lift the PCB up and forwards.
• Take great care not to bend the PCB since this will crack components underneath!

**• On the underside of the PCB, solder the following SM components:**
• 4k7 [472] next to pin 3 of U4 (this enables the J17 menu option).
• 4k7 R457
• 4k7 R460
• Remove R459 [000] and put it in R411 position.
• 10k R459 [103]
• 10k R463
• Remove R458 [000] and discard it.
• 22k R458 [223]
• 390R R410 [391]
• 390R R455
• 1k R443 [102]
• 1k R461                      *This modification is NOT approved by Pace*
• 47nF C191
• 150pF C304
• BC846B Q94
• BC846B Q95
• Remove solder from pads X12, L27, C283

• On top side of board fit:   X12 filter; L27;  C283 (lµF).
• On underside of board fit l0k resistor between C283 (+) and C153 (+).
• Solder a short length of thin wire through TST5 next to L16.
• Check all work then reassemble receiver, leaving top cover off.

**Power on. No LNB connected. Any channel:**
• Press: MENU, 5 (or 4 - PRD800), 2, LEFT, 4, LEFT for audio menu J17 option.
• Adjust L27 until voltage on TST5 wire is 2.33 volts DC.
• Press: NORM

In audio menu, if MONO is selected, option 4 provides PANDA (narrow band), 50µS (wide band) and J17 (wide band). Any one of these options may be selected on any channel.

(J17 is not necessarily correct to specification but sounds good)

*Pace PRD*

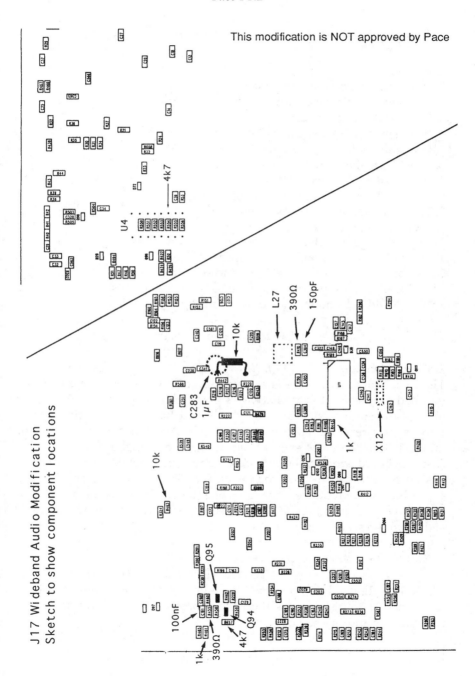

This modification is NOT approved by Pace

J17 Wideband Audio Modification
Sketch to show component locations

page 127

**Frequently Asked Questions - Pace MSS100/MSS228/Prima**

**Contents**
1. Why did my power supply fail?
2. How do I repair the power supply?
3. Can I get extra channels?
4. Are there any "secret" handset codes?
5. I get only a blue screen. What has happened?
6. I get "LNB Short" on the screen - why?
7. Can I use a "Universal" LNB?
8. Why do I get no front panel display?
9. How can I tell how old my receiver is?
10. Why won't my remote control work?
11. Why do I get interference on terrestrial TV pictures?
12. Why do I get "sparklies" on the picture?
13. Excessive contrast level and/or audio interference
14. Why are my TV pictures grainy through the satellite receiver?
15. Can I add a decoder Scart to my Prima?

The following answers apply to BOTH models unless stated otherwise.

*1. Why did my power supply fail?*
The usual cause of failure is a mains electricity power surge. Perhaps you had a power-cut or perhaps you plugged in an electric lawnmower or drill (or similar) nearby or perhaps you have faulty wiring in the plug, socket or somewhere in your house. Another common cause of failure is that the receiver has been dropped or banged heavily. In this case the board around the transformer will be cracked. If the receiver has been subjected to too much heat, the capacitors may fail. The big 47µF/400v is a favourite, together with the smaller ones near it. If the 47µF/400v is marked "LCC" then I recommend you change it immediately as these seem to cause failure.

*2. How do I repair the power supply?*
There is a special IC labelled TOPxxx. This is included in the repair kit SATKIT 8. Remember, most PSU parts are classed as "Safety Critical" components. You MUST use the Pace-approved parts. If you don't you risk damage and fire hazard.

### 3. Can I get extra channels?

Yes for the Prima. An upgrade kit is available from SatCure to give 250 channels.

### 4. Are there any "secret" handset codes?

Yes. The "factory reset" will reset channel 1 only to Sky One. It will also reset the Installation menu settings. It will NOT change the rest of the channels.
Press:

Menu, 0, Store, Right arrow, Left arrow.

Later MSS100 and all Prima
There is a hidden function to align the audio PLL frequency offset in the Prima and later MSS100 that uses the RC-10 handset:
Press "Function", "Menu", "Radio" and "Store".
The message "Please Wait" appears while the audio Phase Lock Loop centre frequency is reset.

Early MSS100 only
Press "Function", "Menu", "Radio" and "Store".
The Audio PLL number will flash on the screen. DO NOT adjust this!
Press the Fav key once. The video level value should be flashing now.
Write down the value and adjust with caution.

### 5. I get only a blue screen. What has happened?

The blue screen appears if there is no signal.
The most obvious cause is that your LNB is not connected. Alternatively, you may have shorted out the LNB cable and damaged something inside the receiver.
Make sure that LNB power is ON in the installation menu.

Prima "No Signal" on blue background.
Audio present if channel tuning menu is selected (audio mutes with blue background).
Look for a dry joint on L305.

MSS100 blue screen "No signal" and/or no RF output
Check for dry joint on U200.
5.625 MHz crystal may be faulty (if marked "IQD")

Corruption of the EEprom contents can cause loss of picture or sound. You can cure this by readjusting the VIDEO VALUE number in the secret menu.

MSS100 Intermittent blue screen "No Signal".
Dry joint on D18

**6. I get "LNB Short" on the screen, even with the LNB disconnected.**
Occasionally this happens if you've selected power for just one LNB in the Installation menu. The simplest way to correct this is to plug the receiver into the mains and press the factory reset sequence. This resets it to "LNB Power 1 & 2".

**7. Can I use a "Universal" LNB?**
Yes. Select tone ON in the second screen of the tuning menu for the appropriate channels.

**8. Why do I get no front panel display?**
In the MSS200, check the solder joints of the LED display itself.
In the MSS300, check the soldering of the surface mount components on the front panel display. There is also an upgrade for early MSS300 which suffer from no display intermittently, when warm. This is explained in "The Satellite Repair Manual."
"No display" can also be caused by a faulty microcontroller and various other things.

**9. How can I tell how old my receiver is?**
The date of manufacture is incorporated in the serial number.
For example: RAAYAH5245xxxxx
The "5" indicates 1995
The "24" indicates week 24 counting from first week in January.
The "5" indicates Friday.

**10. Why doesn't my remote control work?**
Prima uses a different remote control handset from other models.
This control has the code "RC-10" in the bottom right hand corner of the keypad.
The later model MSS100 also uses this remote.

**11. Why do I get interference on Terrestrial TV pictures?**
MSS100 Radiated interference from PSU affecting VHF and UHF reception.

Radiation from the snubber diode can affect VHF and UHF TV reception when ready made RF connecting leads are used. Many of these leads do not have full screening and allow the ingress of interference. Receivers fitted with a new transformer, part number 237-1000201, also require an 82uH inductor to be placed in series with R3 and D8. It is also necessary to change R3 from 22R to 47R. To reduce or remove the emitted radiation the following modifications are advised:

Change C7 (should this be C2 ?) to 1nF 1KV Ceramic Cap. Part No 159-1029951. Fit a 200nH coil, Part No 134-0200080, across track cut between C2 and D5.

Only on units fitted with Transformer, Part No 237-1000201: Change R3 to 47 ohms. Cut track between R3 and D8, and bridge the cut with an 82uH axial lead inductor. (82uH inductor has Part No 134-0820601).

There is also a kit to get rid of "hum bars" on terrestrial pictures. This kit improves protection against high voltage "static" which builds up on your TV aerial during windy/stormy weather and which results in no terrestrial loop-through (very grainy Tv pictures).

**12. Why do I get "sparklies" on the picture?**
Sparklies on picture when receiver is cold.
This is normal. If you use the receiver straight from a cold van or workshop the tuner will take at least half an hour to reach normal operating temperature.
If sparklies are present all the time, read the SPARKLIES page.

**13. MSS100 Excessive contrast level and/or audio interference.**
This problem can be experienced when receiving some transmissions from the ASTRA satellites or on a transmission using 36MHz deviation. An improvement can be gained by accessing a hidden video level adjustment menu using the following steps:

a) Press F, then MENU, then RADIO then STORE on the remote control handset.

b) Press the Fav key once. The video level value should be flashing now.

c) Make a note of the values before alteration. Adjust the VIDEO VALUE number using the left arrow key from 47(Default) to 37 for Ku Band transmissions. If C Band transmissions are being received, adjust from 111 (Default) to 101.

d) Press STORE on the remote control handset to save the new values.

DO NOT adjust the first menu option, Audio PLL unless there is an obvious sound problem and the displayed value is a long way from zero. If any alteration is made to this option by mistake, exit the set-up by pressing 'NORM'.

The adjustment is simple to perform. A change has been implemented on all units which display a date code greater than 6204 to overcome the problem. By way of example, XXXXXX6213XXXXX is new production having the changes incorporated, and will not require adjustment.

You can remove the blue screen and NO SIGNAL screen, to determine if there is a signal, by pressing F followed by STORE.

Early MSS100 Audio distortion on narrow deviation subcarriers, especially 7.90, 8.35 and 8.50 MHz

Fit two 1.4V diodes type BZV86 (Part No 125-0014501) to copper side of PCB under U500, as shown in diagram supplied in Pace Service Matters volume 5. Most units had these fitted in the factory.

**14. Why are my TV pictures grainy through the satellite receiver?**

MSS100 poor RF terrestrial loop through.

Solder pad broken beneath the RF output socket.

Also dead UHF I.C.

There is also a kit to get rid of "hum bars" on terrestrial pictures. This kit improves protection against high voltage "static" which builds up on your TV aerial during windy/stormy weather and which results in no terrestrial loop-through (very grainy Tv pictures).

**15. Can I add a decoder Scart to my Prima?**

Not practical. You would need to fit dozens of surface mount parts.

# Pace MSS100, MSS228 and Prima

Later MSS100 from March 1997 use the Prima remote control marked "RC-10". These receivers have a serial number beginning either PCAAAxxxxxxxxx or NBIOOxxxxxxxxx or letters later in the alphabet. The microcontroller is the Prima micro 809-8661101. For compatibility with Video Plus™ Deluxe equipment you must identify the later MSS100 as a Pace Prima instead.

*Factory reset:*
[MENU] [0] [STORE] [>] [<]. This will reset the Micro but will not alter the user defined channel memories and settings.

**Power Supply Faults**

*Dead power supply:*
Replace U1 (TOP202YA1). Measure all resistors and diodes and replace any found to be faulty (especially R2, 10Ω). Replace any suspect electrolytic capacitors (especially C3, 47µF/400v). Measure fuse. Check board for cracks. SATKIT 8 is available for repairing these models.

*PSU pulses:*
D11 µF5402 (use BYW98-50) or D9 (use BYV96D or BYV37).

*PSU voltages incorrect:*
Some power supplies may be found to be slightly out of tolerance. If so, reduce the value of SMD resistor R3 to 10R 5%.

*No LNB voltage:*
Check "Power on options" menu.
*LNB voltage remains at 13v even for horizontal:*
Check 20v supply from D10 through L4 feeding C12, Q1 and Q2.*

**Audio Faults**

*Audio distortion on peaks:*
Pace recommend the addition of two special 1.4v zeners 125-0014501 BZV86C1v4.
Both anodes go to link 502 adjacent to the 56 pin Sound I.C. STV0056-3.

One cathode goes to pin 2 and the other goes to pin 54 of this I.C.

There is also a hidden function to align the PLL frequency offset in the Prima and later MSS100 that uses the RC-10 handset:
Press "Function", "Menu", "Radio" and "Store".
The message "Please Wait" appears while the audio Phase Lock Loop centre frequency is reset.

*Poor audio on weak stations:*
Try connecting 82pF between pins 23 and 19 of U500.*
*Suggested by Hugh Cocks in "Television" magazine.

*Audio volume too low:*
Check "Power on options" menu.

*Intermittent loss of audio on channel change:*
May be Phase Lock Loop drifting out of lock because of voltage over-shoot. The remedy is to limit the voltage by connecting two surface mount 8v2 5% zener diodes (925-0082511) across capacitors C506 and C507 which are adjacent to U500. The cathode (bar end) of each diode goes to the positive end of each capacitor. Also dry joint on C200.

**Loss of Picture**

*Intermittent blue screen "No Signal".*
Dry joint on D18. Dry joint on L305.

*Permanent blue screen "No Signal".*
Crystal X100 5.625 MHz.

*Blue screen "No signal" and/or no rf output.*
Check for dry joint on U200.

*Blue screen "No Signal".*
It could be that there is a Videocrypt fault. Check that there is video going to the Videocrypt area form U500 pin 7. This is where the video is processed for detection and is the origin of the NO SIGNAL message. You can remove the blue screen and NO SIGNAL screen, to determine if there is a signal, by pressing F followed by STORE.
In the hidden menu the video level default is usually 45-47 but depends

on the dish signal, try making it bigger.

*PRIMA Loss of picture and sound:*
Occasionally the 4MHz clock to U500 (STV0056) may be borderline and cause general malfunction of the IC. Increase the clock amplitude by changing the following parts:

R706 SMD 220R 5% 940-2210501
R208 SMD 2k2 5% 940-2220501
C219 SMD 1p8F 50v 5% ceramic 940-0185301

**Picture Faults**

*Picture rolling intermittently.*
C545.

*PRIMA, MSS228 Patterning on the picture:*
Excessive load on the power supply caused, for example, by damaged Sky cards, can cause instability. Reduce the value of C7 to 220pF 10% ceramic capacitor 159-2219651.

*Excessive contrast level and/or audio interference.*
This problem can be experienced when receiving some transmissions from the ASTRA satellites or on a transmission using 36MHz deviation. An improvement can be gained by accessing a hidden video level adjustment menu using the following steps:

Press F, then Menu, then Radio then Store on the remote control handset. Press the Fav key once. The video level value should be flashing now.

Make a note of the values before alteration. Adjust the VIDEO VALUE number using the left arrow key from 47(Default) to 37 for Ku Band transmissions. If C Band transmissions are being received, adjust from 111 (Default) to 101.
Press STORE on the remote control handset to save the new values.
DO NOT adjust the first menu option, Audio PLL. If any alteration is made to this option by mistake, exit the set-up by pressing 'NORM'.

The adjustment is simple to perform and could be given to a customer

by telephone if the problem should arise. A change has been implemented on all units which display a date code greater than 6204 to overcome
the problem. By way of example, XXXXXXX6213XXXXX is new production having the changes incorporated, and will not require adjustment.

The audio buzz can also be experienced if the on-screen graphics white
level is too high. In this case, change SMD resistor R604 to 680R 5%.

### RF Modulator/Terrestrial Reception Problems

*Hum bars on terrestrial channels.*
From the aerial input pin to ground fit the following two parts:

Prima:
D201 SMD inductor 1.2µH 5% high SRF 230MHz 913-0012501
D202 SMD diode BAV99 dual SOT23 TR 912-0009951.
MSS100:
D24 SMD inductor 1.2µH 5% high SRF 230MHz 913-0012501
D25 SMD diode BAV99 dual SOT23 TR 912-0009951.

On early receivers, scrape away the green resist coating to solder the
parts to the copper ground plane. On later receivers, fit in the spare
positions for D201 and D202 (Leave D202 if already there). D201 may be
vacant or a 1k resistor may be there (replace it with the inductor).
This modification may also improve protection of the TDA8725T against
static discharge from the TV aerial.

This change is valid only for PCB serial numbers ending in 105.
Receivers with serial numbers beginning PCD or NCE already have
these parts fitted.

*Horizontal lines on UHF picture while handset keys pressed:*
Inside the UHF modulator, gently push inductor L201 so it leans
towards the front of the PCB at approximately 45° angle. This minimises
interaction between the data bus and UHF oscillator circuit.

*Poor RF terrestrial loop through.*
Broken pad beneath the RF output socket or
Faulty TDA8725T. Open-circuit R219 39Ω.

*UHF output stuck on channel 44 frequency. Going to a higher number has no effect. Going to a lower number produces oscillation of the UHF carrier:*
C208 10nF SMD.

*Radiation from PSU affecting VHF and UHF reception.*
Radiation from the snubber diode can affect VHF and UHF TV reception when ready made RF connecting leads are used. Many of these leads do not have full screening and allow the ingress of interference. Receivers fitted with a new SMPS transformer, Part Number 237-1000201, also require an 82uH inductor to be placed in series with R3 and D8. It is also necessary to change R3 from 22R to 47R. To reduce or remove the emitted radiation the following modifications are advised:

Change C7 to 1nF 1KV Ceramic Cap. Part No 159-1029951
Fit a 200nH coil, Part No 134-0200080, across track cut between C2 and D5.

*Only on units fitted with SMPS Transformer, Part No 237-1000201:*
Change R3 to 47 ohms. Cut track between R3 and D8, and bridge the cut with an 82uH axial lead inductor. (82uH inductor has Part No 134-0820601).

**Front panel faults**

*All front panel LEDs lit. No functions:*
U700

# Pace MSS200/300/Apollo/Panasonic TU-SD250

(Apollo is virtually identical to the MSS200 but the circuitry for the channel number display, 22kHz tone generator and 12 volt switching is omitted from the printed circuit board (mostly surface mount components).

**Frequently Asked Questions.**

1. Why did my power supply fail?
2. How do I repair the power supply?
3. Can I get extra channels?
4. Are there any "secret" handset codes?
5. I get only a blue screen. What has happened?
6. I get "LNB Short" on the screen - why?
7. Can I use a "Universal" LNB?
8. Why do I get no front panel display?
9. How can I tell how old my receiver is?
10. How can I download the memory?
11. Why do I get no decoder messages on screen?
12. Why do I get "Card Invalid" message?
13. Why doesn't my receiver work with pirate card/PC software?
14. Why do I get picture interference?
15. How do I change the audio bandwidth on MSS300 ?
16. How do I increase the LNB voltage ?
17. How does the search function work?

**1. Why did my power supply fail?**
The usual cause of failure is a mains electricity power surge. Perhaps you had a power-cut or perhaps you plugged in an electric lawnmower or drill (or similar) nearby or perhaps you have faulty wiring in the plug, socket or somewhere in your house. Another common cause of failure is that the receiver has been dropped or banged heavily. In this case the board around the transformer will be cracked. If the receiver has been subjected to too much heat, the capacitors may fail. The big 47μF/400v is a favourite, together with the smaller ones near it. Also check diode D17 for a short circuit.

## 2. How do I repair the power supply?

If the board is definitely not cracked and there are no scorch marks on the mains side of the transformer, simply replace the main switching Transistor, Q1, the large capacitor 47μF/400v, the 22μF and 10μF capacitors (high temperature!). Check R1 which is a special 10 Ohm safety type (DON'T use any other type!) Solder the transformer joints to be sure they are all right. Replace the fuse with an identical type and put everything back together.

*Remember, these are classed as "Safety Critical" components. You MUST use the Pace-approved parts. If you don't you risk damage and fire hazard. A kit (SATKIT 9) is available and reliability kit (RELKIT 9).

## 3. Can I get extra channels?

Yes. There is a special "hack" which can be done with the "Pacelink Pro" computer system. You will need to send your receiver to someone who has this system. Alternatively, simply buy the 250 channel upgrade kit.

## 4. Are there any "secret" handset codes?

Yes. The "factory reset" will reset channel 1 only to Sky One. It will also reset the Installation menu settings. It will NOT change the rest of the channels.
Press:

Menu, 0, Store, Right arrow, Left arrow.

To Authorise card: [F] [9]

To set Channel on after power fail:
[F] [RCL] [x] (where [x] is the channel number).
Repeat this sequence to turn the feature off.

Note: Due to a software conflict, this feature also causes card authorisation (you will see a black background with flashing "P"). To cure this problem, disconnect diode D65 which will disable the card authorise system. The two are never likely to be needed together.

## 5. I get only a blue screen. What has happened?

The blue screen appears if there is no signal.
The most obvious cause is that your LNB is not connected or, on a twin-

input receiver, is connected to the wrong input. Alternatively, you may have shorted out the LNB cable and damaged something inside the receiver. Make sure that LNB power is ON in the installation menu.

**6. I get "LNB Short" on the screen, even with the LNB disconnected.**
If a short circuit has occurred in the LNB cable or connections, it can destroy two surface mount resistors (1R8 near the front edge of the board) and possibly Q25 as well.

**7. Can I use a "Universal" LNB?**
Yes. Select tone ON in the second screen of the tuning menu for the appropriate channels. (This does not work in early Apollo version but an upgrade kit is available).

**8. Why do I get no front panel display?**
In the MSS200, check the solder joints of the LED display itself.
In the MSS300, check the soldering of the surface mount components on the front panel display. There is also an upgrade for early MSS300 which suffer from no display intermittently, when warm. This is explained later. "No display" can also be caused by a faulty microcontroller and various other things.

**9. How can I tell how old my receiver is?**
The date of manufacture is incorporated in the serial number.
For example: RAAYAH5245xxxxx
The "5" indicates 1995
The "24" indicates week 24 counting from first week in January.
The "5" indicates Friday.

**10. How can I download the memory?**
You connect a fully wired Scart to Scart cable between the Decoder sockets of identical MSS receivers then follow the on-screen instructions from the Installation menu. You can not download successfully from dissimilar receivers and, to be certain, you should use this transfer facility only between receivers which have identical microcontroller I.C.s.
If you are going to program a large number of receivers, use a "PaceLink" computer interface from Kesh Electrics.

### 11. Why do I get no decoder messages on screen?

Try setting the contrast higher in the Installation menu.
If this doesn't work, and you have checked the tuning, you probably have a fault in the decoder section or else you have fitted your Scart plug into the wrong socket!

### 12. Why do I get "Card Invalid" message?

Try your card in a different receiver to test it.
Make sure that the card contacts are clean and the card slot spring contacts are clean and not bent or twisted.

### 13. Why doesn't my receiver work with pirate card/PC software ?

I don't know.

### 14. Why do I get picture interference ?

Strong terrestrial signals or a TV amplifier can cause crosstalk. The effect is to cause degradation of the Satellite TV picture through the RF output. Test simply by disconnecting the Aerial input connector. If this cures the fault, fit an attenuator.

Tuning voltage from L26 also supplies the card reader. Picture interference which disappears when the card is removed can be caused by a fault on this 30 volt rail.
You might have tuned the satellite RF output too close to a terrestrial UHF channel frequency.

Your receiver might be running too warm in which case locate it in a cooler place and fit RELKIT 9 and also consider fitting the SatCure "miniature cooling fan."

### 15. How do I change the audio bandwidth on MSS300 ?

Early models did not have audio bandwidth selection. Fit later Micro. Latest models have an additional 600kHz bandwidth option. Fit Micro and later Audio processor IC (both).

### 16. How do I increase the LNB voltage ?

If the LNB 13v supply is too low, you can cure this by changing two zeners.
D33 (6v2) becomes 6v8 2% to increase 13 volt supply.
D32 (5v1) becomes 4v7 2% if necessary to decrease 17 volt supply.

This solves problems if you run the receiver through any sort of splitter.

Explanation: For vertical polarisation, D32 gets shorted out so it affects only horizontal polarisation voltage. D33 is in circuit all the time so it affects BOTH vertical and horizontal polarisation voltages. Alter the values of these zeners to achieve the LNB output voltage that you want. (You can't have more than 13.8v vertical or more than 19v horizontal).

**17. How does the search function work?**
A two-speed search function has always been available on the MSS range of receivers, but is not mentioned in the User Manual. In the Tuning Menu press 'F' to commence the search in 50MHz steps. Press 'F' again to access the 'fine' mode in 1MHz steps.

# Pace MSS200/300/Apollo/Panasonic TU-SD250

## Power Supply faults

*Dead:*
If fuse measures OK, replace C59 (22µF/35v/105°C), C60, and C61 (10µF/50v/105°C). Replace C54 (47µF/400v) capacitor as a precaution if marked "LCC". If fuse is melted, also replace R49, Q5, FS1 and measure other components. Check for dry joints L9/10. Don't confuse "dead" with front panel display not lighting up!

The BUL54AR transistor's gain is not well-defined. Overheating of this transistor may be cured by replacing R62 (68R) with 33R and R51 (15R) with 8R2. Alternatively, fit a BUT11A or MJE18004.

*Apparently Dead but PSU can be heard to start up:*
If no pictures and LNB volts low, C74 1000µF/25v.
If pictures and LNB voltage OK, see "Front Panel Faults".

*Goes bang after complete kit is fitted:*
Check D17 1N5404 for short-circuit. D17 supplies 14v for the LNB supply. Otherwise look for obvious mistakes and measure everything.

*PSU "whistling":*
D9 BYV37 faulty.

*"Stuck in standby" symptom. No response to buttons:*
LNB current detect circuit: R452, R208 (1R8 SMD) or a leaky Q29 (centre front edge of board). Check Q25 (in front of tuner). Otherwise D35.

Tracing "streaky picture" faults and other strange symptoms can be time-consuming. Save time by fitting RELKIT 9 which contains all the electrolytics you are likely to need. (Especially the LOW ESR types).

## Front Panel Faults

*MSS200 no front panel display or missing segments:*
Resolder all pins on LED display. Otherwise, replace display.

*MSS300 no front panel display:*
Early versions use a 22µF electrolytic for C2 on the display panel.

This should be a 1µF/50v multilayer ceramic type.
Resolder any bad joints on surface mount components.
Add 1N4148 diode to front panel. Remove surface mount diode D1.
Note that you can NOT use a transformer from another model.
The MSS300 has an extra winding for the -21v supply to the vacuum
fluorescent display. (If the capacitor or diode on this supply line fails,
you will lose the display and the audio as well).

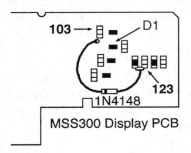

MSS300 Display PCB

*Corruption of front panel display ("junk in display"):*
Newer models having a new type of Infra-Red receiver module fitted
(Sony SBX1910-52) are susceptible to noise and fluctuations on the 5v
supply line. Where problems are encountered, decoupling of the supply
line should be modified as follows:
Change L1 to a l00R 5% 0.25W Carbon film resistor Part No. 140-1012501
Change C12 to 470µF 16V 20% Part No. 155-4771750

*MSS300 segments duplicated in display:*
Vacuum fluorescent display faulty.

*After PSU failure the channel number display no longer works:*
Channel up button does not work. Strobe outputs on Micro Pins 21 to 27
missing.
Replace microcontroller  (809-8663209)

*Stuck in standby:*
R452, R108. (Don't confuse this with a blank display).

*Stuck in standby. Zeros on display:*
Daughter board not making contact with socket or faulty micro.

## Picture Faults

*Blue screen "No Signal":*
If no LNB voltage, check "F" connection inside tuner.
Otherwise check for dry joints on L18, L19 (grey picture floats sideways if blue screen is turned off with F STORE).
If 'scope shows no sync pulses at graphics generator or at U12 (PTV111) then replace U12, 503kHz resonator and all electrolytics around U12.
Also U16 and many other causes!
(blank screen, audio OK with blue screen turned off).
Q42, BC856B

*Blue screen when hot:*
Tuner pin 1 s/c to ground or dry joint on L18, L19 or tuner F pin not soldered.

*Rolling B+W pics:*
U4 micro or dry joint on L18, L19.

*Picture distortion/poor video:*
U16

*No RF output or stuck on channel 69:*
Dry joint on U2 or broken track from transformer pin to D15.

*Severe horizontal streaks on picture:*
C140

*Diagonal Interference lines 2mm apart or herringbone pattern - all sat channels - all outputs:*
C221 near Nicky IC.

*Picture drifts sideways:*
Broken track on U4 or dry joint X3. (Also see decoder faults).

*"Poor video":*
U26

*After warm-up, TV screen shows 00000000 in top left corner:*
(Sound may be affected.)

Replace MSP3400 sound processor. Could also be Nicky I.C. or EEprom.

*Low video level, rolling pictures:*
C238 47μF next to Nicky chip.

*Distorted, blurred picture:*
with multiple "ghost" vertical bars at sharp edges, screen filled with
faint coloured patterning. Symptoms vary with different "DECODER
OUTPUT" settings in "EXTERNAL AV" menu:
C221 (1μF/16V) near to the Nicky chip.

**Audio Faults**

*No audio:*
Usually U14 MSP3400.

*Noise on audio with some TVs:*
Some TVs (notably Hitachi) have a very high audio frequency response
and create background noise from the remains of the high-frequency
switching pulses generated by U14. To cure this fault, replace surface
mount capacitors C265 and C266 (3n3F) with 6n8F. Alternatively, solder
conventional wire ended 3n3 capacitors from pins 28 and 29 of U14 to 0v
on pin 35. These capacitors will now be in parallel with the originals.

Other audio noise effects can be caused by failure of U14, or (rarely)
C192 (39pF) or Q30.

**LNB Supply Faults**

*No LNB voltage or voltage too low:*
Q25 (NPN). I sometimes use a TO220 metal tab replacement which must
be fitted with metal tab to the left (nearest the side panel). The "F" connector joint inside the tuner can break to give the same symptom. Also,
make sure that "LNB POWER" is "ON" in the Installation menu. (I know
all this is obvious but even *I* have been known to forget!)

*LNB Short:*
R452, R208 (1R8 SMD) or a leaky Q29 (centre front edge of board). Q25
(in front of tuner) and D35. If no SMD resistors available, fit a 1Ω fusible
resistor between link LK 110 and the positive leg of C143.

*LNB Short (continued):*
Early receivers that have a date code (the first three digits of the serial number) higher than 433 may supply insufficient current for certain LNBs and devices like the Global Mini Magic: The solution is to solder a 2R2Ω resistor between link LK 110 and the positive leg of C143.

*No 18 volts:*
Check 18 volt supply is reaching Q30 emitter from power supply D16 cathode. H/V switching is controlled by U4 pin 15. Ensure that this control voltage is reaching Q32 base via R215. Q32 controls Q31 which controls Q30. Q30 passes 18 volts to L25 which overrides the 14 volts received via D36. The H/V line also controls Q26 which shorts out D33 (5v1 zener) if V is selected.

*LNB voltage drops when unit tapped:*
L25 dry joint

## Menu Faults

*Menu background grey with some TV receivers:*
The cause is 17.7344MHz colour oscillator tolerance spreads. To ensure that the oscillator runs at the correct frequency, change the trimming capacitors C213 and C214 from 12pF to 8p2F, Pace part no. 950-0825301. Situated next to on-screen display chip U17 (M35010)

Note:
In the tuning mode, you scan up the band by  pressing the button to the right of 'menu'. The receiver may get to around 11.4GHz then jump to the bottom of the scale, at around I0.7GHz. The jump always happens at about 11.4GHz. There is no trouble when scanning down the band.

*Will not tune right down to 700MHz:*
Replace tuner type A5 with later tuner A6. This is not generally a problem as standard LNBs are not designed to work at this low frequency.

## Decoder Faults

*No decoder messages:*
Make sure Contrast is set at 4. If fault remains, check for dry joints on L18, L19 next to X2. Suspect U8 and U16.

*Flickering picture, noise on decoded picture or decoder dropout:*
Replace C319 (220nF) with 47nf and replace R611 (47k) with 120k.
These components affect the clamp level and some experimentation
with values might be needed for best results.

*No decoder messages or dropout when warm:*
C109 (1µF) next to U12 (PTV111). C105 4µ7. U12 may also fail but less
common. X3 Resonator-503 KHZ.

*Will not work with external D2Mac decoder:*
Scope the video waveform from the external decoder socket and at the
same time change the video baseband option on the menu eg PAL,
MAC, CLAMPED, FLAT. If the waveform doesn't change (stays in PAL
mode) replace Q68 and Q69 (BC846B).

*Cross-hatch pattern in areas of saturated colour on decoded channels:*
Change R106 from 620 to 330 ohms 0.1W 5%      Part No 940-3310501

*Ghosting of pictures through decoder (double image):*
U21, Q3

*Tuning menu drifts left. No decoder messages:*
U8

**Decoder operation: Notes.**

Connect TP4 test pin to 0 volts in order to force the video signal through
the decoder.

*U12 PTV111 operation:*
Pin 7 indicates PLL "lock" condition.
Low = no sync pulses and tells the Microcontroller to turn on blue
screen with "no signal" message. Note that U12 produces free running
sync pulses even with no signal input. This helps to prevent decoder
lock-up during channel-change. The H and V sync pulses from U12 are
used by the Videocrypt decoder and by the graphics generator chip,
U17.

*Decoder Scart:*
Pin 12 also acts as a data I/O port and pin 8 as a clock line for data

transfer. These are used for downloading data and for dish positioner control. Pin 12 is a relay driver output.

**U4 microprocessor operation: Notes.**

R84 (47k) pull-down resistor on pin 36 tells the micro that a polariser board is fitted.
Pin 6 is the reset line for power-on reset. It is active low. Faults here can cause resetting of the internal clock.
Pin 14 can be pulled low for "card read" initialisation.
Pin 19 is the Videocrypt reset line.

**Handset Codes**

Factory Reset:    [MENU] [0] [Store] [right arrow] [left arrow]

Authorise card:   [F] [9]

Channel on after power fail:
[F] [RCL] [x] (where [x] is the channel number).
Repeat this sequence to turn the feature off.

Note: Due to a software conflict, this feature also causes card authorisation (you will see a black background with flashing "P"). To cure this problem, disconnect diode D65 which will disable the card authorise system.

**UHF modulator and Terrestrial TV problems:**

Strong terrestrial signals or a TV amplifier can cause crosstalk. The effect is to cause degradation of the Satellite TV picture through the RF output. Test simply by disconnecting the Aerial input connector. If this cures the fault, fit an attenuator.

*Picture Interference:*
Tuning voltage from L26 also supplies the card reader. Picture interference which disappears when the card is removed can be caused by a fault on this 30 volt rail.

*Horizontal lines or venetian blind (Scart pictures OK):*
C48 4µ7F next to RF modulator.

*Interference to terrestrial TV signals:*
Can arise from harmonics of the 28MHz clock generator within the Videocrypt section of the receiver. Careful modification of the circuit can reduce the radiated harmonics.
Change C97 (22pF) to 1K 0.1W 5% SMD resistor Part No. 940-1020501
Change C98 (47pF) to 39pF 50V 5% SMD capacitor Part No. 950-3905501
Change C99 (56pF) to 22pF 50V 5% SMD capacitor Part No.950-2205501

**Miscellaneous:**

*MSS300 Audio Bandwidth:*
Early models did not have audio bandwidth selection. Fit later Micro. Latest models have an additional 600kHz bandwidth option. Fit Micro and Audio processor IC (both).

*Front panel:*
This can cause various faults because it has a microprocessor which polls the buttons. Keep a spare panel in stock for testing faulty receivers.

For testing MSS200/300 always select "clamped" baseband for decoder output and test picture from decoder scart socket. This helps to narrow down the possible faults and shows if the tuner and Nicky IC are OK.

*MSS300 Card Flap not opening when release button is pressed:*
Remove the display panel. Tighten the screw which holds the metal bracket that secures the toothed wheel. Lift the end of the spiral spring back by several teeth on the toothed wheel so that it pulls the card flap open.

MSS466, MSS260/1
*Intermittent loss of PAL audio on channel change from a MAC channel:*
Caused by Phase Lock Loop drifting out of lock because of voltage over-shoot. The remedy is to limit the voltage by connecting two surface mount 8v2 5% zener diodes (925-0082511) across capacitors C506 and C507 which are adjacent to U500. The cathode (bar end) of each diode goes to the positive end of each capacitor.

# Frequently Asked Questions - Pace MSS500/1000
Sony SAT301U, Hitachi SR2070D, Toshiba TS540

Contents
1. Why did my power supply fail?
2. How do I repair the power supply?
3. Can I get extra channels?
4. Can I upgrade my MSS500 to Dolby audio/or to motorised?
5. Are there any "secret" handset codes?
6. I get only a blue screen. What has happened?
7. I get "LNB Short" on the screen - why?
8. Can I use a "Universal" LNB?
9. Why do I get no front panel display (gone dim)?
10. Why does my MSS do strange things?
11. How can I tell how old my receiver is?
12. How can I download the memory?
13. Why do I get no decoder messages on screen?
13a. Why can't I record a picture from the VCR scart?
14. Why do I get "Card Invalid" message?
15. Why do I get picture interference?
16. Where do I get more information/get my PRD repaired?
17. On D2Mac channels, why do I get no menus?
18. How does the Search Function work?
19. Can I have my MSS500/1000 upgraded to internal positioner and 500 channels
20. Why are certain options missing from the Set Up Programmed menu on my 508-1P?
21. How can I prevent the channel name from being displayed permanently on the TV?
22. Can I upgrade my MSS500 to have an internal Pro-Logic processor and D/D2MAC decoder?
23. How do I enter the service menu of my Pace MSS 500?
24. How do I update cards in my D2Mac receiver?

## 1. Why did my power supply fail?

There are no known design faults in this power supply so the usual cause of failure is a mains electricity power surge or overheating. Perhaps you had a power-cut or perhaps you plugged in an electric lawnmower or drill (or similar) nearby or perhaps you have faulty wiring in the plug, socket or somewhere in your house. The only other common cause of failure is that the receiver has been dropped or banged heavily. In this case the board around the transformer will be cracked and the result is often several expensive chips AND the tuner destroyed by high voltages. Repair may not be possible but, if it is, leave it to the experts. A bodge repair can be unsafe.

## 2. How do I repair the power supply?

I recommend that you DO NOT ATTEMPT IT. But you will anyway so: If the board is definitely not cracked and there are no scorch marks on the mains side of the transformer, simply replace the main switching FET with a STP5N90* and check the 27R resistor which feeds it. Solder the transformer joints to be sure they are all right. Replace the fuse with an identical type and put everything back together. If it goes bang, get a qualified repairer to fix it.

*Remember, these are classed as "Safety Critical" components. You MUST use the Pace-approved parts. If you don't you risk damage and fire hazard and could even be prosecuted under the Consumer Protection Act. Yes, I'm trying to scare you.
Use the proper kit. SATKIT 10

Overheating can be solved by fitting our fan kit. This has been used very successfully by lots of people.

## 3. Can I get extra channels?

Do you really need more channels? The very latest model has 500 channels. Pace will upgrade MSS500 to MSS500IP (500 channels with internal positioner) see Q. 19. In theory, older versions can be upgraded but there is no kit. We investigated this and it can be done as a workshop upgrade but there are too many variants to allow a simple kit to be used.

## 4. Can I upgrade my MSS500 to Dolby audio/or to motorised?

In theory, yes, but Pace do NOT offer a Dolby upgrade.
They DO offer a positioner upgrade if you send the receiver to them.

**5. Are there any "secret" handset codes?**

Yes. The "factory reset" will reset channel 1 only to Sky One. It will also reset the Installation menu settings. It will NOT change the rest of the channels.

Press:

Menu, 0, Store, Right arrow, Left arrow.

There is also a secret code which will display the AFC number on screen.

This works on early versions only.

Press:

[F] [I] (that's a letter "eye" for "Information").

Repeat the same button presses to turn this feature off.

Power-on program: Selects the program (channel) that appears when you power up the receiver.

-Press F (function key) and then RCL (recall key)
-Select the program number.
-Press STORE to save.

To disable it, repeat the key combination with the same program number.

Audio frequency indicator:

-Press F (function key) and then RADIO key

You can tell which software version you have by going into:

5. Installation
then
7. Download

Press STORE and the Pace part number of your software comes up at the bottom of the screen. The last three digits are the version number. This won't corrupt your channel settings, by the way, unless you happen to have another Pace receiver linked to your receiver of course!

**6. I get only a blue screen. What has happened?**
The blue screen appears if there is no signal.
The most obvious cause is that your LNB is not connected or, on a twin-input receiver, is connected to the wrong input.

**7. I get "LNB Short" on the screen, even with the LNB disconnected.**
Occasionally this happens if you've selected power for just one LNB in the Installation menu. The simplest way to correct this is to plug the receiver into the mains and press the factory reset sequence. This resets it to "LNB Power 1 & 2". It can also be caused by failure of C11, C12 in the power supply. If this is the case, you should fit RELKIT 10 which contains the Pace recommended upgraded C11, C12 and all the other parts which will have degraded at the same time. The miniature cooling fan kit would also be useful. Note: some people fitted ordinary capacitors and *caused* the above symptom. Use only the approved low ESR capacitors. It saves a lot of problems.

**8. Can I use a "Universal" LNB?**
Yes. Select tone ON in the second screen of the tuning menu for the appropriate channels.

Set it as a Multi tone LNB with 9.750 and 10.6 Lo settings.

In order to have the right frequency displayed, you need the internal positioner micro fitted. This provides new LNB type options. However the 'Universal' setting has a problem; it will not accept high band frequencies above 12500MHz. Use the following settings:

4 Polariser type: Volt
5 LNB: Multi Band Tone
6 Low Band: 9.750 FSS A
7 High Band: 10.600 Var.
You then get the range of:
10.700 - 11.900 Low Band
11.550 - 12.750 High Band.

**9. Why do I get no front panel display?**
Capacitor C2 on the front panel board was prone to failure - especially when the receiver has been "cooked". This capacitor should be replaced with a 1µF/50v multilayer ceramic capacitor. Do not use any other type.

(The original was 22µF electrolytic). SatCure can supply this capacitor as part of the reliability upgrade kit (RELKIT 10) on request, or just send 4 stamps to SatCure for C2 by itself (with instructions).

Removal of the panel is a delicate task which requires the correct tools and careful handling. You need the exact instructions from the service manual. We recommend that this work should be carried out only by persons who are practised in such work. We accept no responsibility for damage which might occur.
However, it is OK to solder the new capacitor to the copper track side of the display panel, across the existing capacitor, without removing the PCB.

### 10. Why does my MSS do strange things?
Occasionally, the rotary switch will stick between contacts. This leaves the microcontroller open to interference and it might change channel or volume all by itself. Give the knob a turn then use the handset to select a channel. An improved rotary switch is available.
Alternatively, some early models had an infra red receiver which was susceptible to interference. This can be replaced with a later type.

### 11. How can I tell how old my receiver is?
The date of manufacture is incorporated in the serial number.
For example: RAAYAH5245xxxxx
The "5" indicates 1995
The "24" indicates week 24 counting from first week in January.
The "5" indicates Friday.
The latest Micro version is ...108. This may be on an upside-down Eprom board or a microcontroller on the main board. (A different version may be used for the motorised "IP" version.) Earlier versions gave no real problems but some customers noticed that the word "MUTE" would appear on video recordings. Also, if mute was not used in timer mode, the loudspeakers might suddenly blast out the sound of "Eurotica" (or whatever) at 1am in the morning! Upgrading is simply a matter of getting the microcontroller or Eprom replaced. However, your customised settings will be lost.

### 12. How can I download the memory?
You connect a fully wired Scart to Scart cable between the Decoder sockets of identical MSS receivers then follow the on-screen instructions

from the Installation menu. You can not download successfully from dissimilar receivers and, to be certain, you should use this transfer facility only between receivers which have identical microcontroller I.C.s. If you are going to program a large number of receivers, try Kesh Electrics in County Fermanagh, Ireland (013656 31449). They have designed a PC Windows program and interface ("Pace Link") to do this. It costs about 200 pounds.

### 13. Why do I get no decoder messages on screen?
Try setting the contrast to 4 in the Installation menu.
If this doesn't work, and you have checked the tuning, you probably have a fault in the decoder section or the video amplifier circuit. Surface mount transistor Q58 may fail (PNP surface mount BC856B - see picture). It often happens gradually and increasing the contrast setting to 8 might fix the fault temporarily. We can supply this part if required. Alternatively, the fault might be cured by fitting RELKIT 10

### 13a. Why can't I record a picture from the VCR scart?
Try replacing Q35 (NPN surface mount BC846B).

### 14. Why do I get "Card Invalid" message?
Try your card in a different receiver to test it.
Make sure that the card contacts are clean and the card slot spring contacts are clean and not bent or twisted.
The ribbon cables which connect the card reader board to the main board can cause this fault (especially the one at the left side - check for continuity). If it's not this then the card reader board probably has a fault.

### 15. Why do I get picture interference?
There are lots of causes. If the interference takes the form of lines across the picture and has only recently become noticeable then (assuming you have not changed anything or moved any cables) it may be that C11 and C12 at the front of the power supply need to be replaced. (Pace supply a higher quality type, included in our reliability upgrade kit RELKIT 6). Do NOT use any other type. If the interference is not caused by these, then the usual causes apply (cheap pre-made RF leads and Scart leads being prime suspects).

## 16. Where do I get more information/get my MSS repaired?
http://www.netcentral.co.uk/satcure/ or contact Pace on 01274 532000
or service@pace.co.uk

## 17. On D2MAC channels why do I get no menus?
The TV is getting simple "loop-through" RGB from the decoder via the
MSS1000. The receiver doesn't have the capability to insert its on screen
graphics/menus in this mode. If you switch to PAL mode, you'll see
your menus and channel idents.

The RGB pins from the decoder SCART just pass directly to the TV
SCART. The decoder takes pin 16 (RGB fast blanking) high. This forces
the TV to RGB input.

Answer: cut pin 16 in the decoder (or TV) SCART lead, and change the
decoder setting as above. This will allow you to watch via composite
video but with menus. If you want RGB quality, select RGB on your TV
but you will lose the menus when you do so. Be aware that the picture
will probably shift sideways when you do this!

## 18. How does the Search Function work?
A two-speed search function has always been available on the MSS
range of receivers, but is not mentioned in the User Manual. In the
Tuning Menu press 'F' to commence the search in 50MHz steps. Press 'F'
again to access the 'fine' mode in 1MHz steps.

## 19. Can I have my MSS500/1000 upgraded
to internal positioner and 500 channel specification?
There is an upgrade which can be organised through Pace Returns
department. There are two upgrade paths that can be taken:
Positioner Only - 80 + VAT. Positioner and 500 Channel - 95 + VAT.
(prices may have changed) Please be advised that the upgrades can be
carried out only in Pace Service Department in Shipley.

## 20. Why are certain options missing from the Set Up Programmed menu on my MSS508-lP?
Options 3, 4 and 5 are removed from the Set Up Programme menu when
the Dish type is set to Fixed in the Input Menu. These options are not
required when the receiver is connected to a fixed dish. The options will
be present when the dish type is set to Steerable.

**21. How can I prevent the channel name from being displayed permanently on the TV screen?**
The Permanent channel name feature can be enabled/disabled by selecting the (i) key then STORE.

**22. Can I upgrade my MSS500 to have an internal Pro-Logic processor and D/D2MAC decoder?**
Unfortunately, these upgrades are not available from Pace, although an internal D2Mac decoder may be available another company.

**23. How do I enter the service menu of my Pace MSS 500?**
Go to: mac installation> 1. type 7 6 5

**24. How do I update cards in my D2Mac receiver?**
To update cards you must do this via the menu for entering new secret codes. This is accessed as follows: Press: MENU 8 Then select "CASS control" (To select an item press arrow up/down to position and arrow right to select). Then select "new secret code" Now you enter 4 digits by selecting each digit with arrow up/down and moving to next digit with arrow right. When the 4th digit has been selected just press arrow right again and the code has been saved. The above procedure must be repeated for each of the 7 codes making up a new Eurocrypt key.

# MSS1000/MSS500/Toshiba TS-540/Sony SAT301U

**Power Supply Faults**

*MSS1000 Psu ticks but will not light up or function:*
Disconnect power supply plug to prologic sound board. If this cures fault, check D54 for s/c. If D54 is OK, replace electrolytic capacitors C5 10µF and C6 100µF/35v. If sound board is faulty, see "Audio Faults".

*PSU voltages low and pulsing rapidly:*
C5 10µF and C6 100µF/35v
Check 10R SMD resistor.

RELKIT 10 contains the recommended low ESR electrolytics which will cure a variety of different symptoms. Save time by replacing these parts first.

*Does not light up or function:*
Check U12A

*Board cracked around transformer near D9 (TL431). PSU whistles or ticks and/or all voltages too high:*
Repair cracked tracks. Replace D9 and optocoupler if necessary. If no tuning voltage check zener diode D18 (27v) for s/c. If no front panel display replace C2 (1µF/50v/ceramic) and TR6 (ZTX314 or ZTX450) NPN medium power on the display board. Also check the negative 21 volt track on the display board (it melts near the ribbon connector). Sometimes the 27R resistor and power MOSFET in the PSU will fail.

If the power supply voltages have remained high for a long time, you might find the F2A fuse melted. Also the big Audio processor IC, tuner, Microcontroller and decoder ICs.

*Premature failure of C216:*
In some units, C216 discolours and/or the top bulges. Reliability can be improved by fitting a different type 1000µF/63v/20% Ultra-low ESR type (857-1086760). This is included in RELKIT 10 from SatCure, together with other parts which often fail due to overheating because of installed position (closed cabinet etc.)

**LNB Supply Faults**

*"LNB short" for no apparent reason:*
C12 1000µF/25v or 35v (very low ESR type).
*LNB short intermittently and only with an LNB connected:*
Change R52 (pin6 of U3) from 5k1 to 15k.

*LNB 1 + 2 "Short Circuit" message:*
U22, U23

**Front Panel Faults**

To initiate a display self-test press:
menu F 6 store
Press norm to exit.

RELKIT 10 contains the recommended low ESR electrolytics which will cure a variety of different symptoms. Save time by replacing these parts first.

*Front panel display dims or disappears:*
Replace C2 (22µF on front panel) with 1µF/50v multilayer ceramic capacitor part number 155-1055751. Do not use any other type!
Otherwise, look for melted track on -21v rail on display board. Also dead Q6 ZTX314 = ZTX450 (on front panel). Consult service manual before attempting to remove front panel display board!

*Stuck in standby, zeros on display:*
Microcontroller daughter board is not making contact with its socket.
Otherwise fault on data lines to EEprom (maybe leakage between links).

*MSS500-IP displays "motor overload" and chinese characters on screen:*
The 500 channel upgrade is incompatible with the microcontroller on the positioner board.
Change positioner micro from 808-8630120 to 809-8633121.

**Audio Faults**

*PSU ticks if sound board supply is connected (see PSU faults first!):*
Replace U11 & U12 on sound board. If s/c remains, replace Q3, Q4 SMD (BC846B marked "BR") and Q6 (BC856B marked "3Bs") on sound board.
If this fails to fix it, try replacing 4v7 zeners D1, D2 (925-0047551).

**See sketch on next page...**

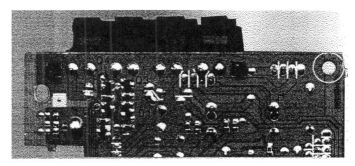

*Intermittent loss of surround sound:*
An insulated link wire had to be fitted to the solder side of the sound board in early models. Most will already have had this modification carried out so this is unlikely to be the cause. MSP3400 is more likely now.

*MSS1000 no audio:*
Disconnect from mains for two minutes. Otherwise replace U22, U18.

*MSS1000 no centre sound in config. No. 3:*
In speaker configuration no 3, one of the two audio channels normally used for Surround sound is switched to carry the centre channel sound. This configuration is normally used where the TV set doesn't provide adequate audio performance. Switching chip U2 carries out the changeover. There have been a few instances where U2 has failed to switch over. To ensure positive switching, R83 on the Dolby® Pro Logic board has been changed from 470kohm to 100kohm. Its full specification is 100kohm, 0.1W, 5% part no. 940-1040501.

*Surround sound comes on during video recording.*
*Mute symbol appears on recordings:*
Fit later software in Eprom number 805-1000108. This software is already present in receivers with serial numbers which begin "PALAE...." (or letters higher in the alphabet).

*Sound muted when returning from a MAC program:*
Replace microprocessor with later masked version.

*MSS1000 No prologic:*
Reset to Config 1 in menu

*MSS1000 Crackling from speakers/distorted audio:*
U14A

*MSS1000 Crackling on audio when Sky card version 10 is inserted:*
Check that C614 has been fitted. It forms part of the high-pass filter preceding Q104. C614 is located on the copper side of the PCB at the extreme edge under L53 and adjacent to X2 and X6.

*Distorted audio or no audio from RF or scart:*
Check C10 100µf 35v.
Also can cause slow display start up or flickering display.

Although the micro detects whether the Dolby Prologic™ board is connected and alters the on-screen menus accordingly, it does NOT route audio to the RF modulator if you remove the Dolby board. To achieve this, you need to change some link wires, thus:

MSS1000 J1, J4 fitted.
MSS500 J2, J3 fitted.
They are all around U18.
This information is especially useful if you scrap the Dolby board and leave the receiver as an MSS500 !! (You wouldn't would you?)

**Picture Faults**

*No picture:*
Check U8 and tuner if LNB voltage is present.

*Lines 1cm apart on every channel:*
Check tuner.

*Picture becomes sparkly intermittently:*
If installation is O.K. and the weather is fine, the tuner may be faulty.

*Dull pictures with no decoder messages (may be intermittent)*
Q58 BC856B (prime suspect)
Q100 BC856B
Q62 BC846B

*No picture from TV Scart (may be intermittent):*
Q40 BC546B. If this transistor has failed, also replace R261 and R263 SMD with higher value resistors 270R 5% (940-2710501) for reliability.

*No picture from VCR Scart (may be intermittent):*
Q35 (BC846B)

*Intermittent (when warm) "No signal" message on coloured background.:*
C208 1µF. X5, 503kHz resonator. U29, PTV111, or...
*If tuning voltage goes up and down in a random fashion:* X3 next to U22.

*Vertical black bar, some 30mm wide on my 13" screen, moves continually from right to left. On-screen channel idents also move right to left.*
*No decoder messages. Occasional vertical roll of picture:*
(From the Aux and Decoder scarts the black bar is not visible.)
Replace the PTV110.

RELKIT 10 contains the recommended low ESR electrolytics which will cure a variety of different symptoms. Save time by replacing these parts first.

**Menu Faults**

*MSS1000 no prologic in menu:*
Check ribbon connections to prologic board. Replace ribbon cables.

*Clock inaccurate:*
Replace C6 (39pF) with 47pF/5% ceramic capacitor (150-4705551).

**Decoder Faults**

*Says "insert card" with card in slot:*
Ribbon Rib7, CA1.

*MSS500/1000 videocrypt messages off-centre or distorted:*
Replace R75 SMD (911) with 1k2/5% (940-1220501)

*No decoder messages:*
Ensure that Contrast is set to level 4 in the installation menu.
Otherwise, replace U9.

*After warm up decoder messages disappear:*
Picture loses V & H sync (turn blue screen off to view).
OK with U29 frozen. Replace C208 1µF next to U29 (PTV111/TEA2130)

*Noisy picture on decoded chans:*
C11, C12. Tuner or U5

*"Card Invalid" message when card is inserted:*
Sometimes without card inserted.
Usually a cracked ribbon cable at the left side of the main PCB but some-times the PTV113 on the card-reader board is dead.

*Cross-hatch pattern in areas of saturated colour on decoded channels:*
Change R62 from 620 to 330 ohms 0.1W 5% Part No. 940-3310501
Change R64 from 470 to 560 ohms 0.1W 5% Part No. 940-5610501

If the decoder circuit is suspect then a signal can be forcedthrough
by pressing: menu 0 store rcl tv sat.
Note this is a toggle command and must be turned off using the same
sequence.

*Flashes "P" below decoder message:*
Faulty U8 PTV112

*Loss of sync. on decoded channels:*
U5, PTV110

**Terrestrial Picture faults**

Interference to terrestrial TV signals can arise from harmonics of the
28MHz clock generator within the Videocrypt section of the receiver.
Careful modification of the circuit can reduce the radiated harmonics.

Change C38 (22pF) to 1K 0.1W 5% SMD resistor Part No. 940-1020501
Change C40 (56pF) to 22pF 50V 5% SMD capacitor Part No. 950-2205501
Change C39 (47pF) to 39pF 50V 5% SMD capacitor Part No. 950-3905501

## Miscellaneous Faults

SPURIOUS CHANNEL OR VOLUME CHANGE

A condition may arise in which the unit changes channel or volume level alters by itself. This can be due to the contacts of the rotary control on the front panel coming to rest in a position in which they are not properly made. The cause of the problem is the detent tabs on the front panel moulding becoming slack. Where troubles of this nature are experienced it is advisable to replace the rotary control.
A new assembly is available with built-in detent springs to overcome this problem.
The fault may also cause random power-up from standby mode.
New control part number: 146-0002421
3 way shrouded header: 161-1020310
A similar fault can be caused by the infra-re sensor fitted to early units. Pace can supply a later version sensor.

*Symptom:*
Test bars on screen and
VCFC1
CAS25
SHIFT :0D
ADJ :24
PATTERN :00
Sound OK. All menus OK. OSD is OK:

Cause: Dry joint on TST1 in the decoder section.

*MSS Remote will not work Sony SAT301U receiver:*
The only answer to this problem is to replace both microcontrollers - one on the main board and one on the front panel display board, with those specified for the identical Pace-badge receiver.

*Garbage in front panel display:*
Early type IR sensor may need to be replaced by later type. Improved capacitor decoupling may be required.

# Chaparral Monterey 20/40

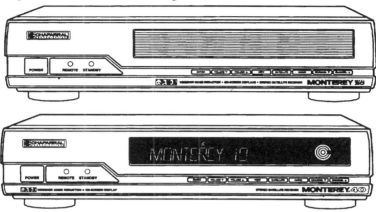

*Power-On light works but TV screen is blank. Pressing channel button pro-*
*duces white patterns on the screen.*
Use Master Clear procedure: Switch mains on. Hold ENTER and VOL-
UME ▲ buttons then press POWER. Wait for a few seconds then press
POWER again.

When accessing menu options 4 to 9 you must enter the pass code 2 3 4
5.

## Setting up to use a RAI decoder or Videocrypt decoder
Example:
Select EUTELSAT F2
Select RAI UNO (at a time when video is encrypted) then press
MENU
6
▼         [CONFIGURE]
〉         SWAP to find [INPUT-1]
ENTER
〉         SWAP to find [TYPE: DESCRAM TYPE D]  (TYPE A for
Videocrypt)
MENU
7
▼         [SOURCE]
〉         SWAP to find [INPUT-1]

> A kit incorporating new front
> panel is available to convert
> a Monterey 20 to a 40.

ENTER

Notes:

Check decoder operation for Rai Due, also, since encryption method varies.

RAI decoder "SATVIEW" type needs a scart to phono lead. The red phono plug goes to 1 VIDEO on the Monterey 40 and the black goes to OUTPUT DESC 1.

(If input/output No. 1 is already in use then configure for a different number).

## Voltage Switching modification

Later Chaparral software allows the DC output voltage on the lower LNB port to be switched between 13v and 18v by appropriate menu selection. It is more useful to switch the voltage on the upper port because this port supports a wideband LNB.

The modification is simply to locate Diode D148 and D142 close to it then cut and resolder one leg of each diode to the position of the other so that the diodes are then crossed over each other.

Note: References to Ports A and B respectively in the menus will now be wrong.

Ensure that the later software is actually fitted or the modification will not work.

Press the following button sequence:

SAT

MESSAGE

AUDIO

SELECT

Select Menu 6 "Receiver Setup"

Before modification

**Port A** (top) gives:

18 volts regardless of the option set on the menu line "13v"

**Port B** (bottom) gives:

13 volts when VERTICAL is selected on the menu line "13v"

18 volts when HORIZONTAL is selected.

After modification
**Port A** (top) gives:

| | |
|---|---|
| 13 volts | (13v VERTICAL selected in the menu) |
| 18 volts | (13v HORIZONTAL) |
| 18 volts | (13v 4 GHZ) |
| 13 volts | (13v 11 GHZ) |
| 18 volts | (13v 12 GHZ) |
| 18 volts | (13v DBS) |
| 18 volts | (13v OFF) |

**Port B** (bottom) gives:
18 volts    (*regardless of menu option selected for* 13v)

### Testing With an Actuator

Connect the motor wires to the two terminals which sit alone at the rear of the receiver. Connect the two reed switch pulse wires to 'SENSE' and 'GND' which are connectors 2 and 4 (counting from top left of the block of 8 connectors).

Connect a TV set and tune to match receiver output. Select MENU 6. Enter the pass code 2345 and reselect the menu if necessary. Follow the menu instructions to set the East/West limits and drive the actuator east or west to test the function.

# Chaparral Cheyenne Using with a decoder

Select the scrambled channel and set the audio frequency which can not be altered once the descrambler is selected. Do this by pressing [MODE] until AUDIO FREQUENCY is displayed on the screen. Change the frequency if necessary (usually 6.50 is correct) and press [STORE].
Press [A] [F] [6] [3]
Press and hold [9] to give a black background to the graphics.
Move the arrow on the screen down to "USE DESCRAMBLER" by using the arrow keys to the right of the [MODE] button.
Press [1] to select then [STORE] then [0] to remove the black screen.
(The screen will remain black until the decoder is connected.)
Use a SCART to VIDEO phono lead to connect the decoder.

# Echostar Variants

*Much of the information in this section has been reproduced by kind permission of ECHOSPHERE INTERNATIONAL on the understanding that repairs and modifications be carried out only by approved distributors or service centres of Echosphere. Some of the material is original and may not necessarily be endorsed by Echosphere.*

# Echostar SR-4500

*Limited channel range — typically will only tune up to channel 25.*
Measure voltage on diode CR17 cathode / C88+ / CR18 cathode which should be about 54vDC. If not then replace C87 (100µF, 100v). Similar fault may be caused by C88 short circuit.

*No channels. Raster shows faint lines or sparkles as each channel is selected. Signal strength LEDs all light to indicate maximum even with no LNB input.*
Replace capacitor C160 (47µF/35v) inside demodulator. If that fails then it is likely that at least one other capacitor has also failed. At this stage you might find it more efficient simply to replace the entire demodulator. This fault is often caused by overheating and occurs more often in receivers which have been used on 240 volt mains with 220v selected.

Sometimes the demodulator will oscillate due to too much gain in the amplifier stages. If this is the case, change the emitter resistors R114 (for Q102) and R130 (for Q107) from 10Ω to 39Ω.

### To Clear Memory
Erase Satellite 01
Press [EAST][WEST][STORE] all together.
Hold them during countdown to zero.
Continue to hold them during three more fast countdowns.

*Lock light is on:*
Press "lock" then 4 3 7. Otherwise, replace 28C16 EEprom.

*Won't tune higher than mid FSS band:*
Check Tuner Vcc, should be approx 30V. If low replace C87 and C88 (lOOuF/lOOV!).

## Demodulator

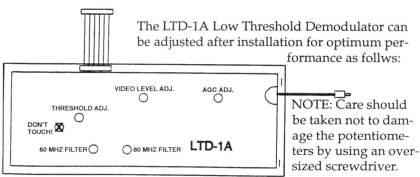

The LTD-1A Low Threshold Demodulator can be adjusted after installation for optimum performance as follws:

NOTE: Care should be taken not to damage the potentiometers by using an oversized screwdriver.

### 1. THRESHOLD ADJUSTMENT
Turning the (1 turn) threshold adjustment potentiometer clockwise or counter clockwise. This adjustment will tune the demodulator from white to black sparklies. A plasbc alignment tool is suggested for this adjustment. The pobntiometer should be set so that there is an equal amount of black and whib sparklies in the video on a weak signal.

### 2. VIDEO LEVEL ADJUSTMENT
Increases or decreases the MAC and Baseband video output level. Only adjust when required.

### 3. AGC ADJUSTMENT
Increases or decreases the AGC voltage. This signal is used for an inclined orbit antenna positioner which requires the AGC voltage for signal strength. The typical output voltage is in the range of 100 to 400mV. Only adjust this potentiometer when required.

### 4. ADJUSTMENTS IN CASE OF POOR AUDIO PERFORMANCE
When the Low Threshold circuit is switched ON and poor audio is detected, there are two possible problems:

If the THRESHOLD ADJUSTMENT has been set to the narrowest position, turn the potenbometer until the audio is free from distortion. Incorrect adjustment of the 60 and 80 MHz filters. (These are factory set to the optimal setting for normal use). Adjust the 80MHz filter first. Tum the 80MHz adjustment to minimise the distortion then turn the 60MHz adjustment until the audio distortion disappears.

## SR-4500 BASEBAND LEVEL ADJUSTMENT

In some rare cases a customer using the SR-4500 together with a BaseBand type of decoder might experience the following:

1. Video picture too bright or too dark
2. BaseBand decoder not working properly

This can easily be corrected by adjusting the video/baseband level with the BaseBand potentiometer which can easily be reached through the bottom plate underneath the receiver. Turning the BB-potmeter Clockwise will increase the brightness and vice versa.

Note: - The Composite BaseBand Level adj. poten- tiometer has an effect on the BaseBand out- put as well as the Video output level. The Video Level Adj. potmeter affects only the Video Level.

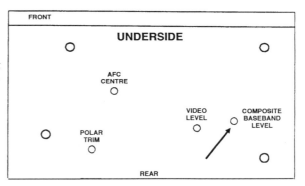

### Connecting a decoder

Make up suitable leads and connect the decoder as shown below. The SR4500 has no video input so you must feed the decoded video sig- nal into a Video recorder instead.

Select "Ext" or "Aux" or "AV" on the Video Recorder.

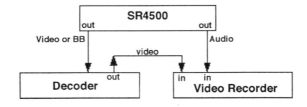

# Echostar SR5500

*Switching mains on occasionally causes failure of Power Supply Unit.*
There are two fuses behind the mains switch cover. The left hand fuse is
designed to melt, in the event of a mains surge, and will protect the
power supply itself from failure. The right hand fuse protects the positioner transformer. Always replace a fuse with an identical one.

*Dead:*
Check fuses. Later models blew the 1A for no apparent reason - Check if
S.M.P. running. If so, positioner transformer o/c or poor connection
(processor monitors the positioner supply: no voltage = no function/dis-
play.) Replace C12/13 (1OOuF 35V 105°C low ESR)
Replace R1/R2 (11OK/1OOK High Voltage)
Check large smoothing capacitors C101, C102 for splits or bulges.
The transistor (FET) is an IRFBE30 but a BUZ80A will work perfectly.

*PSU trips:*
Check the two 6v8/1W3 zeners hidden amongst the toroidal inductors.

*Hum bars seen across picture:*
Replace C101 (220uF 25V) and C 102 (100uF 25V) -noise on 12V rail.
Also if pictures are poor check 20V tuner rail- most likely low.

There is a 1A fuse next to the transistor. Replace this with a BUSS1A;
replace the ferrite beads on its lead. Some models use a low value resistor instead. A 0R22 fusible resistor from an SS9000 seems OK.

Monitor the DC voltage on the large power supply connector on the
main board, third pin from the left. Adjust the potentiometer (anticlockwise to reduce) on the power supply board until the voltage reading is
5.0 volts. (Power supplies made after August 1992 have <u>no</u> adjuster).
Measure the voltage on the centre of the left hand of the two potentiometers on the front panel PCB and adjust it to 1.4 volts or until the on-
screen graphics are centralised. Adjust the voltage on the other potentiometer to read 3.95 volts. If a Sharp tuner is fitted you must interrupt
the brown supply wire close to the tuner and insert a 470µH choke.
Failure to do so could result in fine white horizontal line interference on
the picture. A capacitor may also be required between the tuner-side of

the choke and 0 volts. This modification is not required for the later AT2352 tuner made by Astec.

**WARNING:**
PSU capacitors hold charge for a long time after disconnection.

*Actuator will not move:*
Check fuses. Check 24v transformer. Check relay board.

**<u>Adaptation of the favourite video programme in the later versions of the SR-5500</u>** (such as channels on Astra 1B).
Type in channels as usual (video, polarity etc.)
Access the favourite programme list.
Find vacant numbers on the list (there should be gaps everywhere) and write the numbers down on paper.
Exit the menu and tune in to an unallocated channel.
Press the Favourite button once, followed by one of the unused numbers.
Press STORE. The graphics will then indicate how to enter a new name.
Use the channel up/down buttons and the tuning left/right buttons to assign this channel a name; e.g. "EUROSPORT/N3" or similar.
Press STORE.

**<u>Eprom Versions for the SR-5500</u>**
The existing Eprom version can be displayed on the first line of the Status Menu by pressing [EXTRA FEATURES] followed by [5] on the Remote Control.
**IMPORTANT:** The replacement of older Eprom versions may be carried out only in accordance with the following list:

| <u>Old Eprom version</u> | <u>May be replaced with</u> |
| --- | --- |
| 1.02, 1.11S or 1.22ES | 1.26EA2 |
| 1.22EA | 1.26EA |
| 1.21IS or 1.22IS | 1.26IS |
| 1.22IA | 1.26IA |
| 2.03 or later | Used in the SR-5500 |

PLUS. Provides direct numeric frequency entry and menus include features to control the internal ferrite polariser and LNB voltage switching circuitry of the PLUS version. May be used in a receiver with either ASTEC *or* SHARP tuner version to replace *any* previous software.

Note: The default setting is for a SHARP tuner. For an ASTEC tuner then you must select tuner type 1 thus:

Press [Extra Features]
select [3]     Installation
enter password  7907878
select [1]     System setup
select [7]     Tuner type — 1
Store the change.

In addition, for pre - SR5500 PLUS receivers you will need to press [5] to select 13/18v PRESENT...NO and also press [6] for FERRITE....OFF (but read notes below).

**Versions 2.05 and 2.06**......................................... A slight upgrade from 2.03 in that the radio channel list is updated and the Polarity Peaking software is improved.
An extra digit is provided for direct frequency entry.

**Version 2.10 April 1995.** FSS tuning range 10700 to 11999
Quatro & Triple Band LNB DRO of 9750 and 10 MHz (limited range).

### Useful Information
*Installation access code:*  7907878

*External decoder:*
On selected channel press [Tuning Select]: enter 94 to toggle.

*Inverted video output:*
On selected channel press [Tuning Select]: enter 96 to toggle.

Later SR-5500 versions have the ASTEC AT2352 tuner and software version 1.26EA2 (or later). A Technical Bulletin dated **06-06-91** describes the new features. You may also need the Technical Bulletin dated **05-31-91** entitled "SR-5500 Triple Band Operation - Astec Tuner Version".

IMPORTANT!
*After fitting updated Eprom you must CLEAR memory.*
*Then you must CLEAR ALL MEMORY as follows:*
[Extra Features], [5] status, [Enter], [Enter], [<] tuning, [Enter].

A simple internal modification gives a 13/17 volt option if you upgrade the Eprom to 2.07 or a later version.

You will need the following parts:

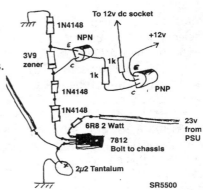

7812 regulator with insulating kit
A 3v9 400mW zener diode.
Three 1N4148 or 1N914 silicon diodes.
Two 1k 0.25W resistors.
A 6R8 2 Watt resistor.
A BC547B or any general purpose NPN silicon transistor.
A BC557B or any general purpose PNP silicon transistor.
A 2u2F/25v tantalum bead capacitor.
Thin, multistrand, insulated wire.
A voltmeter.

1. Bolt the 7812 to the base plate with insulating kit.
2. Solder the 6R8/2W resistor to the input leg of the 7812.
3. Using the voltmeter, locate the wire which feeds 23 volts to the tuner.
4. Cut this wire close to the 7812 regulator and connect it to the resistor.
5. Connect the tuner end of the wire to the 7812 output leg.
6. Connect the positive wire of the 2u2F capacitor to the 7812 output leg.
7. Connect the other wire of the 2u2F capacitor to 0 volts (tuner box).
8. Connect the three diodes and zener in line as shown.
9. Connect them between the middle leg of the 7812 and 0 volts (tuner ).
10. Connect the two transistors and two 1k resistors as shown.
11. Connect a wire from the 1k resistor to the 12v dc socket on rear panel
12. Connect a wire from the the PNP transistor emitter wire to 12v link.
(The link next to transistor Q13 on the main board carries 12 volts. Measure it to be certain).

In the SYSTEM SETUP menu make sure that "13/18v Present" is "YES".
In the LNB Configuration menu, select the appropriate LNB.
To set the polarisation for each channel, press "TUNING SELECT" button 5 times.
Press "FORMAT" button to toggle H-V.
Press "STORE".

*Memory loss*

Memory loss in the SR-5500 can have many reasons —
A loose or empty battery The battery should read at least 3.0 volts (3.2v new).
Memory loss caused by power interruption.
For the latter cause, a remedy is available in the form of a package which includes an MC34064 — an under voltage sensing circuit designed specifically for use as a reset controller in microprocessor systems. When this circuit is mounted in the SR-5500, the gate array U-6 will be reset before a voltage drop can affect memory.
New software fitted without a complete Hard Reset being carried out (this is *not* simply "Clear All Memory". See note elsewhere in this section.)

Please contact your dealer for Technical Bulletin **TB SR-55 91.5** which describes the modification in full.

*Echostar Satellite Interface Module will not work correctly*
Please ask your dealer for a copy of the Technical Bulletin (no reference number) which deals specifically with this unit. You may also need the Technical Bulletin dated **05-31-91** entitled "SR-5500 Triple Band Operation - Astec Tuner Version" which shows a diagram with the interface connections.

*Blank screen with rolling graphics on every channel:*
Usually caused by lack of -5v from power supply. Lack of voltage may be caused by the demise of C106 and diode CR103. At this stage the power supply should undergo complete upgrade or it will fail again in the near future.
The power supply voltages should be your first measurement with any fault on the SR5500.

Front

23.1
-5.1
5.1
11.6
0.0
-12.3

**Power supply connector voltages on main board**

*Polarisation reverts back, 3 seconds after change:*
In the Installation Menu, select FERRITE ON. If you select the OFF option, the polariser signal remains on just long enough to work a mechanical polarotor.

*Tunes only every 4th or 5th channel:*
Replace SAA1057 at the side of the tuner module.

*SR5500 changes channel by itself:*
Check 5v rail. Should be 5.05v. Cover IR sensor. If that cures it, the cause is sunlight or other light source. Otherwise, disconnect IR sensor plug; if that cures it, replace IR sensor. Otherwise, replace 100 pin gate array IC.

*SR5500 loses sat position by several counts:*
Ensure correct screened ribbon cable is used and screen is connected to 0v ground ONLY at receiver end (not at dish). Otherwise, check tightness of actuator bolts. Otherwise, replace reed switch in actuator.

**Threshold Extension Filter for SR-5500**

The Threshold Extension Filter is available from your local Echostar Dealer and is an accessory which can be added to the SR-5500 receiver. It is a variable bandwidth filter, designed to be field adjusted for 1.F. bandwidths between approx. 9 MHz and 22 MHz. The filter is intended to be adjusted once to a given bandwidth and then switched in and out by using the code "99" on the SR-5500 hand held remote control. The filter can be attached to SR-5500 receivers in lieu of an 1.F. looping plug which is standard on later models. The looping plug is a wire connecting together two of the five pins in a Berg-stick type header. The plug is positioned inside the SR-5500, on the opposite end of the tuner from the tuner's input ports.
     To install the filter, the looping plug is removed. A hole should be made in the chassis to give access to the single adjusting screw on one side of the filter. The filter is then installed in its place. The single adjusbng screw on the filter should face the left hand (seen from the front) vertical part of the metal chassis. The two adjusting screws on the other side of the filter should face inside the receiver.
     To adjust the filter to an optimum bandwidth for the chosen video carrier, a small non-metalic srewdriver is supplied. Both the filter bandwidth (by means of the single screw) as well as its frequency setting (by using the two inner screws) should be adjusted empirically to effect the best picture.
     After installation and adjustment the filter is then fixed to the chassis of the receiver by means of a small clip so it will not shake loose and become detached from the five pin header.

# Echostar SR-5500 Plus

This unit is factory configured for 13/18v switching to the LNB inputs *instead* of a 12v output on the accessory jack. If you want the 12v output *instead* of the 13/18v switching capability, simply lift the jumper on the tuner board and move it to position 2 which is furthest from the ribbon cable. In the installation menu change the 13/18v option from YES to NO.

The SR-5500 Plus has a ferrite polariser interface board fitted internally as standard. If the unit is to be used with a mechanical polariser *or with any magnetic polariser other than that made by Echostar* simply connect the plug from the polariser terminals directly to the Relay board socket, bypassing the polariser board.
In the installation menu change the FERRITE option to OFF, unless the receiver is to be used in conjunction with an interface which utilises the pulse output, in which case leave the option ON.

Polariser skew tuning

On a selected channel:
press [TUNING SELECT]
press [STORE]

The optimum polarity setting will be found and stored automatically for this channel.

On all channels for this satellite:
press [TUNING SELECT]
press [ENTER]
press [STORE]

All horizontal channels will be set to the optimum polarity found on the current channel and all vertical channels will be offset by 90°.

To set various satellites:
press [ENTER]
type the number of the satellite or select it with the tuning keys
press [STORE]

# Interface Module

The Interface Module allows you to use the SR-4500 or SR-5500 with the following system configurations:

Two single band LNBs (operating in different frequency bands) with either ferrite or servo polarisers.
One dual band LNB with either a ferrite or servo polariser.
One or two dual polarity LNBs (no polarisers).

Once the interface module is connected, the FSS/DBS button (on either the SR-5500 remore control or the SR-4500 front panel) will select the appropriate frequency band (either FSS/DBS or FSS/Telecom). The SKEW and polarity functions in the receiver continue to operate as usual and can be used to "fine tune" or reverse the polarity angle for the best possible reception.

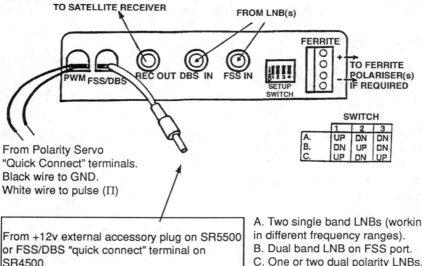

From Polarity Servo
"Quick Connect" terminals.
Black wire to GND.
White wire to pulse (Π)

From +12v external accessory plug on SR5500 or FSS/DBS "quick connect" terminal on SR4500.

For the SR4500:
Cut the connector from the wires.
Strip 1mm of insulation from the ends.
Connect black wire to the ground terminal.
Connect the red wire to the FSS/DBS terminal.

A. Two single band LNBs (working in different frequency ranges).
B. Dual band LNB on FSS port.
C. One or two dual polarity LNBs.

Switch 4:
Up = 10 mA ferrite polariser
Dn = 35 mA ferrite polariser

Disregard this setting if you are not using a ferrite polariser.

PWM Input - If your system includes a ferrite polariser, these two wires should be connected to your satellite receiver's POLARITY SERVO terminal strip (labeled "ROTOR" on the SR4500). The black wire shoula be connected to the GND terminal and the white wire should be connected to the PULSE (P) terminal. When these wires are connected, the interface module will accept the receivers Pulse Width Modulated (PWM) servo output and convert it to the appropriate control current for the FERRITE Output.

FERRITE Output - These two terminals are provided for connecting the interface module to a ferrite polariser. If your system is equipped with one or more ferrite polarisers, connect the wires from the polarisers to the FERRITE terminals on the interface box. If the polariser wires are marked "+" and "-," connect each wire to the appropriate terminal. If your polariser wires are not marked, connect the wires arbitrarily and then test the system to make sure you have video. If you do not receive video once your installation is complete, you may need to reverse the wires connected to the FERRITE terminals.

If the feedhorn(s) in your system are equipped with mechanical servo polarisers, no connections are made to the interface module's FERRITE terminals. Mechanical servo polariser wires should be connected directly to the back of the satellite receiver.

FSS/DBS Input - These wires should be connected to either the FSS/DBS terminal on the SR4500, or the +12 volt External Accessory plug on the SR-5500. Connect the red wire to the central (red) terminal of the separate plug and the black wire to the outer (black) terminal of the plug. If you're connecting an SR4500, strip approximately 1.0 cm of insulation from the wire ends. The red wire should be connected to the FSS/DBS terminal, and the black wire should be connected to GND. If the FSS/D8S button on either the SR-5500 remote control or the SR4500 front panel does not appear to operate correctly after the interface module is connected, the FSS/DBS input wires may be attached to the satellite receiver incorrectly. If you experience this problem, reverse the FSS/DBS wires and test the system's operation again.

REC OUT - This coaxial connector provides the Intermediate Frequency (IF) output to your receiver. Use a short coaxial cable (not included) to attach the interface box to the "IF" input on the SR4500, or to PORT A (the upper IF port) on the SR-5500. (The interface box will not operate correctly if it's connected to PORT B (the lower IF port) on the SR-5500.) FSS IN and DBS IN - These inputs are provided for connecting your LNB(s) to the satellite interface module. The FSS IN port should be used for either an FSS or dual band LNB. The DBS port should be used for either a DBS or Telecom LNB.

SET-UP Switches - These switches are used to set up the interface module to operate in different types of system configurations. The illustration on the previous page shows how to set the switches for your system.

SPECIAL NOTES CONCERNING THE SR-5500

1. The software in your SR-5500 must be dated later than October 1989 to ensure the proper operation of the interface module. Check the date of your software by pressing [EXTRA FEATURES], and then selecting option [5] (for STATUS). After verifying the date on this display, press [CANCEL] twice to exit from the Extra Features mode.

3. The REC OUTPUT of the interface module must be connected to PORT A (the upper IF port) on the back of the SR-5500. (On some receivers this port is labeled "FSS.")

4. The SR-5500 "SYSTEM SETUP" option must be programmed for "INTERFACE ON." To verify or change this SYSTEM SETUP option:
a Press [EXTRA FEATURES]
b. Press [3] to select "INSTALLATION."
c. Enter the password (if applicable)
d. Press [1 ] to select "SYSTEM SETUP."
e. Press [6I to switch the "INTERFACE" option on.
f. Use the [CANCEL] button to exit from the Extra Features mode.

## SR 5500 ASTEC TUNER VERSION

The Astec tuner differs from the former (Sharp) tuners in the following points:

The video bandwidth of this tuner can be selected in three steps being 27, 21 and 17 MHz. The normal bandwidth is 27 MHz to which all channels have been preset. The 21 MHz bandwidth is selected by means of the direct entry code [00] for the Bandwidth Reduction Filter (BRF), whereas the narrow filter of 17 MHz is selected with the direct entry code [99] for the Threshold Extension Filter (TEF).
A separate Threshold Extension Filter can not be used.

The signal strength indication now is divided in steps from 0-256. This giving a higher resolution and more accurate automatic peaking of polarity and dish position.

The voltage supply to the lower (DBS) port is only available when the frequency band of the LNB connected to this port has been selected. This prevents interference from the other LNB.
For Dual band LNBs and a dual polarity LNB the use of a Satellite Interface is still required.

In the new software version for this receiver ( 1.26EA2 onwards) a function is incorporated to select the correct input port for either a DBS or Telecom LNB.

The Triple Band Operation solution with a Dual band FSS/DBS LNB combined with a single Telecom LNB, (or, which is new, a Dual band Band FSS/TEL LNB combined with a DBS LNB), mounted on a Ferrite Orthomode Feed no longer requires an additional C/Ku switch.

If you have changed the video and/or audio frequency of a program, the name of the video or audio program, or the name of a satellite, and have stored this information, the original frequencies and names can now be retrieved by selecting the same channel or satellite again and pressing the following direct entry code: for the frequency
[4I[9] + [STORE]
for the program name [5][0] + [STORE]
for the satellite name [5][1] + [STORE]

## Triple band configuration.

The items required are as follows:
a) 1 SR-5500 provided with 1990 or later software version
b) 1 Satellite Interface Unit
c) 1 C/Ku switch
d) 1 FSS/DBS Dual Band LNB
e) 1 Telecom LNB
f) 1 Ferrite Orthomode Feed

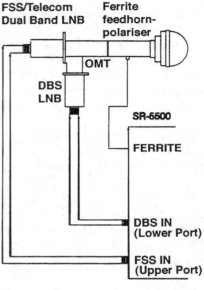

The above items are configured as shown in the attached diagram. The 0/12 V line of the receiver controls both the C/Ku switch as well as the satellite interface simultaneously, such that when FSS or DBS is selected, Telecom is switched off and vice versa. This is to prevent interference between these bands.

Please note the following points:

1. Due to the software configuration of the SR-5500 this design will work only with an FSS/DBS dual band LNB and a single band Telecom LNB.

2. The dip switches of the satellite interface must be set for dual band operation as indicated in the attached diagram.

3. In the On Screen Graphics menu the Satellite Interface should be kept in the OFF state. This enables the lower port, allowing triple band operation.

4. To prevent cross-polarization on the DBS bands a dielectric plate should be inserted inside the feedhom in front of the ferrite polarizer. This is to separate between left hand and right hand polarized signals.The hood of the feedhorn should be carefully taken off to insert and align the dielectric plate properly Then the cap should be glued to the feedhorn again to prevent moisture ingress.

## SR-5500 plus Triple Band Operation with 950-1750 MHz tuner

The items required are as follows:

a) 1 SR-5500 provided with Ferrite polarizer control and 13l18v switching, with 2.03EE or later software version.
b) 1 FSS/TELECOM (or FSS/DBS) Dual Band LNB
c) 1 DBS (or Telecom) Single Band LNB
d) 1 Ferrite Orthomode Feed

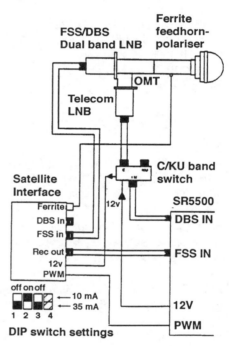

Please note the following points:

In the On Screen Graphics EXTRA FEATURES menu select:
3-INSTALLATION
1-SYSTEM SETUP
2-LNB CONFIGURATION
4-0RTHO MODE
2-FERRITE ORTHO
1 (or 2 for the LNB selection indicated above in brackets) and several times press CANCEL to return.

# Echostar
# SR6500/7700

*SR6500/7700 PSU dead:*
Large capacitor C8 marked "GLORIA" may fail. Copper tracks may
melt. Remove damaged +ve tracks and replace with insulated wires
beneath the board.
Replace the I.C. with a UC3844.
Replace the capacitor C8 with a 150µF/400v/105°C.
CR5 1N4006 may be s/c.
Q1, Q7 BUZ80A may be s/c.
BR1 may be s/c.

Akit is available (SATKIT 13)

Notes:
R11 = 10R, R14 = 1R, R9 = 1k2 1206, Q3, Q10 = "2F" 2N2907 or "T8"
BSR16 PNP, Q2 = "1P" 2N2222 or "U8" BSR14 NPN. R5 is 2 x 100k =
200k 350v. BR1 is 600v/8A.

*Standby light on but no functions*
If not power supply, try replacing the two software Eproms. (Later versions are available).

On "Golden" series SR6500, measure R168 in the power supply. If it is
greater than 14k2, replace it.

*Handset not working*
If no LEDs light on handset, remove the battery cover and the batteries.
Ensure that switches 1 and 6 are ON and the others are OFF.
Replace the batteries.
Flick switch 5 ON then immediately OFF.
Press [SPEED] (left hand LED flickers).
Press [AUTH] (all four LEDs light).

Consult user handbook for instructions on how to set the handset for
use with your particular receiver.

*Channels do not match up with frequencies selected.*
The LNB offset "DRO" must be set to match the LNB in use. Some "Triple-Band Extended" LNBs, for instance, need an offset of 9750.00 instead of 1000.00 and the receiver must be set accordingly. This option is already set and may be selected in the SR7700 without further problem. In earlier receivers, however, only ordinary "Triple Band" option exists and must be customised to match an unusual LNB.
Such customisation *must* be carried out before any other option is set, including the setting of East/West limits!

*Skew adjustment insufficient.*
Unless you are using an Echostar polariser you may need to select the 85mA option in the menu.

*Skew value will not store.*
With a ferrite polariser the timed polariser option must be OFF.

*Left audio produces a vacuum cleaner noise:*
C74 3µ3F/35v.

SR-6500 connected to a DR-70 Mac decoder may give poor audio on DMAC channels. To cure this, remove the audio board. Locate inductor L19 on the right side of the board. Solder a wire across it. Replace the audio board.

**Hard Reset for SR6500/7700/8700**
Reset the receiver as described in the manual.
Select a language.
[CANCEL] back to the Extra Features menu.
Press the lower left button on the handset.
Press [STORE].
Press [ENTER].
Now the MAIN TEST menu will appear.
Press the tuning [<] button.
Press [ENTER}.
The RAM will be erased.

SR7700: Auto tracking problem. This receiver has a system that enables satellite tracking on installation after East, West, centre satellites have been stored. The system does not work fully if the centre stored satellite is not near enough to the centre of the arc.This is fully explained in the instruction manual. May also be some software problems.

ECHOSTAR SR7700 ( and possibly SR8700 )
*"LINE CLOCK FAILURE" flashes on screen when unit turned on or channels changed:*
Cure: R1 (1 meg) on power supply high or o\c

# Echostar SR8700

In many respects this is similar to the SR7700 receiver but there are major differences, not least of which is the power supply..

*PSU dead:*
R16 and R17 (100k/350v) towards the centre of the PSU board.
(The going rate for this repair is currently around £65.00 and some dealers are still fitting the wrong type of resistor! It is *most* important that these resistors are rated at 350 volts. Available from SatCure).

The D2Mac version has an interesting problem:
Selecting Composite Video gives NO Scart output on this model.
If you want to connect an external VideoCrypt decoder via Scart you must do it like this.

Press Tuning and select Ext 1 or 2 as appropriate for Scart.
Press MENU and select Installation then AV Setup.
Select MAC baseband for Scart output.
Store these settings.

On the Videocrypt decoder put the deemphasis switch ON.
Connect Scart to Scart.

*Clock loses 2 hours per day:*
In the Installation menu, press STORE and hold it.
You can toggle between 50Hz and 60Hz mains.

# Echostar SR5700

*Will not respond to handset even with new batteries:*
(maybe after mains failure).
Hold Standby button on handset whilst plugging receiver into mains power. Release Standby button. Handset should now work normally.

*Pal I/G adjustment:*
Some models have a jump link at the rear inside the modulator. Versions without this have a software control (I am told). Code 80?

# Echostar SR800

Insufficient LNB current available:
Replace RT5002 (300mA PTC) with a 400mA PTC device such as Raychem RXE-040.

# Echostar SR80

Shows blue screen for a few seconds with external decoder:
Replace R173 (220k) with 4M7. Replace C137 (4u7F) with 1nF.

# Echostar SR50

18 volt LNB feed gives less than 17 volts:
Replace R501 (1k4) with a 6v8 zener. Situated left rear corner near modulator.

# Uniden UST-7007

*Blows main fuse.*
See end of UST-8008 section.

*Frequency tunes in large steps. Unable to fine tune some channels.*
DBS has been selected instead of ECS. Press "DBS" button until display reads "ECS" then press MEMO button. Do this for every affected channel. (With DBS selected, frequency steps are ~ 4MHz. For ECS, frequency goes in 1MHz steps).

*No LNB voltage*
Check switch setting on rear panel. Left position is 0 volt. Centre is 18 volts. Right is 15v for ECS and 18v for DBS.
Check Voltages from transformer secondary on J401.
Check fuses F401 and F402.
Check bridge rectifier behind F401.
Ensure voltage is reaching IC115 with 12 volts ₀ᵥ coming out. (IC115 is in the centre of the panel, adjacent to the right of the mains transformer.
Check voltages on Q112, Q145 and IC116 (near the rear panel switch).

0v    18v    15v ECS / 18v DBS

*Panel display shows stars.*
Replace Microprocessor IC113.

*No tuning voltage or no variation in tuning voltage.*
Check C108, C109, C111 and IC102.

*Intermittent picture or intermittent sound.*
Dry joints on Scart, R.F. modulator or relays.

*Intermittent dead.*
Dry joints on power supply.

Note: When working on main PCB, <u>always</u> disconnect the plug from the power supply board. The high voltage stored in the smoothing capacitor is easily shorted to the 5 volt line and will destroy the microprocessor.

*Destroys LNB.*
Intermittent shorted turns on mains transformer primary.

*Intermittent patterning.*
Replace modulator.

*Poor pictures:*
Replace capacitors inside tuner.

> The RF modulator from a Pace SS9200 fits and has the bonus of a test signal switch.

*Videocrypt decoder does not work.*
An internal modification is possible to allow the decoder to work. The TV must be connected to the RF output socket because the decoded picture is not routed via the TV SCART.

If the UST-92 D2MAC transcoder is connected, the TV must be connected to the UST-92 TV SCART socket (or RF socket on later models) because the D2MAC picture is not routed to the receiver TV SCART or to the RF output. You must select [MAC] on the receiver front panel button.

# Uniden UST-8008

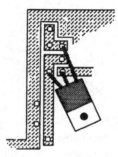

*No polariser output.*
Q801 tends to overheat. Sometimes it goes short circuit and sometimes it melts the solder and falls out. I always replace it with a BD936 or TIP32A on the upper (track) side of the PCB as shown in the sketch. Fit double-sided foam adhesive tape beneath transistor.

*Polariser skew insufficient.*
Replace one of the two large resistors (100Ω) with 47Ω 0.5W (R828 or R834). You can check the polariser current by fitting a 68Ω 2 Watt resistor to the polariser terminals on the rear panel. Adjusting the skew to maximum should give a reading of at least 8 volts across the resistor.

*No LNB voltage with 15V selected by switch.*
Replace fuse F401 (T1A) with T2A fuse. If still no LNB voltage, check inside the tuner; the track breaks where the "F" connector is soldered. If T2A fuse melts the mains transformer may have an intermittent fault.

*Won't light up. PSU etc. OK:*
Replace 2 x 1uF adjacent to IC1

### Modifying the UST-8008 for 14v/18v switching

Disconnect the power supply from the main
board.
Locate pin 7 of IC804 on polariser board.
Solder a wire to it and feed the wire through
the main board to the underside.

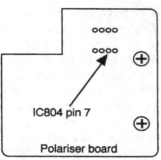

Remove the 7815 regulator (the front one of
three on the aluminium divider wall) and
refit it with an insulating kit. Do not resolder
the centre leg.

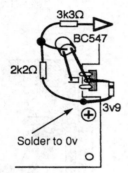

Fit transistor, 3v9 zener and resistors as shown.
Connect the wire to the 3k3Ω resistor. Connect
power supply. Select +++ for 14v and - - - for 18v.

*No tuning voltage.*
Check D405 (27 volt zener).

*No voltage from transformer.*
Replace transformer.

| VRMS | J401 |
|------|------|
| 18.6 | ○ ○ |
| 30.6 | ○ ○ |
| 12.6 | ○ ○ |
| 24.7 | ○ ○ |

*Low video gain. Poor, unlocked pictures:*
Replace 10µF capacitor inside the tuner (front right side).
Test this by warming the capacitor with a soldering iron.

*Tuning problems.*
Check C106, C107, C108.

*Blows main fuse.*
Remove and discard the large capacitor which is close to the fuse.
If the fuse still blows, renew the transformer.

### Using External decoder

Connect decoder to the right hand SCART socket as viewed from front.
Open flap and press [AUX] until you see [A1] indicated. Press [MEMO].
Repeat for each scrambled channel.

# UNIDEN UST-92

The UST-92 is designed to work with Uniden receivers.
Although it may work satisfactorily with other makes of receiver, consistent operation can not be guaranteed. In particular, it will not work correctly unless the receiver has the correct MAC de-emphasised baseband output available.

**The UST-92 will usually not work with Pace or Monterey receivers.**

Note: Later UST-92 decoders include Eurocrypt. Of the earlier types, only those of "series 7" can be modified to incorporate Eurocrypt.

Note: Eprom versions prior to v5.03 may not support Filmnet encryption reliably.
    (The Eprom must be a fast access, 120nS, type 27C512).

## Upgrading the UST-92

Disconnect the mains supply and remove the cover.
Remove the "jumper" link located in front of the 8 pin I.C. at the front of the unit.
Replace the existing EPROM with the new (version 5.03 or later).
Reconnect the mains.
Press [STANDBY]
Press [SELECT]
With the menu cursor highlighting SERVICE press [SELECT]
With the menu cursor highlighting DEFAULT VALUES press [SELECT]
Disconnect the mains.
Reconnect the mains. Set the VCO adjustement as follows:
Press [STANDBY]
With the menu cursor highlighting SERVICE press [SELECT]
With the menu cursor highlighting VCO ADJUSTMENT press [SELECT]
Use ▲ and ▼ to minimise the scrolling of the picture.
Replace the "jumper" link and press [SELECT].

*Will not descramble D2MAC channels:*
If the decoder is genuinely faulty (i.e. it used to work with the same receiver and the receiver tuner is O.K.), replace I.C. marked DMA2286.

# UNIDEN UST-771

*No drive East or West.*

Most faults are caused by incorrect installation.

Replace Q109 even if it measures correctly.

Check Q110, Q105 and Q106 for short circuit.

Check cut-out which goes open circuit.

Check D120, D121, D119 which go short circuit.

Check Opto couplers IC108 and IC109 which go open circuit.

*Loses memory.*

Measure battery cell on the main board. When new this is 3.2 volts. Causes problem if less than 2.8 volts. Replace if less than 3 volts. Cut tags of existing cell, leaving them as long as possible. Solder tags of new battery to tags still in board. Saves the trouble of taking out the board and also allows the largest size of cell to be fitted for longer life.

*Loses memory after mains failure.*

On early versions, remove the wire link between R164 and pin 33 (end pin) of the microprocessor.

On later versions, cut the track which forms the same connection.

# Maspro SRE-90S

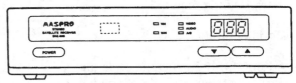

*Very low audio.*
Check Q206; a 2SC3311 near phono sockets. May be replaced with a BC238 or similar.

*No audio.*
Check X201 oscillation on pins 1 & 14 of IC204 (LC7215). If no oscillation, replace X201 with an 11.160 MHz crystal.

*Buzzing on audio which varies with video level.*
Turn yellow adjuster in RF modulator. (Also see next page).

*No polarity switching (15v only)*
Ensure that the label on the rear specifies 14/18v switching. Early versions provided 15 volts only!

*No polariser control:*
When vertical polarity is selected (with polariser or 100Ω resistor connected) a hum bar breaks up the picture. The -12 volt rail on Link W344 (alongside the tuner) will show a pronounced "ripple" on the oscilloscope.
Replace C407 (100µF/35v) next to IC405 on the right hand edge of the P.C.B.

*Will not store:*
The SRE-90R has fixed channels above channel 26 and parameters can not be changed.

*Black & white sparklies on Astra 1B (esp. 18 & 30).*

Adjust trimmer in tuner module (uppermost of pair).

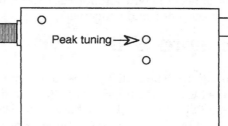

Peak tuning ➡ O

*Maspro SRE90 very sparkly pictures since Jan 95 as if tuner failing:*
Astra 1D filter required.

### Modifications

Adding 13/17v switching capability.
Carry out the modifications shown
in the sketch in order to use a
switching type LNB.

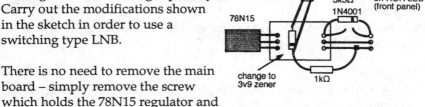

There is no need to remove the main
board – simply remove the screw
which holds the 78N15 regulator and
bend the tiny board upwards to give access to the solder joints.

The zener diode must be fitted the *opposite way round* to the existing
diode, as shown in the sketch.

Solder the BC547 transistor to the legs of the zener diode.

Solder the 1N4001 rectifier across the link wire then cut the link.

The 3k3Ω resistor is soldered to the middle leg of the transistor and a
wire is connected from the resistor to the thin track on the front panel
(the track which is connected to the LED marked "HOR" on the panel).

### Using with External Decoder

Use a SCART to SCART lead to connect videocrypt decoder but modify
the lead at the receiver end if a buzzing is detected on audio:–

Disconnect the wires from pins 3 and 6 and cut them short.
Connect pins 3 and 6 together.

# Maspro ST8

To call up the installation menu you put the receiver in standby, then
press the channel up/down buttons simultaneously.
Dead PSU? Replace FA5304 I.C., 2SK1545 FET available from Electrotech
Ticking PSU? check large rectifier diodes at front of PSU.

# NEC 3022

### Fitting External Decoder

Open the front panel.
Select each encrypted channel in turn and press
[PROG]
[SHIFT] until I/E appears.
Use up/down buttons to select video.
[PROG] to store.

Connect decoder with a SCART to "D" plug lead as used with Amstrad
SRX200.

# NEC 4012

*No LNB voltage*
Replace R605 with a 1Ω 0.5W resistor (easiest to crimp it around the legs
of the existing resistor and solder it – a terrible "bodge" but saves
removing the entire board.
(R605 sits just left of centre near the front edge of the board, behind the
plug and socket designated "TB".)

*Dead:*
Replace large electrolytics & bridge rectifiers.

# Connexions SRT40

*TV pictures poor. Satellite pictures O.K.*
Check 12 volt supply from D601. If missing, replace R601 (180Ω/0.5W), D601 (12v zener), C602 (100µF/16v). If 12 volt supply is O.K. replace RF modulator.

# CX95A / Echostar SR-70VC

*Card will not go in slot.*
Remove cover and re-position any wires which obscure the slot.

*Hiss but no audio from RF output. Scart output audio OK.*
Some receivers intended for export are adjusted for PAL G. Remove the top cover. Remove the tuner nut and all screws from the rear cover. Hinge down the rear cover and adjust the tiny slotted adjuster nearest the test switch in the RF modulator, with a jewellers screwdriver, until clear audio is heard.

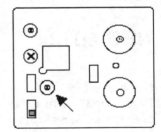

*Receiver will not light up.*
No 5 volt on U601.
OK when decoder board unplugged.
Check all small yellow decoupling capacitors on the decoder board for a brown stain which indicates internal short circuit. Replace any faulty capacitor.

### Lost Some Channels or Settings?

Factory Reset:
Hold ▼ and ▲ and reconnect mains power.
Continue to hold ▼ and ▲ until [SEL] appears in the LED display.
Release the buttons and [PR2] appears in the display.
Press ▼ and [PR1] appears.
Press STANDBY and the display will count down.
Reset sequence is now complete.
(PR1 for English; PR2 for German settings).

The sketch is intended to show the approximate voltage measurements.

*Receiver "dead".*
*Does not light up.*
*5 volt missing from*
*U601. Fuse may have*
*melted:*
Disconnect decoder board then replace any melted fuses. If the receiver now lights up, check decoder board I.C. decoupling capacitors for brown marks indicating internal short circuit.

*Blows fuse:*
Check all large black diodes for short circuit

*18 volts too low:*
Replace R609 (780R) with 1k (centre of board near front).

220nF C126 beneath videocrypt board can fail and cause picture problems.

**CX95A / SR-70VC power supply section**

*No Decoder messages and won't decode:*
IL01 - I.C. (TEA2029C) on Decoder PCB.

Note: Spare parts are available from PROTEL in London.

# Videocrypt decoder SVA1

**The information given in this section is intended to help you to decide whether the unit is beyond economic repair. You must <u>not</u> attempt to repair a Videocrypt decoder yourself.**

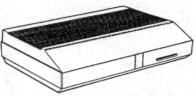

**Under the licensing agreement with Thomson plc only authorised repair centres are permitted to repair these decoders. Each authorised repair centre must satisfy very stringent requirements relating to test equipment and facilities. Only authorised repair centres may purchase the special gate array and card reader I.C.s from the manufacturers.**

*Decoder works intermittently (encrypted video keeps flashing back on screen).*
Also may appear simply as intermittent streaks across the screen. Adjust PP02 in PSU section anticlockwise. A minimum value of 4.80 volts on TP01 is recommended. (If adjusted too far, screen message becomes faint.) Suspect TEA2029C or diodes DW01 and DW02. Putting two 1N4148 in series for DW01 can help.

*Blank screen.*

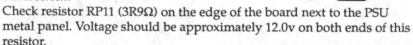

Check resistor RP11 (3R9Ω) on the edge of the board next to the PSU metal panel. Voltage should be approximately 12.0v on both ends of this resistor.
Check board for cracked tracks — a common problem.
Check 5 volts on DP09 cathode/link J130 or DP10 cathode. If very low or zero, check DP09 (2v7 zener), RP44 (0Ω22) and DP10 (5v6 zener). DP09 goes high causing DP10 to short circuit and burn out RP44. Check 28MHz crystal.
Failure of 74LS541N can also cause blank screen.

*Completely dead.*
Check fuses.
Check board for cracked track leading to mains input side of transformer.
Check transformer pin solder joints which break under 50Hz vibration or dropping.

*Broad, horizontal black and white bands on screen.*
Electrolytic capacitor (CP01 4700µF/16v) in power supply is loose or
faulty.

*Messages appear and decodes non-card channels but card won't work.*
Look for cracked track near to fixing screw nearest card reader.

*No messages. Picture remains scrambled.*
If TP03 collector gives 16v instead of 12v, check DP11 (6v8 zener). Also
check TV04 transistor near SCART socket and check 100Ω resistor
beneath TV04. If these are OK, check TA01 and TA02 which often fail.
Finally, suspect IV02.

*Descrambled picture quality poor, streaky colours, perhaps worsening with time.*
Check 28.000MHz crystal by tapping and with freezer aerosol. Measure
frequency which should be within 0.001MHz of 28.000. Similar symptoms caused by 1V01.

*Horizontal alternate lines missing.*
1V02 or 1V03 faulty.

*Messages O.K. but vertical white lines on screen.*
Suspect 1V02 or IV03 line memory I.C.

*Black line down side of screen.*
Suspect IV02 or IV03 line memory I.C.

*Light sparkles on poor picture:*
Suspect capacitor CA12

*No graphics.*
Suspect 1W05, 1W03 and 1V01. Check TV19 for short circuit.
Pins 37 and 39 of I.C. 1W03 should have positive going pulses. If pulses
are negative going then suspect I.C. 1W01.

*Message reads "Card Invalid".**
Make sure that the card really is valid!

Broken tracks to - and adjacent to - TP05 (front left corner).
Card detector contacts inside card holder dirty or bent. Check RP12 for
dry joint. Check zener DP15. Check zener DP16. Check IW05. If message
appears even without card then switch contacts at the rear of the card
reader may not be touching each other.

*Message "No tokens left".\**
Look for broken track in power supply area.

*Message "No programmes remaining".\**
Check for 3v on pin 38 and 5v on pin 12 of 1WC5.
Check for 5v on link 246 with card present.

---

*These faults can often be cured simply by connecting a 270Ω
resistor between link J130 and the link J107 near to the front edge of
the board. **Magic!***

---

*White spots in centre region of the picture:*
May be caused by failure of CA02 electrolytic which may also be associated with the failure of TA04.

*Over bright picture:*
IV06 can cause this fault.

*After repair, 5 volt rail remains well above 5 volts:*
Replace DP28 (7v5 zener).

*Intermittent scrambling when hot:*
Suspect IW02, DW01 and DW02.

*Does not light up. No 12v on TP03:*
Check DP21, DP11 for s/c. RP39 o/c or dry joint.

## Useful voltage measurements

|       | B     | C     | E     |
|-------|-------|-------|-------|
| **TP01** | 8.4   | 5.05  | 9.16  |
| **TP05** | 0.0   | 12.2  | 0.15  |
| **TP09** | 0.0   | 37.6  | 0.0   |
| **TP03** | 15.8  | 12.2  | 16.5  |

(PP02 adjusts 5 volt output).

*See also the SRD400 section which lists many Videocrypt™ faults.*

Rear View of Decoder SCART

| 1 | Audio out RH |
|---|---|
| 2 | Audio in RH |
| 3 | Audio out LH |
| 4 | Audio earth |
| 5 | |
| 6 | Audio in LH |
| 7 | |
| 8 | AV switching |

0v out = internal bypass

12v out = select external videocrypt

| 17 | Video out earth |
|----|----|
| 18 | Video in earth |
| 19 | Video out |
| 20 | Baseband in |
| 21 | Common earth |

# Ferguson SRD4

*Unable to remove parental lock.*
Perform factory reset, by pressing the following button sequence:
STANDBY
ENTER (for 10 seconds)
9
A
6
9
A

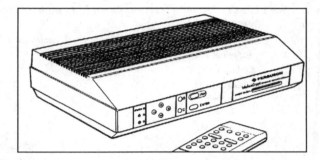

To bypass the PIN
9
A
6
9

*Power supply whistles in standby*
Replace DP13 (a 3v9 zener diode).

*Dead (PSU won't start up. May be intermittent):*
CP08 (220µF/25v)
TP12 BUT11A or similar
DP21 3v9 400mW
DP13 3v9 1w3
IP01 UC3842.

Fit SATKIT 11 to fix dead PSU.
RELKIT 11 will get rid of most
"streaky picture" faults.

*No video signal*
Check LNB connection. Check "F" connector socket is connected to the
main board.
If no 14v on LV15 next to tuner – replace PNP transistors TP71 (and some-
times TP73) at the front of the power supply (use FXT749).
Possibly CP69 (1,000uF, 25V), DP69 (BA158) and DP72 (1N4007).
Otherwise:
Replace surface mount I.C. beneath the tuner (use one from an old SRB1
(BSB receiver). Remove the tuner daughter board and resolder dry joints
on the underside. Replace this daughter board with one from an SRB1.

*Standby light OK but no lights or functions when not in standby*
No 5v on LV14 next to tuner – replace TP77. Clean decoder connectors.

*No LNB voltage*
Check "F" connector joint. Check large blue disc PTC resistor RP63.
TP64 switches 13/17v, controlled by TP75, TP67 from pin 11 of SMD I.C.
beneath the tuner section. If pin 11 track o/c then LNB voltage stays 13v.

*LNB voltage more than 20 volts*
Replace DP64 7.5 v zener (6v8 is OK).

*Sparkly pictures (both black and white sparklies):*
Replace "MN" 4 legged SMD beneath tuner next to "F" connector with
"C1C" device from a Hitachi BF9 tuner.
Otherwise replace tuner inner module.

# Ferguson SRD6

*To reset PIN number:*
Turn off mains
Press & hold Standby
Turn on mains
Hold Standby for at least 6 seconds
Main "Satellite menu" will appear
Press [2] to select the line "child lock"
Enter new PIN.

*No pictures:*
Check IM05 TEA6417B on daughter board. ("low cost video switching
module")
Baseband should go into pin 1.
Video should come out of pin 16.

# Zeta-1000L/BEST Galaxy-2022L

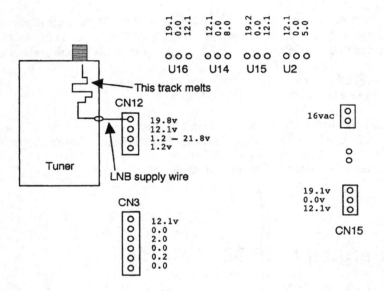

The sketch indicates voltage measuring points.

*No LNB voltage.*
Remove tuner and check track which carries current feed to the socket. Repair track if damaged keeping dimensions the same as original. Fit a 630mA fuse in the yellow feed wire between CN12 and the tuner to minimise future damage.

*Switching LNB voltage.*
It is possible to switch the LNB voltage between the 19 volt and the 12 volt supply lines. See Drake ESR324E for details of a similar modification.

# Drake ESR324E

*Adding a videocrypt decoder loop-through.*
Carry out modification 1. shown in the sketch.
The video level must be reduced by turning the potentiometer anticlock-wise.
Video is taken out via the VIDEO phono socket and back in via the TM socket.
If the videocrypt is disconnected, link TM and VIDEO sockets together. (Note that the picture will be dull without the decoder in line since the video level has been reduced).

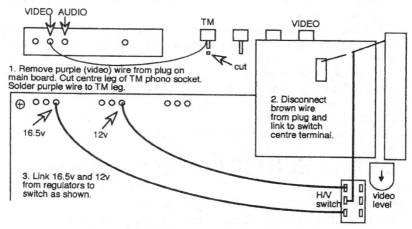

*Adding 12/16 volt switching for a marconi type LNB:*
Carry out the modifications shown as 2. and 3.

# Drake 250S

*Losing positions/channel data:*
I.C. U116(28C16) EEPROM.

# Drake ESR2000mac and ESR800mac

*Here's how to get into the secret Menus of the internal Macab Mac200:*
press "Cancel" "4" "5" "6"

# Drake ESR-250E

Speed up tuning for a full-band LNB.
The tuning-in of the upper bands (DBS and TELECOM) will be required,
due to the difference in the local oscillator frequency of this LNB.
Find a spare channel to be assigned (e.g. M6 CHANNEL 73).
Enter set-up mode L (modify channel).
Select 1 — High-voltage supply.
Select 2 — IF frequency.
Press 0 0 on the remote. The receiver will now start to scan, quickly,
achieving a full scan in approximately 20 seconds. The polarity switches
after each scan.
When the desired channel is viewed momentarily, press STORE immedi-
ately. The receiver will continue to scan but the frequency will be stored
in memory.
Exit scan mode by pressing the Volume Down button then fine-tune as
normal. Set all the other parameters for the channel and store them.

*Blows main fuse at rear of unit:*
Check all diodes on the left side of the main board for short-circuit.

# DRAKE ESR100 (= Arcon Titan S)

*LED display shows "dE5" and nothing functions:*
The Drake has an 8 section dipswitch on the rear panel.
The "Datentransfer" switch is in the wrong position.
(I think the microprocessor just waits for downloading).

# ITT Nokia SAT 1100
### Salora 5902

*No polariser output.*
Broken tracks where the Polariser
output socket is soldered to the PCB. If the screw which supports the
phono sockets is lost then the same track break can occur there, too.
To test polariser output, connect a 68Ω resistor across the socket terminals. Measure the voltage across it which should be 0v when POL 0 is
selected and approximately 9v when POL 9 is selected. There should be
steps of roughly 1 volt inbetween when POL + (other numeric key) are
pressed. Pressing TUNE + or - will alter the voltage in smaller steps.
The Nokia SAT 1100 changes the LNB voltage from 14v to 18v according
to the polariser selection. The changeover point is between P4 and P5.
This model has 14/18v marked on the rear panel.

*Decoder won't work.*
Press [0] three times to select external loop-through. Store this setting
for each appropriate channel by pressing STORE followed by the two-
digit channel number within eight seconds.

*Blank screen on some channels.*
The above selection for external loop-through has been stored but no
external unit is fitted (or may be fitted but not switched on). Press [0]
three times to de-select external loop-through and store the setting.

If the blank screen remains, the problem may be caused by failure of a
transistor: try connecting together links JS28 and JS29 (next to a hole in
the centre of the board). If the picture appears, the surface mount PNP
transistor connected to these two links beneath the board has failed. It
can be replaced with a conventional FXT749 soldered to the copper pads
or you may get away with leaving JS28 and JS29 connected together!

*Sound but no picture.*
Look for broken 0v tracks beneath phono sockets.

*No LNB voltage:*
There should be 25 volts going into IT02 and 18 volts coming out and
going via copper tracks and links to the tuner. The tuner pins, if not
cropped short, can touch the chassis and short the voltage out.

## Adding 13/18v switching capability to early models.

The sketches show an under-board view of the modifications required. The method uses a 7812 voltage regulator in place of the existing 7818 fixed-voltage regulator, and a transistor to reduce the resistance when 13 volts is required. Almost any NPN transistor will suffice. The transistor is mounted through existing holes in the board. The resistors are soldered beneath the board.

A track must be cut and *the new regulator must be insulated from the heatsink.*, either by using a plastic encapsulated regulator (as used in Amstrad SRD400) or by fitting an insulator kit or by cutting the copper away from each copper leg of the heatsink then bridging the resultant earth-rail break with wire.

13 or 17 volt LNB voltage is now selected for each channel by choosing either pol 0 for Vertical or, for Horizontal, any other pol (1 — 9). eg. press [POL] [0] [STORE] then the two digit channel number.

*Stuck in standby:*
IC10 SAA1251

*No picture, no LNB volts:*
CT09 100nF

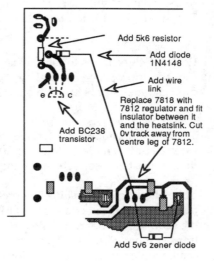

Add 5k6 resistor
Add diode 1N4148
Add wire link
Replace 7818 with 7812 regulator and fit insulator between it and the heatsink. Cut 0v track away from centre leg of 7812.
Add BC238 transistor
Add 5v6 zener diode

### Salora SRV1150 type 6241

*No signal to TV.*
Replace transistor T30 (TIP32A) PNP. Check IC13 (7805) solder joints.

*No video/blank screen.*
Replace C50, 2200µF/16v.

To use an external decoder, this model requires modification or else route the signal via a video recorder.

# Nokia SAT1700

*Dead*
Check PCB fuse FP01.
Check for dry joints on LP07, LP08.
In the MkII you may need to replace the following:
DP02 BZX83C30
DP06 BZX55B12
DP07,8,10,19  1N4148
DP09 BZX83C15
TPO1,5  BC857B
TP02,3  BC847B
TP04 MOSFET P6N60F1
FUSE 500mA recommended
RP17  2K7 SMD 5% 0.25W
RP30  22R SMD 5% 0.25W
RP18  1R5 5% 0.25W Flame Retardant
TL431 adjustable zener reference
IP01 Optocoupler (CNY17-1Z)

There is no factory reset function. An external programming box may be purchased in order to reprogram the unit.

*After warm-up, the PSU whistles and horizontal lines appear on the screen on vertical channels only:*
Optocoupler IP01 CNY17-1Z.

*No LNB voltage*
If only port 1 affected, replace DB61. If only port 2 is affected, replace DB62. If both ports affected, replace RB64 (1Ω1).
Note: LNB voltage can also be turned off in the Service Menu so check this first!

LNB volts will not go below 16.5
IP02

*Blank screen when MENU button pressed*
Check AF51 crystal operation.

*Misspelt graphics*
Check AF51 crystal for dry joints.

*No picture from RF and TV Scart but OK from AUX Scart:*
TF31 (BC547B surface mount) use BC847C.

*No output from RF modulator but OK from SCART socket*
Check for voltage on capacitors C81 and C82 at the side of the modulator. If no voltage, replace TP07 in the power supply.

*To change from fine tune value back to AFC, select CHANNEL in the menu:*
Press [FP+] then [FP-]
Press STORE
Enter the three digit channel number
Press [TV/SAT]

*No pictures on lower frequency channels (or drifts off when warm):*
Early tuners would not tune lower than Astra 1a. Replace tuner panel.
Receivers with serial numbers 149628 to 159888 were affected.

*Picture drifts in and out every few seconds (especially ASTRA 1C):*
Channel polarity is reversed. (Early receivers had all Astra 1C channels
reversed).
Later receivers had this corrected and the carton is marked (NP).

*Intermittent or no decoding. Faint messages. Or completely blank screen:*
Improve 5v connection by soldering a wire from J48 to pin 7 of decoder
board connector. Clean connector with WD-40.

*LNB volts switch 16.5 - 17.0 only:*
Replace IP02.

*Some channels are very sparkly:*
In the menu, select CHANNEL and press [FP+] then [FP-]. Press STORE
then enter the three-digit channel number. Press [TV/SAT] to exit from
the menu.
If this fails to correct the problem, in the menu, deselect the AFC and
fine tune until picture is clear, then store.

To select/deselect RADIO press the [--/---] button while the appropriate
line is selected in the Audio menu. (Obvious, wasn't it!)

*Not sure what the symptom is but here's the cure!*
Link beneath decoder board J72.
10 way connector pin 10 high (5v)
If micro not reset = 0v therefore micro faulty.
micro order code 64-80130-01
AF51 crystal

## Secret Handset Codes

To enter the Service Mode, press the following button sequence, quickly:

| STORE | -/-- | TV/SAT |
|-------|------|--------|

If [ERR] message appears, cancel by pressing TV/SAT then try again.
Once in the service mode, you can alter such features as PIN number,
actual video level and other program codes.

### Nokia SAT1700 mk II used with D2MAC decoder

Press [MENU] [P+] [FP+] to select installation menu on screen
Press [P+] [P-] until the DECODER line is selected on the screen menu
Press [FP+] until this line reads d3
Press [STORE] then enter the channel number (3 digits).
Press [TV/SAT] to confirm changes and to exit menu mode.

### NOKIA 5918 D2MAC DECODER (3002CS)

*Blank screen. Unable to access main menu:*
Replace NVram followed by master reset then adjusted items in service
menu and main menu.

*The 3002CS uses the TV SCART socket for its satellite receiver connection!*

Connect 3002CS to TV using SCART - SCART or RF output. With the
3002CS handset press: [MENU] [P+] [FP+] [P+] [P+] [P+] and press
[FP+] to set Baseband output to SCART. The next line down - Baseband
Deemphasis - may be set to MAC or FLAT to correspond to the receiver
output. You may need to return to this, later. Now connect TV to satellite
receiver. Connect the satellite receiver Decoder Output to the TV Scart
socket of the 3002CS.

Set the satellite-receiver for EXT AV on a D2MAC channel. Set the receiver baseband deemphasis to MAC or FLAT. You may need to change this setting on both receiver and 3002CS to get a reliable picture. Note that some pirate cards may not work.

Some receivers will not give a satisfactory MAC deemphasised output. PRD without 2GHz written on the serial number label can be a problem. Early Pace receivers can also give intermittent results. Where this is the case, set the receiver to give PAL deemphasis and alter the 3002CS wiring as follows:

Inside the 3002CS "TV" socket Scart plug, cut the wire from pin 20. Extend this wire to a Phono plug in the BASEBAND IN socket of the 3002CS.

Set the 3002CS Installation menu Baseband input to "Phono."
Set the 3002CS Installation menu "TV switch" option to "On."
(See the following page for more detailed instructions).

**Nokia SAT1800 with 3002CS D2Mac decoder (5918).**

Connect the 3002CS to the TV via the Scart socket labelled "TV" or via an RF lead (tune the TV to the RF output).
Press:
[Menu] button to see the menu.
[P+] until the word "Installation" is highlighted.
[FP+] to show the Installation menu
[P+] until the words "Baseband input" are highlighted (select "Phono")
(PAL deemphasis is always selected automatically for Phono input.
For Scart socket input, Flat or Mac deemphasis may be selected).
[P+] until the words "TV switch" are highlighted (select "On")
[STORE] to store these settings.
[TV/SAT] to exit the menu.

Connect the SAT1800 to the TV and select each D2Mac channel in turn.
Press:
[down arrow] to highlight "Channel Set-up".
[OK]
[down button] to highlight "Decoder".
[down arrow] to select "d3".

[OK]
[OK]
[TV/SAT]
[TV/SAT] to exit the menu.

Modify a Scart to Scart lead as follows:
Inside one plug, cut the wire which goes to pin 20. Extend this wire by 200mm and fit a Phono (cinch) plug to it. Label this plug "TV 3002CS." Label the other Scart plug "Decoder Scart SAT1800."

Connect the SAT1800 to the 3002CS using the modified Scart lead. The modified Scart plug goes to the "TV" Scart socket on the 3002CS. The Phono plug goes to the "IN Baseband" socket. The other Scart plug goes to the "Decoder Scart" socket on the SAT1800.

With a D2Mac channel selected you should see the message "No smart card in slot" after a few seconds. Press the green handset button to select left or right card slot and insert the smart card.

**Nokia SAT800 with 3002CS D2Mac decoder (5918).**

Set each D2Mac channel to decoder type "D3" by pressing SETUP 5 times then using arrow keys. Press "store" 3 times. Set the 3002CS decoder as for SAT1800 and use the modified Scart lead.

---

**Nokia d2mac decoder reset and SVA1 5volt line**
On the Nokia 5815 D2mac decoder, and using the twin pic pcb, when changing from any of the 3 TV3 channels to either Filmnet + or TV1000 or vice-versa the decoder does not issue a reset to the card.

The only way to get the reset is to either pull the card/interface out and put it back or to put the decoder into and out of standby using the remote control or the pushbutton on the front. This then makes the decoder issue a reset.

If you put a led onto the reset line, you will see the led flash when a reset is issued.

5volt -------/ \ / \ / \ / \ /-----()----- reset line.

2k2 resistor  led

From: bl@aerostar.win-uk.net (B L)

# Nokia SAT2202

*Blank screen. No 12 volts from TP08 beneath decoder board:*
Replace TP08 with a PNP transistor rated at 1A/800mW or higher.
An FXT749 will do but the lead configuration is different.
Also, replace RP36 with 330Ω.

*Timer fault:*
Replace Eprom on decoder board with version 2.09 or later.

An Eprom kit is available for the SAT2200 to upgrade it for DMAC as
well as D2MAC reception. Order mod kit 58631093.
This replaces 262-5337-02.


# Nokia 5152 Positioner

To install:
Hold up/down buttons and apply mains power.
The display will show [-].
Press [0] on the remote to select Nokia 1700/2202 and wait 2 seconds.
To clear memory press Memory button for 2 seconds then release.
The display will show ---.
Wait 15 seconds.
Exit service mode by disconnecting mains power.
Reconnect mains.
Set West limit and press Memory button.
Set East limit and store.

# Nokia SAT800/PAL203

*SAT800+ dead:*
R525 (383k) o/c or TS7 (BC857) leaky

Modification of output stage for baseband signal.
Symptom: D2Mac scrambles intermittently.
Cause: BB signal is too high for the output stage.
Remedy: Replace chip resistor RE85 (150R) with 100R.

Connecting SAT800 to D2Mac decoder 5918/3002
SAT800/PAL203 delivers a baseband signal with PAL deemphasis. A
MAC decoder connected to it must be able to handle PAL deemphasis.
Decoder 3002 has a phono socket for PAL baseband. A scart cable must
be modified as follows: Cut wiire from pin 20. Extend this wire to the
centre pin of a phono plug. Fit this end of the cable to the 3002 decoder.

Nokia Sat 800 no sound on Granada Plus or Foxkids

Go to the page with decoder option, and set it to the same value as for
all other channels, D1 I think (you have a choice of None and D1 to D4)

# SAT780

The first 50 (approx) channels are "locked."
To enable/disable this tuning lock, do this:

Using remote control, enter service mode
Store, Mute, TV/SAT

Setup, Setup, Setup

(The front panel display indicates lock or unluck status with a symbol)

Press
6    to toggle lock on/off
Press
Store   to confirm change.

# Philips STU824

Faults as per PRD900 but uses a different microcontroller.

Factory reset:
Short pins 6 & 7 on the 24C16 EEprom.
Connect mains power.
"-E2" appears in display.
Remove short circuit.
To turn IR remote operation off press:
[standby] and [up] and connect mains power.
To turn IR remote operation on press:
[standby] and [down] and connect mains power.

Faulty or intermittent remote operation may be caused by a bad solder joint on the Infra Red receiver.
Some problems can be solved by replacing the 24C16 EEprom.

# Philips Filmnet BBD-901

See separate section further on

# Philips STU909

Very little information on this D2Mac model.
However, SATKIT 22 is available to fix a dead power supply.
A 500 channel memory upgrade was made available but no information about this at the time of writing. Please check by email.

# Mimtec NIMBUS

Mimtec company went out of business at the end of 1997.

*Parental Lock set.*
Press SETUP
The display will show COdE
Enter 2 7 1 8 2 within 3 seconds.
The display will flash PIN and 9999 alternately.
Enter 9 9 9 9
Press STORE

# Mimtec SPIRIT

*Single hum bar moves up/down picture.*
*transformer hum.*
This fault may not occur until after a warm-up period.
Replace bridge rectifier D4 with a higher rated device.

Power supply notes:
(Also used in
Manhattan
Videocrypt decoder).

T5 is an N-MOS
transistor.
D15 is a Schottky
diode.
T11 is N-MOS type
IRFZ14

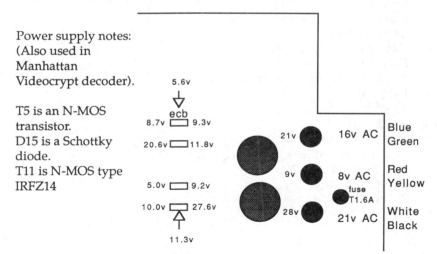

# Mimtec Premier

*Different brightness levels between satellite & T.V.*
Change R94 (750Ω) to 680Ω (located left of R84). On main PCB locate R15 (link) and replace with 15Ω resistor. Use oscilloscope to check at TP Vin = 0.9v peak to peak (R15 on interface board) then adjust preset on decoder PCB to equalise brightness between scrambled and unscrambled pictures.

Receiver completely dead.
Replace internal 630mA fuse. This fault is caused by the use of an electric drill, lawn mower or vacuum cleaner in a nearby socket.

Sorensen power supply blows up:

**A kit is available SATKIT 15.**
Mimtec "Sorensen" PSU No. 2090236  repair kit
IC1 TEA2018A
D10 10v zener
D5 1N4148
D22 BYV95B (Secondary diode s/c is common.)
C7 10uF/50v
C9 1uF/50v
C25 1nF
C6 220uF/25v
C26 100nF/50v multi-ceramic
C8 470pF/50v
TR1 MJE18004/BUT11A/BUL54AR
FS1 T500mA
R2,R3 47k/0.75W/350v
R6 1R fusible
R7,R11 4R7 fusible
Measure D6 - D9 for s/c
D1 - D3 1N4007
OC1 CNY17-1G
R12 100R
R40 10R

LNB voltage problems, check:
TR4,5,6  BC547
TR2  BC557
TR3  BD536
Adjuster next to R35

**Mimtec Premiere 2**
To bypass the decoder, remove the plug marked "VC" and join the copper pads on the edge of the board next to the "VC" socket, thus: 1&2 and 9&11, counting from the front.
Connect link LK4 near IC5. Cut link 3 and reconnect link 2 (near the RF modulator).
TR16 and TR17 on the decoder interface board can die, causing blank screen.

*Picture pulls and does not decode:*
On main board, try changing
C85 (1000uF/16v)
C86 (220uF/16v)
L8 (220uH)
VCR Loop Through
C1
C3 1000uF/16v

# JSR3300

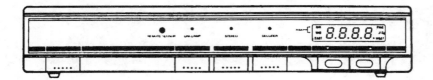

*Modification for external decoder to reduce video level*
The small potentiometer nearest the tuner sets the video level but
adjustment will affect the picture on internal signals as well as those
routed externally. The following modification reduces only externally
routed video signals and overcomes the problem of excessive brightness
and/or buzzing on audio when a decoder or transcoder is connected.

Locate link J5 which is next to the SCART socket and is the longest link
of three. Solder a 330Ω resistor across the link then cut the link in half.

Alternatively, solder the resistor into the SCART lead wire which goes to
pin 20 of the receiver SCART plug.

### Mains Voltage Selection
For 240 volt operation the red wire from the transformer (not the white)
should be connected to the fuse holder. Take care to insulate well!

### Audio loop
When an external decoder is used and DECODER is selected from the
handset, both video and audio are routed out via the SCART socket.
Most decoders loop the audio back but, for those which don't, link
together pin 3 and pin 6 in the SCART plug (receiver end).

### Twin LNB inputs
The two LNB inputs both remain powered up regardless of which is
selected.
This fact can cause a problem when a Telecom LNB is used. The local
oscillator in the Telecom LNB transmits a signal which blanks out the
Movie Channel on Astra.

*Changes channel by itself when knocked or vibrated.*
Check all internal connectors are tight.

*Audio when test signal is on but no video.*
Video invert switch on rear panel is easily damaged and can cause this fault.

*Handset STORE button will not work.*
The store button is a tiny rubber "sausage" which is easily pushed too far in.
Use a pin carefully to hook it back into place or unclip the handset halves and reposition the rubber piece in its guiding ring.

*Does odd things when changing channel from 1 - 99 - 98 etc:*
Press internal reset button and re-program. May be caused by mains interference.

*Dead:*
The 220v. mains transformer is prone to failure on this model.

*Fuse melted. Transformer hums when fuse replaced:*
Check large diodes D504 to D507.

> The JSR2200 (single LNB input version) has an internal link to select inverted video.

# Technisat VC2002S

*Lights up but no RF or Scart out:*
If F601 or F602 630ma fuse is blown, replace diodes
CR605,604,606,607,601,600,602,603,608,609, all with BYV95A then
replace T630 ma fuse.

# Technisat 3004

*Does not light up or goes off when LNB connected:*
Replace C710 (33uF/400v/85C)
I use a 47uF/400v from a Pace receiver. This is much larger so I use a
cable-tie to secure it to the rear left corner of the PCB, using two existing
holes. I fix it so the pins face left and solder wires from the pins to the
holes in the PCB. Then I finish off by securing everything with hot melt
glue. It doesn't look very pretty but it's safe and it works!

*Picture might develop horizontal lines and might disappear to leave a turquoise
raster and sound:*
Surface mount transistor, T106, near the tuner. This is labelled "F3" and
it's an NPN transistor. I use an FMMT2369A from a Pace PRD.

Various models of technisat receivers lock up in standby. Cure ( and I
have no idea why it works ): reverse batteries in remote control and
press any button then re insert batterys correctly and voila it all works.

# Tatung models

TRX1801 "Early Bird", TRX1081/V and Decca DRX1851
*Modifying a SCART-SCART lead for connecting a videocrypt decoder.*
At the receiver end, disconnect the wire from pin 15 in the plug and cut
short.
Disconnect the wire from pin 19 and reconnect to pin 15.
Link pins 13 and 10.
Label each plug to avoid reversing the lead which would damage the
decoder!

De-emphasis switch on SVA1 decoder should be set to IN.

TRX1081/V and DRX1851 might show horizontal interference lines and will need to be modified internally by a Tatung authorised dealer.

<u>TRX1801/22</u>    <u>TRX1802</u>    <u>DRX1851/22</u>    <u>DRX1852</u>
These receivers use a standard SCART-SCART for videocrypt.
De-emphasis switch on SVA1 decoder should be set to OUT.

**Faults**

We have not had many in for repair but a problem we have seen is failure of one or more of the rectifier diodes, usually accompanied by a melted fuse on the board.

The 630mA fuse may be replaced with a T1A fuse if it keeps melting. This is quite safe to do and is often necessary if the receiver is used with a modern LNB which draws more current.

Tatung TRX3901

No decoder messages
Replace TEA2029C and associated capacitors.

In Lock Mode but code not known:
Slide back ttop cover approx 100mm.
Find main micro on front display panel.
To the left of this micro are two test pins.
Switch receiver on.
Short-circuit the test pins and maintain the short.
Press Display button once only.
Locate C716 on display panel and momentarily short-circuit it.
All segments of display will light from right to left then timer mode is seen.
Remove short-circuit from test pins.
Receiver is now reset.
Audio will be muted on channels 33 to 48. Reset them with remote control.

# CAMBRIDGE RD480 EXTRA (Finlux 480)

## Frequently Asked Questions

**1. Why can't I receive "Sky Movies Gold" or "Zee TV" or....?**

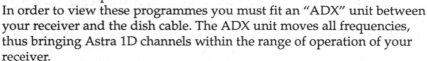

These channels are transmitted by the fourth Astra satellite called "Astra 1D".
The channel frequencies are lower than your receiver can accept.
In order to view these programmes you must fit an "ADX" unit between your receiver and the dish cable. The ADX unit moves all frequencies, thus bringing Astra 1D channels within the range of operation of your receiver.

**2. How do I re-tune channels?**

There is a fine tune facility (read section 2.1.5) but you can't tune a channel to a different programme. However, you can select ANY program to be on the first eight channel numbers ("Favourite channels" P1 - P8). See User Manual (available from SatCure 01270 753311).

**3. How do I use a D2Mac decoder?**

The RD480 is not designed to work with a D2Mac decoder. However, it will work with some models. The RD480 has *no* Mac baseband output so it will work only with a decoder which accepts PAL input. You should take your receiver to a satellite specialist and get him to provide a D2Mac decoder which is compatible. Be sure to ask for a demonstration of the decoder with your own receiver. Be sure to buy the same connecting lead and the decoder which are actually used in the demonstration. Bear in mind that a smart card may not be available for the programmes you want to watch. Ask your dealer about this.

**4. How do I listen to satellite radio programmes in stereo?**

Connect the audio outputs to the "Aux" or "CD" input on your Hi-Fi amplifier. Select the appropriate audio frequency on the appropriate satellite channel (see section 2.1.3). You do not need to have the TV switched on to listen to satellite radio if you connect the receiver to your Hi-Fi system.

## 5. How do I watch programmes from "Hot Bird" as well as Astra?

You need a larger dish with two "LNBs"
fitted to it. In addition you will need a
switching unit to select the satellite whose
programmes you want to watch at any time.
There are semi-automatic switching units
which fit on the dish. Alternatively, you can
run two cables from the dish and use a
"manually operated A-B switch" next to
your receiver. The best method is to use the
proper µVH7 switching unit which can be
programmed on a "per channel" basis.

## 6. How do I get the on-screen menu for my satellite receiver?

The RD480 does not have this facility. To set the various features you
should refer to the User Manual (available from SatCure).

## 7. Why do I get intermittent "Card Invalid" message?

The series 10 SKY card seems prone to this on certain receivers.
Make sure that the card contacts are clean and the card slot spring contacts are clean and not bent or twisted.
If this doesn't help, provided that you occasionally get a picture when
you insert the card (even if momentarily), then try scraping the black
spot off the card. This works 100% for me.

THIS MOD IS NOT APPROVED BY SKY

*"Card Invalid"* :
Resolder surface mount capacitor C240 beneath the card reader.

PARENTAL LOCK — *receiver will not come out of standby*
Perform factory reset if the PIN is not known:
- Disconnect mains power.
- Hold ▼ button (▲ button for Germany)
- Reconnect mains power.
- Release ▼ button.
- Wait while default settings are loaded into memory.

*Removal of cover:*
Disconnect the mains supply. Use cutters or pliers to pull out the four
rubber feet. Unscrew the six #1 pozidriv screws located in the holes. Lift
off the top cover. (Spray feet with WD-40 to make replacement easy).

*Removal of board:*   Remove the six #0 pozidriv screws which retain the board. The two front screws also secure the front panel. Lift out the board complete with front panel, rear panel and tuner. Take great care not to twist the ribbon cables which are easily damaged.

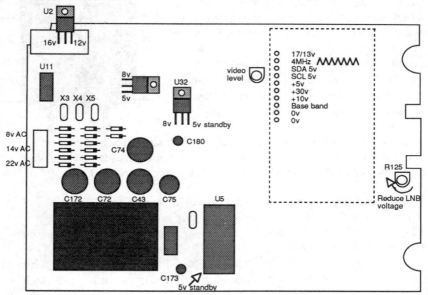

*Display flashes SC.*
Indicates a short circuit on the LNB input. Some early production had an incorrect type of R125 (LNB voltage adjuster) fitted. The centre leg of this could touch the copper on the top surface of the P.C.B. and cause a short circuit — often intermittent. Remove solder with desoldering braid and lever R125 upwards slightly to eliminate the fault. R125 is located at the far right hand side (viewed from the front). Resolder R125 with the minimum amount of solder.
(Cambridge recommend replacing R125 with the correct type.) If the fault *still* occurs, try disconnecting the rear wire in the tuner ribbon cable by using desoldering braid. If this cures the fault, replace the tuner.

*Almost blank screen, perhaps with some flashing lines:*
Check 10v to tuner from U2 via D50 and D51. If O.K. replace tuner. Take care not to damage the ribbon cable. If no 10v replace both diodes (BAS16 marked "A6") beneath the board. Otherwise, replace the two 100µF electrolytic capacitors inside the tuner module.

*Jumps some channels when pressing up/down buttons:*
A channel "skip" feature is incorporated and may have been programmed by the user. Use the factory reset to erase channel skips.

*Will not respond to handset:*
Broken ribbon connector PL3 from the front panel. The wire at the far
left of the cable is usually at fault.

*A single hum bar travels down the picture after warm-up:*
Replace *all* of the 1N4003 diodes in three rows at the left of the main
board unless you can isolate the one diode which is the culprit.

*Apparently dead but transformer output voltages O.K.*
Check 5 volt standby regulator U32. If very hot and no 5 volts then a
short circuit on the 5 volt line is indicated. Disconnect 5 volt feed to the
UHF modulator (the end pin nearest to the mains cable entry) or remove
the UHF modulator altogether. If 5 volts is then correct, replace UHF
modulator. If not, replace regulator U32 (LM2940CT 5.0v). This regulator
self-protects and will not usually fail. If still no 5 volts then isolate components on the 5 volt standby track until you find the culprit: U5 pins 20
and 21; C173 (100µF); C180 (47µF); C205 (100nF surface mounted
beneath U32).

*Only channels P1 to P8 can be selected or incorrect channels after reset:*
Replace the EEPROM "U100" which is an 8 pin surface mount 24C02
beneath the main board, near to the tuner ribbon connector. Do factory
reset. On very early versions the I.C. was on the tuner assembly itself. If
this fails to cure the fault, replace the microprocessor.

*Sound but just a blank screen:*
1uH choke L7 in the video feed through the deemphasis network open-
circuit.

*Almost blank screen from TV scart. OK from decoder scart:*
Q22 BC846.

*Picture breaks up. Stuck on one frequency. Hum on audio:*
If 5 volts from U3 too low (measure) then check Q44. It is fed with 8
volts and drops this to 5 volts when turned on by Q43. If Q43 is o/c then
the voltage from Q44 will be zero or too low. If Q43 has a partial fault

you might find that the 5 volt rail slowly increases. Q43 is PNP (BC856B will do).

*Won't go above a certain frequency. Some Astra 1B channels missing:*
The tuner gets a supply of around 35 volts from C172. If this is low, replace C172 (2200µF/35v) and ALL 1n4003 diodes (fourteen of them). Cut each diode lead close to the top surface of the board. Use solder wick to remove solder from each hole. Carefully remove the leads.

## Audio Problems

*Modification to obtain 6.65MHz audio on channel A7.*
Replace crystal nearest the heatsink (18.432MHz) with 17.360MHz.

*Audio A1 fades to a hiss after warm-up:*
Replace 17.714 MHz crystal X4.

*Audio has loud hiss in background – may be intermittent when tapped.*
Check soldering of surface mount tantalum capacitor beneath the board.

*Audio on CNN has "sibilance."*
Check dish alignment – interference from Eutelsat 16°E will cause this.

For fault-finding purposes, it is useful to note that three pins on the microprocessor control the selection of audio crystal, as follows:

Pin 28=5v   selects X4 (17.714) via R8 and D26. Audio 1, 3 and 4.
Pin 27=5v   selects X3 (18.074) via R6 and D27. Audio 2, 5 and 6.
Pin 26=5v   selects X5 (18.434) via R4 and D25. Audio 7, 8 and 9.

Note: The mains transformer has tags for selection of either 220 volts or 240 volts

*Useful tip:*
Spray rubber feet with WD-40™ to facilitate replacement.

*Please Wait" flashes rapidly but decoding is very intermittent:*
TCE10705400 decoder chip.

*Cambridge*

# CAMBRIDGE ARD200 Akai SX1000,
## BT SVS200, Alba SR7000, JVC TU-AD1000

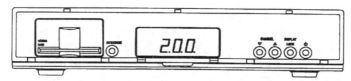

**Secret Button Codes**

*Factory reset.* All program ident graphics will be deleted!
The only way to regain them is to download the information from
another receiver or re-program each channel manually.
Hold channel DOWN button and plug receiver into mains.
Release button and wait 25 seconds.

*Set video level for decoder if no messages or intermittent:*
Hold [MUTE] and [↻] on handset (displays video level 1 to 8).
Select correct level (4 recommended) with arrow buttons.
Hold [▲] on receiver and press [STORE] on handset.
Also set video level to 4 in the LNB menu.

The ARD200 and SVS200 are factory set to use an Enhanced LNB.
If you use a standard (non-Astra 1D) LNB, reprogram by using the
following sequence:

| MENU | ........................................shows main menu |
|---|---|
| 3 | ........................................shows programming menu |
| 0  0  0  0 | .....four digit code |
| ▼ | ........................................shows menu 2 |
| 6 | ........................................shows LNB setup menu |
| ▲ | ........................................changes 9.75 to 10.0 |
| STO | ........................................returns to programming menu |
| 0 | ........................................exits menu |

## Power Supply Faults

*Receiver will not light up:*
Replace fuse. If no output from power supply, replace power supply I.C. U14 (an MA2810, order code ICCS5629). If the varistor MOV1 has failed, (a V275LS4) the receiver may be tested without it. Its function is to break down and melt the fuse if a mains voltage surge occurs.

*All PSU voltages too low:*
Replace U15 (CNY17F-2), U16 (TL431) then Q53 (BC546B) if still faulty.

*Front panel lights up but no picture, sound or LNB voltage:*
Check Q21 (large surface mount PNP transistor near centre of board). If no 5v output from its collector (large tag) then TR21 is probably dead. This can be caused by a mains surge, a shorted RF Modulator or a shorted Tuner. Even after replacing these you may find that the LM317 is also damaged and the decoder does not work!

*Receiver will not come out of standby:*
Parental lock may be activated. To clear, perform the factory reset if the pin number is not known. With unit disconnected from the the mains power hold the channel down button, wait while default settings are loaded into memory.
Note: factory reset will remove all alterations stored by the user. Otherwise, replace MPU ICCS5579.

## Picture Faults

*Poor pictures from RF. OK from Scart:*
Try replacing the 1µF/50v electrolytic inside the Modulator just above the video input pin. (From Hugh Cocks).

## Decoder Faults

*Streaky decoded pictures:*
Replace C177 100uF on decoder board.

*"Card Invalid":*
Look for dry joints on surface mount capacitors C76, C77 on the main board (beneath the decoder board). Scrape black spot off SKY card.

*Kills Sky cards:*
Locate Q44, Q45 and Q46 which are located beneath the position where the Sky card sits. Solder together the two adjacent legs (b-e) on each transistor. This prevents Vpp from exceeding 5 volts on the card.

*Using a D2-Mac decoder:*
"Sometimes it takes a long time for the picture to lock up. Sometimes the system doesn't decode at all."

1. Use a fully-wired Scart cable, not the video-plus-audio type.
2. Call up option 7 in the installation menu and select BBAND video on the DECoder output then press STORE
3. Call up the LNB setup menu, option 6, and select VID LVL on LNB A. Reduce the level to 4,3,2 or 1 (the lower the better, consistent with a good picture).
4. Select channel setup (option 2) and if necessary set the source to DECoder.

**Miscellaneous Faults**

*Clock will not store so timer function can not be used:*
Replace MPU ICCS5579. This square 128 pin IC causes a lot of erratic problems which may be function control: i.e cannot change channel or switch out of standby.

*Channels mixed up, switches to standby when channels are changed. Other strange responses may occur:*
Replace U1 MPU ICCS5579 a 128 pin surface mount ASIC situated on the main PCB. A faulty ASIC is a common cause of problems with this receiver (blank screen, no decoder messages, no menu etc.)

*Notes:*
The 128 pin ASIC can not easily be removed without the proper equipment. Usually when failure of this IC is suspected, the receiver is scrapped.
Cambridge spares: Try South Coast Technology in Portsmouth or SatCure (see Appendix). An RD480 User Handbook, which includes full tuning details plus channel frequency listings for Standard, Enhanced LNB and ADX systems, is also available from SatCure.

# Alba SAT4501/4502/4503

*Will not respond to remote control. Front panel LED may flash*
Replace microprocessor which is in a socket behind the front panel PCB.
Micro part number A00Z861000 (Z8610A)

Various strange faults ranging from flashing LEDs, to failure to store settings, to P.F. displayed (power fail) for no apparent reason are all down
to a faulty processor.

Check the secondary winding plug/pcb socket for melt down/poor
grounding- hard wire if bad. Also C308/C311 for degradation caused by
poor ventilation.

*Positioner, Dead - Transformer winding fuse o/c:*
Replace transformer.

*LED lights, but shuts down SAT45XX receiver when connected:*
Two diodes not shown on original schematic- 6.2V 1.3W Zener across
Vcc and Gnd may be s/c.(other diode is lN4148 anode to Gnd, Cathode
to junction of R511/D505) Both added for safety reasons.

*Alba Sat 300:-Mod for poor recording:*
Fit s/c link across R19 (15Ω) near T2 and 100pf ceramic cap across R9
(68k) near T1. Also remove R77 near T2 Adj video gain.

*Alba Sat 300:-Saturated reds, and lines:*
Reduce video level with internal adjuster.

# Bush IRD155

*Won't come out of standby:*
Check R505/507 (120K), C512 (33uF/25V) and also C508/509 (luF/5OV)
-very similar to the Amstrad SRD500.
SATKIT 19 will fix a dead power supply.
Parts available from Bush/Alba (see appendix).

# PALCOM SL4000 and SL650IRD

Servicing Tips — kindly supplied by Palcom (Distribution) Ltd, 142 High Street, Yiewsley, Middlesex. UB17 7BD. Tel: 0895 431633.

SL4000 only

*Blue screen and graphics but no picture:*
Early versions suffered in manufacture from a wrong value resistor (R606). If this is open circuit - approx 25 volts one side and zero the other - replace with a 27Ω 0.5W resistor. Also replace the 1.6A fuse if this has blown.

*Unit will not respond to handset commands.*
Check 1.6A fuse.

SL4000 and SL650IRD

*When a blue screen is displayed on a TV the unit will not respond to the handset.*
In a few circumstances where the TV screen is a very bright blue, the infra-red sensor is blinded by the TV. This might happen if the receiver is placed to the TV and, in particular, underneath the TV. Solutions are to move the receiver further away or, in the short term, to use the front panel buttons to select another channel.

*Unit dead:*
Check fuses but also check that the white edge connectors are clipped fully into place. These connectors feed the voltage rails to the main panel and to the tuner board.

*Noisy picture and horizontal lines across the screen.*
This could be a faulty tuner unit. To confirm, remove the receiver lid and tap the top of the tuner can with a screwdriver. If the picture starts to break up then the tuner almost certainly has a fault. Return the receiver to your dealer for replacement of the tuner.

## Using an External Decoder with SL4000

Select the desired channel.
Open store facility. Press recessed store once; select a new channel number (say 1_0_0.) Wait four seconds until the flash rate of the numbers changes then press store again. The channel is now available on both 100 and 101.

Now change the remaining parameters on channel 100 as appropriate:
8 — Decoder — Pal RCA
15 — Audio — 7.02
17 — B/width — 150kHz    and press store twice.
The connections to be made on the SL4000 are Video In and Unclamp Out. These are RCA Phono sockets. See page 4 of the Instruction Manual.

You will need a connecting lead with 2 Phono plugs on one end and a SCART plug on the other. If a blank screen appears then swap the two Phono plugs.

The switch on the external decoder should be left in the ON position unless you are connecting a SKY decoder through the "SAVE" decoder, when the switch must be used to select or deselect the decoder, accordingly.

# PALCOM SL-500

*No LNB voltage from port "A".*
Check R441 ($1\Omega5$) next to Q420 which is bolted to the heat sink.

Erase memory:
[MODE] [POWER] off [ERASE] [POWER] on

Factory Reset:
Mains off, hold [up][down] and switch mains on.
Select appropriate mode (full configuration or just tuner reset)
Press [POWER] on remote control.

# GRUNDIG STR-20

*No LNB voltage:*
Check 0R22Ω resistor at the back of the power supply section.

### Modification to provide 13/17v switching

Glue a miniature 12 volt relay to the rear panel behind the power supply. Connect the make contacts across R645 in the power supply which should be 5k6Ω. (Some versions used 4k7Ω). Turn R647 fully anticlockwise. Connect one end of the relay coil to ground (GND terminal on the rear panel). Connect the other end of the relay coil either to the terminal marked POL or, if available, the 12 volt switching terminal.

The relay is now operated by selection of polarity or by the 12 volt input switch, both of which functions are set by buttons on the front panel. The relay selects either 13 volts or (approximately) 16.3 volts. Program each channel according to the polarity required.

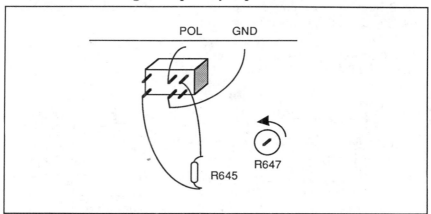

### Using an external Decoder

Use a standard SCART to "D" connector. Early models had no "D" socket (although, at the time, this was available as an after-market modification if required).

*Dead:*
Replace fuse and BU508A transistor.

# GRUNDIG GRD150/250/280/300
## JVC C-200/STU-200

*Receiver dead:*
Check the solder joints of the mains input socket.
Replace fuse (T1A).
Sometimes BUZ80A also fails.
A power supply repair kit is available (SATKIT 20).

*Stuck in standby, timer light flashing (normal):*
Look for broken tracks adjacent to tuner solder lugs. D223, leaky.
Otherwise suspect EEprom (must be preprogrammed).

*Rasping noise. Hum bars present on the video display:*
Replace the 47uF,400V reservoir capacitor.

*No pictures or a single picture (being the bottom of the Astra 1D band):*
LNB installation menu. Make sure that you type in either 10.000 or
09.750 - don't forget the leading zero!

*PSU tripping:*
D205 BA157 leaky

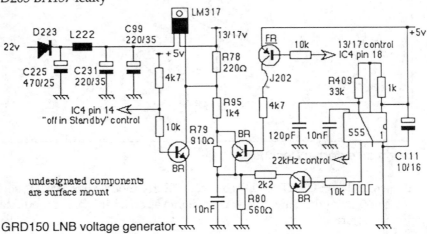

GRD150 LNB voltage generator

*LNB voltage stays at 13 volts:*
PNP surface mount transistor marked "FR" (see circuit, below).

*Handset melts:*
The handset battery clips can move and touch each other.

*Beeping sound from TV when SKY card is inserted:*
Solder a 100nF capacitor between links J72 and J80 behind the card holder.

*Blank screen on Sky channels only:*
L11 open circuit or ASIC fault or bad decoder board connector.

*No satellite RF output. Pics & audio ok from scart. UHF pics OK:*
If no switched 5v at C78+ leg then replace Q222 (PNP) BC327.

*No decoder messages when hot:*
Microcontroller or Decoder fault or bad decoder board connector.

*No decoder messages or intermittent messages.*
*Possibly also ragged channel names – tearing/unreadable:*
IC7 (PTV111) or C37 next to it (4µ7). Note PTV111 = TEA2130.
Bad decoder board connector.

*Horizontal lines on decoded pictures:*
PTV110

*Black screen with on screen graphics:*
Micro, 12MHz crystal, 12v regulator situated under decoder board.

## Secret Codes

Service codes are listed at the SatCure web site.

*Pin number:* 2355
*Astra reset code:* 2601
Unfortunately, the system wipes out all channel names at the same time.

GRD300
*Poor pictures looks like weak signal:*
Check the video bandwidth setting.

A Service manual for Grundig GRD150/200/300 and Minerva models is available form Grove Farm Publications, Grove Farm, Long Lane, Barnby in The Willows, Notts. NG24 2SG. Send £14.95 plus £1 postage.

## GRD150 Audio improvement Modification

Replace C28 electrolytic with 470µF/16v if not already this value.
Replace C24 and C32 with 100nF.
Add 12pF across R41 and R42.

If L4 and L7 are NOT 4µ7H then also:

Replace R40 and R43 with 47k.
Replace R44 and R117 with 680k.
Replace C23 and C25 with 22pF.

## GRD150/250 Add a decoder connector.

Fit diode 1N4148 in positions D15 and D20 (8 positions in a row).
This tells the Micro "you are a 250".
Remove memory chip IC10 (2586).
Fit 24C16) in position IC11 - NOT IN POSITION IC10 !
This gives 250 chans - DO AN ASTRA RESET.
At this point you have 250 chans and can name about 200.
The menus also offer a decoder option now.. and LNB1 and 2.
List of parts that need to be added..
C15 10uF
R10 1K
R13 150R
R24 100R
Q3 BC847 SMD
Q14 BC847 SMD
R118 100R
R119 75R
R176,7 1K
R420,1,2,3 470R
R432 75R
SCART SOCKET
ALL RESISTORS SURFACE MOUNT.
Remove blue twisted pair of wires by scart sockets.
*Written by Andrew Jardine*

# Grundig GRD300

Similar to GRD150 and earlier models but with the following differences.

*To change the modulator output from PAL I to PAL G for export:*
The PIN is 3105
Once in the service menu there is an option near the bottom for the RF modulator sound.
It just requires reducing by 1, from 001 to 000, then just press store.
The sound offset will have changed from 6.0 to 5.5MHz next time it's turned on from standby.

BTW, be careful with the rest of the settings, apparently you can damage the receiver by incorrect settings on some of these.

*Vac Fluorescent display shows only faint horizontal bars. Receiver works OK:*
Loose wire under display connector on main board.

*Vac Fluorescent display not working:*
Replace all 10µF on display board and C104 (2200uF) on main board.

*To adjust the RF modulator UHF channel:*

1) Put the receiver in standby.
2) Press and hold [STORE] for about six seconds, until the display changes to 'Cxx' - where 'xx' is the current channel number.
3) Use [P+] and [P-] (or the number keys) to select the output channel you require.

4) Press [STORE] to memorise the setting.

*Order codes for pre-programmed EEproms and microcontrollers:*
GRD200 EEprom 73771-200-05 Micro 73771-280-11
GRD280 EEprom 73771-280-15 Micro 73771-280-11 (the same)
GRD300 EEprom 73771-300-06 Micro 73771-300-07

## STR2200S

*STR2200S muted audio or short burst of sound when changing channel:*
Add 8v2 SMD zeners across C427 an C436, anode to -ve of capacitors.

## Minerva SAT5000, Matsui RD600

Similar to the Grundig GRD150 but uses the "Omni" chassis.
*Pin number:* 2580
*Astra reset code:* 1937

*PSU failure:*
Usually just the fuse (T1A) and Q201 (BUZ80A)
A power supply repair kit is available (SATKIT 20).

*Will not light up but PSU OK:*
12MHz crystal

*No RF output:*
Check fuse F201 (F250mA wire leaded type)
Note: Matsui RD600 does not have this fuse.
If fuse is OK, see if RF Modulator screw turns without stopping - a sure
sign that it has been "screwed".

*Oblong pattern of white dots on all Sky channels:*
PTV114

## GSR1 mkII

*Distorted audio:*
IC400 STV0055A

## Toshiba BTR5

### Using External Decoder
Connect decoder using a SCART to SCART lead.
Set [A OUT] switch to [VIDEO].
Set receiver [MODE] switch on rear panel to [PROGRAM] position.
Press [SELECT] to set mode to AUTO.
Set receiver [MODE] switch on rear panel to [RECEIVE] position.

*Poor or no pictures:*
Replace the three 47µF capacitors inside the IF module which is soldered
into the main board and connected via a coax cable to the tuner.

# BT SVS300/ HOUSTON 1002

*Similar to Amstrad SRD540*
Power supply repair kit available (SATKIT 17).

*No video or poor video:*
C113 located near VR101.

*No video. Audio with test bar on:*
C126.

Capacitor negative (stripe) end is indicaded by a shaded semicircle in these receivers!

*Low video level/ blue screen/ jumping pictures:*
Replace C220 (220µF/16v) near centre of main board.

**For decoder faults see SVS250 section**
Decoder repair kit for SVS250 and SVS300 RELKIT 17.

# BT SVS250/ Matsui OP10

(This model was built by the manufacturer of the "Oritron", "Aegir", "Dixi" and "Lenco" D2Mac decoders - "Orient Power Video Manufacturing Ltd.").

**Power supply faults**

*Dead:*
Replace fuse 250mA

*Dead:*
F401 (T500mA) or slack fuseholder.
Q403, Q402 or transformer primary o/c (measure between live & neutral pins on mains plug).

*F402 keeps melting:*
C412 and Q401

*Internal mains hum:*
Resolder connections on power input socket.

*No tuning supply:*
C134, C135 next to tuner or R408 (listed in manual as 2k2 should be 220R/2Watt).

*Tuning supply rises to 40v:*
Z401.

**LNB voltage faults**

*"LNB SHORT" on front panel display:*
Check 12v rail; if low, disconnect decoder board. If 12v now OK, replace C51.
Otherwise Q406. Also check IR sensor centre leg. A short from here to 0v can cause the symptom, sometimes intermittent.
Otherwise U401 regulator on front heatsink or R407 (1R).

*No LNB voltage (no warning display):*
Press LNB on remote; press Up or Down to show "L" on front panel display. Press STORE. Three dashes will appear briefly then display turns to normal with LNB voltage on.

*No 18v LNB voltage:*
Q404, U201, Z402, D411 and D420

*Horizontal voltages too high:*
(Middle pin of U401 = 16v instead of 7v2)
Z402.

*Intermittent vertical channels:*
Voltages 16/23v.
D407 dry joints.

*22kHz tone set to ON:*
Press BAND to toggle then STORE.

## Picture faults

*Black/dark video:*
U102 BA7645.

*\*Video multiplexer U102 BA7645 unavailable:*
Bypass it altogether by first cutting out the 12V feed which is a link near this IC, then linking pins I and 10 together. After this mod is done, all the channels will go through the decoder board and the lock facility will not work.

*Herringbone pattern:*
*Customer described it as "colour running" or "it looks like a thumbprint":*
May occur only on one polarisation.
C413 100nF increase to 220nF.
C460 (100µF) next to the heatsink fit 220µF.
*Intermittent rolling of picture to complete loss of picture:*
C166 on main PCB 220uF/16v.

*Herringbone pattern/video distortion:*
Q404, C460.
*Blank screen some channels all the time.*
*Blank screen when channel changing:*
C173 47nF (green polyester) SVS250.

*No video or poor video:*
C113 located near VR101. SVS300

*No output from RF Modulator; Blank screen from Scart:*
D419 (1N4148) o/c causing no 5V supply.

*Severe hum bar on picture:*
R408 (220R/2Watt) cooked, Z401 leaky.

*Hum bar with buzzing superimposed on audio, sometimes after a few hours:*
D405, D406 and C406.

*Bars across picture:*
U203.

*Two vertical white lines on screen. No pictures. Looks like test bars:*
Dry joints on pin 37 of micro or faulty micro.

*Two squiggly vertical bars (intermittent):*
C406.

*White lines on all channels (may be intermittent):*
Dry joints on or near C404.

**Decoder faults**

*No decoder messages after 3 - 5 minutes:*
C45 1uF/50v just to the right of U6 (PTV111).
C38 33nF polyester just to the left of U6.
Could also be C65, C37, C34, VR101 video gain adjuster, EEprom, C52, D15, Ceramic resonator XT2. Also electrolytic capacitors close to D15 (rear right corner of decoder). Intermittent no decoder messages - conductive glue on ceramic resonator.
A decoder repair kit is available (RELKIT 17). This fixes most decoder problems and also picture problems, too.
*No decoder messages:*
PL1/2 dry joints.

*Lines on decoded channels:*
PTV110 or U102 BA7645.*see later note about U102

*Lines on decoded channels and floating white band on clear channels:*
C409.

*Decoder messages unstable on decoded channels:*
Locate R66 on Videocrypt board. Solder a 10k in parallel.

*Random display of "Push button to transfer":*
Poor connection of 5V regulator.

*Card invalid when a good card is inserted:*
(No 3.5Mhz output from PTV110 - should be divided down from the 28Mhz signal).
PTV110

*Intermittent decoder:*
D9 in the decoder (rare).

If you are not getting decoder messages, check pin 11 of PLI. If it is tog-gling between logic high and logic low when changing from a clear to an encrypted channel the decoder board is probably working. The fault may lie with the EEprom. Sometimes when changing the EEprom you have to tune everything in. To get past this problem, simply disconnect pin 2 of U102, so everything is routed through the decoder board, but the lock facility will still work.

**Display faults**

*Out of range bars in display:*
The LNB offset may read 25.38 and if corrected it can't be stored.
EEprom, main micro  or audio IC U301 TDA6160.
Note: The EEprom is connected to pin 10 of the TV Scart socket.
Disconnect this pin since some TVs put a voltage on pin 10 and destroy the EEprom immediately!

*"Push button to transfer":*
Cut off and discard the 6v regulator connector and hard-wire direct to the regulator.

*Poor RF loop-through. Snowy terrestrial pictures:*
Remove cover of modulator then either
a) replace R56 (120R) with 56R or
b) connect a 100R resistor in parallel with R56.

*Patterning on terrestrial channels (especially UHF 39 - 51):*
Connect a 56pF capacitor between R188 and R182 of the main PCB (near RF modulator).

**Remote control Faults**

*No remote functions:*
SR201 sensor faulty.

*Handset inoperative:*
Resonator inside handset.

*Won't store changes:*
U201.

## Audio faults

*No audio:*
IC301 or U304 or U301 TDA6160 FM demodulator..

*Poor audio:*
RF modulator.

*Hissing audio:*
C313.

## Front panel faults

*Power but no display:*
U201.

*Blank raster:*
U201 or Q104 or U402 12v regulator.

*Faulty panel display:*
Display faulty.

*3 horizontal dashes one above the other on left of display (="overflow"):*
U202 EEprom.
Note U202 EEprom is a 24C04 but a 24C08 or 24C16 will do. There is no factory reset so you must reprogram every channel by hand. This is best done by setting channel 1 then copying it to the rest and finally adjusting frequency and polarisation for each channel. Alternatively, I can supply a pre-programmed EEprom.

*3 bars on display:*
C134 or U301 audio IC.

*Goes into C-Band when warm:*
D101, D102 fitted incorrectly.

# Aegir, Oritron, Dixi & Lenco D2Mac

The handset works best when held at least 6 feet away from the decoder because of the way the lens works. Putting sellotape over the lens might usefully shorten the range.
Using a SCART to four phono plug lead.
In the D2MAC menu leave RCA socket selected as standard.
Connect SCART plug to decoder out on receiver.

*Connect phonos:*
B/B IN socket to VIDEO OUT wire, VIDEO OUT socket to VIDEO IN wire.
R AUDIO OUT socket to AUDIO IN L wire. R AUDIO OUT socket to AUDIO IN R wire.

*If you use a SCART-SCART lead:*
Press MENU on the handset then ENTER (several times) until you see "RCA".
Press the "UP" button to change the socket setting from RCA to SCART then press STORE.
If there is no video output from the SCART (blank screen) you may need to press the "0" (AV) button on the handset. If possible, set the receiver AV source to EXTERNAL instead of AUTO. You must set the receiver AV source to MAC (except SRD510/520/550).

If possible, set all non-D2MAC channels to INTERNAL instead of AUTO. Set the receiver baseband output to MAC instead of PAL and make sure that the MAC baseband signal goes to pin 19 of the SCART. (On Amstrad SRD510/520/550 it comes out on pin 12 of the Decoder SCART so you must remove the wire from pin 12 of the SCART plug and discard this wire. Move the wire from pin 19 to pin 12, then label the plug "Receiver End")

Note: The picture quality from the SRD may be poor, with "ghosting". It can take up to half a minute for the decoder to "lock on" DO NOT set the Amstrad to MAC in the menu - leave it as PAL.

For some receivers you might have to remove the cover from the D2MAC decoder and change link J14 from its left position (looking from the front) to its right position. This link affects the baseband filtering and can prevent the decoder from "locking on" to the encoded picture. The DMAC decoder is unlikely to work reliably with some Pace receivers unless they have a 2GHz tuner fitted because the bandwidth of the baseband signal from the tuner is too narrow.

Link J14 is a black "saddle" which is to be found next to the silver colour crystal at the left hand side.

Note: The RF output socket on the decoder uses PAL G standard for export so there is no audio. This is not a problem if you use only SCART connections.

Warning! If a pirate card is used with the decoder then the sharp edge may damage the card-reader contacts. In addition, card contacts which are not gold-plated may put solder onto the gold-plated card-reader contacts. The long-term effect may be unreliable connections which result in messages such as "CHECK THE CARD" even with a good card. Such problems are not covered by warranty.

# Churchill & Optimac D2Mac decoders

1. The Churchill power supply is similar to the Pace PRD type.
A repair kit is available from SatCure

A power supply that whistles is about to fail! Disconnect the power cord and do not reconnect it until the unit has been repaired. At this stage you can probably fix it simply by fitting three capacitors.

2. The Optimac power supply uses a transformer which occasionally fails.

3. The main problems with the Churchill are bad connections or corrosion in the IC sockets.
A special extractor tool is available from SatCure for the square chips.

The chips *can* and do fail but fault-finding is usually a complicated business.

In order of likelihood, you could try replacing the following chips:

DMA2286
DMA2281
CCU3000

4. The Remote Control Handset is available from SatCure.

5. Churchill Service Menu
Normal - 8 - Normal - 9 to access service menu from serial number 94003 onwards.
You may need to do this several times before it works.
For early models you must link 2 of 3 pins next to Eprom & press menu.

6. Churchill serial number label
Prefix NM means No Modulator
Prefix PD means PAL/D2MAC deemphasis selection on SCART pins, see 7.

7. The later Churchill will accept either D2Mac or PAL input
Connections to pins 10 and 12 must be shorted together for PAL (read the label on the back).

# Philips CTU900 D2Mac decoder

The CTU900 is actually a D2Mac cable TV box. It was not intended for use with a satellite receiver and, as a result, has some inherent problems which have been solved by a BBC video engineer. He has given permission to publish this information here.

The CTU900 is mostly held together with moulded clips. Remove the three rear panel screws, unclip the metal panel and take it off. Now you can see the other plastic clips which hold the base and cover together. These are underneath near the front. There is one central clip and one near each side. Release these and the front panel and top panel will slide forward away from the base panel. Take care!

The D2Mac board is mounted on pillars. Squeeze the tips of the four pillars with pliers and lift the board up off the connector pins.

**1. The CTU900 will not work with certain cards.**

The cure is quite simple. If you look at the card slot unit on the front panel, you will see a ribbon cable which connects it to the main board. Just in front of the ribbon cable is a link wire marked 9202. Solder a 56R resistor across this link wire then cut the link in the middle so it leaves the resistor in circuit.

Another point has come to my attention regarding the replacement of link 9202 with 56R (original 39R suggestion did not always work), in the card reader's Vcc to card: The "multimac" remote control update of cards may not work. The original resistor was added because a certain late night programme had a batch of faulty?? cards, but remote control update folk will have to replace the link.

**2. The Picture is "grainy".**

On the D2Mac board, locate the TEA6420 I.C. The front right corner pin is number 1. About 12mm further to the right is a tubular electrolytic capacitor labelled C2341. Solder a 56pF capacitor from TEA6420 pin 1 to the nearest wire of C2341 (doesn't matter which end).

**3. The Picture "flickers".**

On the D2Mac board, locate capacitor C2327. This is a 0.47µF block polyester capacitor (situated between two electrolytics) about 10mm x 6mm. Remove it and replace it with 100nF/63v polyester capacitor. Of course you can adjust this value: try 220nF or 68nF if flicker still exists.

**4. I can't get a picture because the CTU900 won't give 12v on pin 8 of the Scart.**

On the main board next to the TV Scart socket, locate R3122 (75R resistor). Cut one wire so R3122 is not connected. Now solder a wire from pin 20 on the TV Scart socket to pin 20 on the VCR Scart socket. Connect the satellite receiver decoder socket to the CTU900 TV Scart socket. With the CTU900 in standby you can watch normal PAL programmes. To descramble a D2Mac channel simply turn the CTU900 on. Note: the TV "PAL RGB" option under Menu - Install - TV must be set to "PAL".

**5. Service Menu**

Enter by pressing [TV DEC] [P+] [P-] [Clock-button] [I-II]. Complete each adjustment by pressing "OK". Exit by pressing "Standby". VCO adjust is code 150. BER (Bit Error Rate) is code 200. Drives and cut offs for colour can be accessed by code 170 but BEWARE: once you enter code 170, all cutoffs are reset to FF - even if you don't change anything! So, unless your colour balance is very very bad, DON'T enter code 170. http://www.netcentral.co.uk/satcure/

**6. Where do I buy the parts for these modifications?**

Just send four 26p stamps to SatCure, PO Box 12, Sandbach, CW11 1XA

**7. Who can do the work for me?**

ASTRA-TECH in Swansea sell CTU900 already upgraded. Phone (01792) 701719 for prices. Please DON'T expect them to discuss modifications or technical matters. They specialise in selling new and used receivers and new satellite equipment.

SATFIX in Swansea offer a full range of modifications for the CTU900. They also specialise in D2Mac receiver repairs.
To arrange for them to do the work, phone (01792) 781673
Note: They will NOT supply parts or give you technical help so please do not contact them unless you want your CTU900 professionally upgraded. They may not accept any decoder for repair if it has been messed with. If you can carry out the modifications yourself, that's fine, but if you mess it up, don't expect SATFIX or SATCURE to bail you out.

**8. Is there an English language manual?**

No but Satellite Surplus in Telford can supply a useful information sheet.
(01952) 598173

**9. PAL baseband mod**

On the main board replace R3051 (100R) with a 1k resistor + 470pF capacitor in parallel and terminate inboard end to chassis with 300R.

I disconnected the VCR remote control Phono socket to use as a switch so that I could select MAC or PAL baseband externally by inserting a phono shorting plug. I did this by removing link 9574 and cutting zener 6056. Then I wired chassis end of 300R to the phono socket inner connection.

### 10. Flat baseband mod

On the main board replace R3051 (100R) with a 430R resistor and terminate inboard end to chassis with a 560R and 180pF capacitor in series. I disconnected the VCR remote control Phono socket to use as a switch so that I could select MAC or PAL baseband externally by inserting a phono shorting plug. I did this by removing link 9574 and cutting zener 6056. Then I wired chassis end of 560R+180pF to the phono socket inner connection."

PAL, Mac and Flat
If you want access to all three of these, you'll have to fit a switch and figure it out from the above!

### 11. The Ultimate Auto Mac switching

On the main board next to the TV Scart socket, locate R3122 (75R resistor). Cut one wire so R3122 is not connected. Now solder a wire from pin 20 on the TV Scart socket to pin 20 on the VCR Scart socket.

Remove resistor R3062 (220R to VCR Scart pin 8) and link pin 8 on VCR Scart socket to pin 8 on TV Scart socket. (This allows the use of either Scart socket).

Cut R3083 (56k) at end furthest away from Scarts and wire the cut end to R3068 (68R) at end furthest away from the Scarts (don't cut R3068).

(This mod is using TV Scart pin 16 - fast blanking - to switch Scart pin 8 to 12v when decoder is actually decoding a MAC signal.)

Ensure that "RGB" is selected under "Menu" "Installation" "TV" "PAL/RGB".

The VCR Scart must be used for normal "PAL" including recording. The

TV Scart can be used for those who have "RGB" capable TV sets where the host satellite receiver is capable of linking RGB through AND uses Scart leads. Beware!... "RGB" will cause loss of menus on Pace receivers while receiving MAC signals.

You might also want to do the following mod (you might not when you've read it!)

To keep PAL signal on pin 19 of TV Scart even when "RGB" is selected:

1. Remove link 9025.
2. Cut track on SMD R3093/R3094 side of C2020 (470nF) - (SMD resistors are both 470R).
3. Link SMD R3093 (150R)/R3077 (120R) [pad from pin 27 on header from Mac board] to C2819 (470nF) end of removed link 9025 and to C2020 (470nF) cut track end.

**Questions via email:**

*I have read your CTU900 mods page with much interest.*
*Using my CTU900:*
*Selecting either Eurocrypt-M or Eurocrypt-S channels, there is no problem, the card switches between either system automatically. The problem is in using Eurocrypt-S2 channels, such as Canal+*
*To switch between TV1000 (Eurocrypt-S) and Canal+ (Eurocrypt-S2) I have to follow the procedure:*
*Enter 2227 into the code update, then remove my MULTIMAC2.12 Gold card then replace it.*
*To change back to Eurocrypt- M/S, I have to enter 1117, then remove/replace card.*
*Is there a mod so that it will change automatically for either system?*

Regarding your Eurocrypt M&S and S2 query: The pirate card software writers have been writing code that can be updated using the "original parental lockout" secret code programming using the set's remote control, when the broadcasters changed--worked well too.

This information is stored on the smart card in the MAC system. (One example of this software is called Multimac by M. Steigen). Now, when Canal+ Scand. came along using the new "S2" cards, problems occurred with some decoders changing over, so the card progammers decided to use the codes 1117 to force card into the M&S mode and 2227 for S2. Other codes are used as well. (Note: not all decoders have the facility for changing the secret code, eg Visiopass).

*After receiving the unit I switched one of the choices in a menu to D2MAC from PAL and now I cannot get a picture at all. Which sequence of key presses will get me out of this hole?*
*I use Scart between my Pace MSS508IP and CTU900.*

Oh, boy. Now I even have to read the User Manual to you.
On page 15 it tells you to press MENU. (This gets you the menu).
As you can see from the nice picture on page 15, "Installation of decoder" is on the fourth line down so you press the cursor DOWN button three times to get there.
Press OK. That gets you into the installation menu.
Now skip to page 43 where there is a pretty picture of the Installation menu.
PAL/MAC is on the third line down so you press the DOWN arrow twice to get there.
Now press the RIGHT arrow to alter it MAC -> PAL or whatever.
To exit press MENU then OFF.

*Can I fit a second card reader to my CTU900?*

A. I have not done any serious research, but observations suggest that one would have to fit

a. Card Reader.
b. TDA 8000 card reader interface + all the associated SMD components, (The circuits I have do not show details for the second card reader even though the designer laid provision on the pcb).

*Will the software/firmware in the eprom (27C2001) support this facility?*

We think so.
*Just to let you know that I have carried out mods 1, 2, 3, and 11 (Auto Mac switching), and they all work fine. Now I can leave my receiver channel setup in AUTO mode for input, and the CTU900 will switch it as necessary when receiving a Mac signal. From Paul*

Thanks, Paul. Glad to hear there's someone out there who can follow instructions!

*A number of weeks ago a Philips d2 mac decoder model CTU900 was purchased new. It worked / works well with an old Pace 9200 series receiver. Connection made via a 21 pin scart lead. & configured the menu as ext decoder etc etc.*
*As this receiver is getting a little tired a new receiver etc. was recently purchased. A Nokia Satscan 1800, with 80cm steerable dish.*
*Upon connecting the d2 mac to this receiver it was as if the video was not being routed through the decoder. The menu / set up seemed to be configured correctly on the sat receiver.*
*Having questioned the supplier about this problem (having purchased both items from there) we had drawn a blank.*
*Our d2 mac instruction sheet ( CTU900 ) mentioned a slider switch on the rear to select differing base band inputs. This switch does not appear on our decoder (instruction sheet has company name "The perfect signal Ltd" printed on it. Maybe importers name?)*
*It appeared that the Nokia was performing in a different way from the old Pace 9200 which definitely works ok with d2 mac.*
*We took a look at your notes above and thankfully found the answer. We carried out the baseband mods to the philips CTU900 as advised and it came good for us. One silly thing that fooled us was that, when we had set the modified equipment up, the osd message said "card poorly inserted" & it did not decode. The answer was that the card has to go in downside up, or is that upside down? when compared with a sat receiver/decoder. The contacts have to face upwards. Strange but true.*

Thanks, guys.

*From Nat:*
*The file on modifications for the Philips CTU 900, how much of it is applicable to the philips CTU902? I spoke to someone at T.P.S. (in what satellite) and they said the picture can be modified to output RGB on the scart, as the picture is a bit grainy at the moment. Do you know of any mods for the CTU902?*

The CTU 902 is a close cousin to the Visiopass even the software from a Visiopass will run in a 902. (Although remote control codes are different).
The main differences are a PAL coder fitted (instead of a secam coder - the pal coder board was fitted after they were shipped into UK) and of

course a cable tuner only - Visiopasses also had a sat tuner option.

First, regarding "coarse noise": Make sure you are feeding "MAC BB from the host satellite receiver. If you only have "Flat BB" available, replace (R) 3028 (100R) with a 330R and at inboard end (junction to [C] 2007 100nF) connect a series 560R-180pF to chassis. Of course a weak signal will give noise.

As regards using the "Tv" scart to get RGB: it's ok but pin 19 has mixed syncs on it in the "RGB" state the same as the CTU900, and the BB must go in on "VCR" (Magnetophone) scart.

I modified quite a number of Visiopasses to do "the full works" a la CTU900 but I never wrote the mods down - I assume the mods will directly fit the 902 as well, but I would have to get one on the bench to refine if required.

Ken

# Philips "Filmnet" BBD 901

Note: Philips "Filmnet" BBD 900
This is a similar but earlier D2MAC decoder, having only a one-card
reader (at the front), and there is no remote control infrared
receiver incorporated. The software is a little different.

**Problem Solver**

*No picture on D2MAC programme:*
Check in Installations menu, that the decoder is set up to
recognise the input, you use (Scart or Phono).

*Poorly decoded picture on D2MAC programme:*
Check that the input signal deemphasis corresponds to the one selected
in the Installation menu. Check that selection connection between
decoder and satellite receiver is in order. Check all connections to the
satellite receiver. Check that the satellite receiver is tuned exactly into
the channel. Look in user instructions for your satellite receiver if above
does not help.

*Picture not decoded:*
Check the card.
Check deemphasis.
Check that you have tuned into a D2MAC programme
(check information menu)

*Message on screen "No access" or "Ingen adgang":*
Subscription for the payment channel has ended.
Incorrect settings in receiver or decoder.
Check the user instructions.

*Message on screen "Check card" or "Kontroller kortet":*
Check that card is correctly inserted into decoder and is
the right way up. The contacts should be uppermost.

*Television wants to be able to view satellite programmes:*
Remove control voltage to TV by pressing MENU OFF.

*Crackling sound on audio:*
Incorrect baseband input selection. Check menus.
Otherwise faulty chip.

*Picture has green tint:*
Use modified handset to access Service Mode.
Set Green Cut to a lower value.

*Remote Control Handset :*
Philips part number RC6932/01
Order code 4822-218-21137 from Willow Vale Electronics.
Fax: ++44 118 986 7188 (UK 0118 986 7188)
Price approximately 34.00 ukp.

*Picture shifted left or right leaving narrow blank strip:*
Go into "service-mode" on your BD901 by holding (+) and (-) while
plugging the mains.
Use your remote or step your way thru with menu/+/- and use Mode
220 (write eprom adresses).
Select address 057 and write 046,
Select address 058 and write 061
Select address 059 and write 255.

*Alternatively, if this doesn't work:*
Corruption of EEprom. Replace IC7518.
(You can use 24C04, 24C08 or 24C16)
Warning! VCO may then have to be reset in the Service Mode so you
will need a remote control. Also, SCART (default =RCA) may need to be
selected in on-screen menu.

*Keeps asking to be tuned to a Filmnet broadcast with a valid card:*
Set the 901 into the service mode (power off, press and hold the + and -
buttons, power on keep holding the buttons until service mode is seen at
top of screen). Using the handset, enter
220 (EEPROM write mode) then 100 (address) then 000 (new setting).
Repeat this again i.e
220, 120, 000 where 120 is the new location.
Press standby to exit. Before you power off, look at the strange menus.

*Picture drifts across screen or reluctant to lock and stay decoded:*
VCO Adjustment. Original handset needed. Enter service mode
as above, key in 150 (PLL adjustment mode) use + and - buttons on
handset to change value, menu to store.

**SECRET SERVICE MODE**

The service mode can be used only with a remote control handset.
To access the service mode, disconnect the mains power from the
decoder.
Press MENU+ and MENU- and hold them while you reconnect the
mains power.
After a few seconds you will see "SERVICE MODE" and the Eprom version at the top of the screen, with the status/command line at the bottom of the screen.

To enter a command you must press a three-digit code on the handset.

*Here is a list of codes:*

100 RST CARD = 0 (maybe this resets the secret code?)
110 VPP CARD = 5 (set card Vpp to 5 volts)
111 VPP CARD = 15
120 READ CARD INT: 1
130 READ FRONT CARD IN: 1
140 INT PATTERN ON (blank screen)
141 INT PATTERN OFF (normal screen)
150 VCO SET (press + or - on the handset until scrambled picture is still.
then press MENU on the handset then STANDBY).
160 TDA8540 Out0 with Gain X
170 ADJUST WHITE (this resets the picture colour balance. Press MENU
then STANDBY) You can also adjust the colour balance. For example, if
you want less green press MENU until you see GREEN CUT FF. Press
the - button to reduce FF to about CF.Press MENU repeatedly until you
see "DONE". Then press STANDBY.
Warning! Each time you press 1 7 0 you will reset the colours to standard!
181 TPU PATTERN ON (white oblong in centre of screen).
180 TPU PATTERN OFF (white oblong removed).
190 CONFIGURATION 1

200 READ BER (Bit Error Rate)

210 (exits Service Mode - function not known).

220 WR EEPROM ADDR: (allows you to write EEprom address with hex number).

230 LEDS =

241 WR IMBUS ADDR:

250 CTRL - AUDIO = 0

261 (blank green screen)

260 DSY = 0 (normal screen)

270 (exits Service Mode - function not known).

280 SIGNAL PRESENCE = 0

290 TDA8540 Out0 Enable =

300 (blank screen)?

310 Init D2MAC and Sound =

321 VCO INPUT 0 LEVEL = C441

322 VCO INPUT 2 LEVEL = F70A

340 PRESET AY AP B

350 FRONT CARD SELECTED

351 BACK CARD SELECTED

**Use these ONLY if you understand what you are doing!**

### Setting up Philips BBD901 (Filmnet) D2MAC decoder

Connect decoder to receiver via SCART socket

Press [MENU] and [MENU SELECT] buttons simultaneously

Press [MENU SELECT]

Press [MENU +] until language is selected and press [MENU SELECT]

Press [MENU +] until input via SCART is selected and press [MENU SELECT]

Press [MENU +] until D2MAC deemphasis is selected and press [MENU SELECT]

Press [MENU +] until SCART connected to tuner is selected and press [MENU SELECT]

Note: The Filmnet software requires the decoder to "see" a Filmnet transmission each week for a few seconds. For Pace receivers you may have to select PAL output for best results.

An English language User Manual is available from SatCure.

**What is Digital Satellite Television?**

© Chris Muriel. 1998

Contents
1) What is MPEG ?
2) Modulation Schemes ?
3) What is DVB ?
4) Simple Block Diagram of digital receiver.
5) What equipment do I need ?
6) Info on some digital receivers available in Europe.
7) Where can I find appropriate channel listings ?
8) Further information sources & url's

1) MPEG stands for Moving (or Motion) Picture Experts Group & is an organisation of interested parties. It's run in similar manner to JPEG (Joint Picture Experts Group) -JPEG being for still images; there is also a standard known as M-JPEG (Moving JPEG) but this is intended more for the needs of the security industry. MPEG describes a form of compression for digital data where the data represents moving images of a TV like-nature. The standard also allows for audio data streams synchronised with the video. MPEG1 is common on IBM PCs (& other platforms) using *. mpg files. Xing, Mediamatics & other companies supply software players for these and all but the cheapest PC VGA cards seem to have some hardware support for MPEG1 files; normally you need a Pentium PC to have much chance of playing MPEG1 files at reasonable speeds (25 frames per second or more). Anyway, MPEG1 isn't used for satellite TV; the industry needed a faster, more flexible & efficient method. For broadcast use, less tendency to pixellation or "blockiness" was desired with fewer "artifacts" -technical/marketing term for unwanted material on the screen (that's a bit like calling a software bug an "anomaly" ! ! ).

Now what the satellite industry wanted was to squeeze more channels into the bandwidth taken up by a satellite transponder. Analogue satellite TV uses around 36 MHz of bandwidth for its FM video + audio FM subcarriers; this is for each channel. So the operators want to put 5, 10 or more separate channels, via a digital data stream into a similar bandwidth. This allows many more channels or needs fewer satellites to transmit a given number of channels.

To give flexibility, the actual compression ratio can be varied between "Studio Quality" & "Video recorder quality".

Studio needs 12 MBits/second data, broadcast needs 8 MBits, VHS needs 2 MBits/s. I don't want this FAQ to become too technical but read DVBFAQ. TXT from Markus Kuhn for technical info. Just remember that the compression ratio can be varied to cope with the needs of the supplier of the video information. The digital data from several channels can be multiplexed into an MPEG Transport Stream, along with various (compressed) audio channels (which can include digital surround sound & multiple languages). Incidentally MPEG1. 5 is a hybrid (falling between 1 & 2) but any MPEG2 receiver should be backwards compatible with older MPEG revisions. 1 interesting point is that you can't compress "noise" with current MPEG schemes. Imagine watching a film via digital (MPEG) satellite TV where, within the plot of the film, the camera zooms in to show a TV screen switched on but with no antenna connected. You expect to see nothing but noise ("snow)" on the picture. This signal is entirely random & so can't be compressed -there's no repeating pattern/redundancy in the signal. Apparently a future MPEG version (MPEG3 or 4 ???) will have some kind of algorithm built in to get around this problem. MPEG2 is also used for DVD (digital video disk) & other digital video delivery systems including cable & fibre.

## 2) Modulation

The real world is analogue so we have to find a way of transmitting our MPEG2 transport stream as information on a (non-digital) carrier wave. A traditional analogue satellite transmission varies a carrier FREQUENCY in sympathy with the video signal -"frequency modulation" or FM. Similar to this, one can vary the PHASE instead of the frequency - "Phase Modulation". Now we could code our digital signal (which consists of simply binary or "ones & zeros") directly as phase modulation in which case 0 degrees (our carrier reference frequency) could represent a binary 0, whilst 180 degrees phase shift=binary 1; there would be a practical difficulty in keeping track & always changing 180 degrees as there will be natural phase variations over the transmission path. To solve this we can instead make the phase changes cumulative - i. e. make the phase changes refer to the previously signalled state rather than 0/180 degrees absolute. This is known as DPSK - differential phase shift keying. Now those of you who know of schemes used for digital transmis-

sion, in modems for example, will know that DPSK is somewhat ineffi-
cient.

There are various schemes that allow the data rate to be doubled,
quadrupled (or more) whilst maintaining the original signalling rate.

Thus Quaternary (or Quadrature) phase shift keying uses a 2-bit symbol
(instead of previously described 1-bit) based on 4 possible phases.

At the same time, 0 degrees is avoided to prevent long periods of
unmodulated carrier which could cause problems in part of the circuitry
-too complex to discuss here. So we use typically 45, 135, 225 & 315
degrees. We now have a greater data rate in bits per second than our
actual baud (signalling) rate.

This can, in fact be further extended by using a constellation of 8 or 16
phases & beyond -although tolerance to noise (required signal to noise
ratio for a suitably low bit error rate) & to interference increases as the
data rate rises. [This is one reason why computer modems have trouble
at high data rates on a poor line & your 33K modem ends up communi-
cating at 9600 or less].

Other digital transmission media can still use MPEG2 but change from
QPSK to a different modulation scheme. Normally this is QAM for cable
(although QPSK can be used for the return path back to the operator)
whilst digital terrestrial TV will use CODFM -coded orthogonal digital
frequency modulation.

The choice of type of modulation is made based on the sort of problems
most prevalent for the medium, e. g. terrestrial is more subject to multi-
path interference ("ghosting" in analogue TV) & CODFM is fairly resis-
tant to this. For a good, more technical description of QPSK etc. try the
following URL: http://www.coolstf.com/mpeg

## 3) DVB

Like MPEG groups there is a DVB group - Digital Video Broadcast,
made up of interested parties, sharing information & setting the standards. It's somewhat like the VESA group for PC graphics. DVB was set
up by the EBU (European Broadcast Union) to set the standards for digi-

tal video transmission. They have published these via ETSI (European Telecommunications Standards Institute) who also set standards for devices such as GSM telephones. In fact there are several DVB standards for different transmission media. Some of these are: DVB-S Satellite DVB-C Cable DVB-T Terrestrial DVB-SI Specification for Service Information DVB-CI Common Interface for conditional access. They've settled on using a subset of MPEG2 for their compression of the video & audio. I've pasted in below a definition of the requirements to be met to claim that your IRD (Integrated Receiver Decoder i. e. satellite box) is DVB compatible. To be DVB compliant a Satellite or a Cable receiver must, according to DVB Document A001-revision 1, at least fulfil the following key features:

**Systems**
- MPEG-2 Transport Stream is used
- Service information is based on MPEG-2 Program Specific Information
- Scrambling is as defined by CA Technical Group
- Conditional Access uses the MPEG-2 CA_descriptor * Video
- MPEG-2 Main Profile at Main Level is used (1. 5-15 MBits/s)
- The frame rate is 25 Hz
- Encoded pictures may have either 4:3, 16:9 or 2. 21:1 aspect ratio (4:3 is the normal TV format, 16:9 is the wide screen format and 2. 21:1 is the cinemascope format that is use in the movie theatres)
- IRDs will support 4:3 and 16:9 and optionally 2. 21:1 aspect ratios o IRDs must support the use of pan and scan vectors to allow a 4:3 monitor to give a full-screen display of a 16:9 coded picture
- IRDs must support a full screen display of 720 x 576 pixels (and a nominal full-screen display of 704 x 576) o IRDs must provide appropriate up conversion to produce a full-screen display of 544 x 576 and 480 x 576 and a nominal full-screen display of 352 x 576 and 352 x 288 pixels.

**Audio**
- MPEG-2 Layer I and Layer II must be supported by the IRD
- The use of Layer II is recommended for the encoded bitstream
- IRDs must support single channel, dual channel, joint stereo and the extraction of at least a stereo pair from MPEG-2 compatible multichannel audio o IRDs must support sampling rates of 32 kHz, 44. 1 kHz and 48 kHz
- The encoded bitstream will not use emphasis

Note that American DSS, DirecTV etc. systems are NOT DVB-compliant & won't work in Europe. I do know of an attempt by someone in the USA to modify a European Nokia digital receiver to decode DigiCypher2 transmissions - but, at the time of writing, this has not been successful.

## 4) Block Diagram

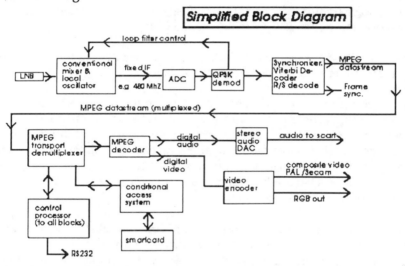

**Simplified Block Diagram**

Some observations on the above diagram : DAC = Digital-to-analogue converter; ADC = Analogue-to-digital converter. The video encoder typically contains 4 or more DACs which have to run at video rates & quality. This infers 8 bit video DACs (not cheap). 3 are needed for RGB; another is needed for composite video out (PAL or SECAM). Some use 10 bit DAC's & the difference *may* be visible by viewing sharp transitions like black to white - hint : have a look at the On Screen Display if you want to try to spot this effect. For simplicity I have not included the conditional access module. Complex ICs are needed for many of these blocks. A QPSK demodulator/ADC/Viterbi decoder can easily cost around $20-$25 in manufacturers volumes! The MPEG transport demultiplexer & decoders cost even more! I haven't included the CPU & memory (usually around 1-3Meg. is needed & some of this may be fast, expensive SRAM). Perhaps you can now see why the digital receivers cost a lot more than the analogue ones! ! ! It's worth noting that on Astra, a Network Information Table (NIT) is transmitted every 10 seconds on every DVB/MPEG transponder. The information sent includes the FEC, S/R, frequencies etc.

## 5) Equipment Needed

First of all, a universal LNB is recommended as digital receivers for Europe are optimised for use with these. A universal LNB will have low phase noise (required so as not to confuse the QPSK modulator) & 2 local oscillators, 1 at 9.75 GHz & 1 at 10.6 GHz.

The default is to enable the 9.75 GHz osc. whilst a 22KHz tone generated by the receiver enables the 10.6 GHz oscillator.

Any receiver made for European digital reception may work up to a point *but* (big problem) many receivers are sold for use on a particular operator's "bouquet" (multiplex) of channels & often have internal software that prevents your receiving anything else! ! ! ! All Pace receivers up to late 1997 seem to suffer from this and, according to a recent French magazine report, so do the Sagem boxes sold for the French TPS (Television Par satellit) bouquet.

You also need the relevant Conditional Access Module (CAM) for any subscription channel along with appropriate smart card (which could include a pirate card - these started to appear in summer 1997 although many were knocked out via ECMs from the operators).

There are several different conditional access schemes in use by the different operators & each system needs the relevant CAM (as well as the smart card for subscription channels). IRDETO is the commonest in Europe.

DVB-CI was a "cop-out" in that they could have specified that all DVB receivers used the same form of conditional access.

Instead they paralleled the situation that occurs in analogue satellite transmissions i.e. many different systems co-exist.

This kept the status quo with the operators (& Hollywood) but runs totally against EU open market policy. Only the CAM interface is covered by the DVB spec. - so they can use their own proprietary encryption systems.

In Spain the 3 digital satellite operators were each going to use a different encryption method. However, the Spanish authorities stepped in & forced them all to agree to use the same system. This promotes healthy competition, allowing the Spanish consumer to buy one digital receiver & choose to take 1, 2 or 3 subscriptions (involving 1, 2 or 3 smartcards) but they will all work on the one receiver & CAM. If you want to complain, I suggest those in Europe write to their Euro MP (officially known as "MEP") ! IRDETO - used by Kirch/DF1, Nethold/Multichoice, Telepiu, M-Net (C-band) SECA - French. Used by Canal Plus/CSN (Canal Satellite Numerique) Also known as "MediaGuard". Also used by the German Premiere bouquet. Viaccess -Used by TPS (Television Par Satellit), French Bouquet which can be found on Hotbird 2 (13 degrees east). Also AB-Sat on the same satellite. Cryptoworks -Used by RTL (Austria/Switzerland). Cryptoworks is a trademark of Philips. Conax - Used by Canal Plus for Scandinavian packages.

The CAM modules use PCMCIA connections - a technology borrowed from laptop computers.

This should allow you to unplug one module & insert another to switch from, for example, IRDETO to Viaccess. However this isn't a simple 5-minute task & the internal software isn't guaranteed to support the change! ! Add to that the difficulty in easily obtaining CAM modules other than the one supplied within the IRD, so this isn't going to be an easy option for most people.

## 6) Some receiver information

Some of this info I have collected from others, info on the Pace DVR500, D-Box, Nokia 9200 & Seleco is from my own personal experience. The latest receivers do now have teletext -although not all operators or channels send teletext data. Also look out for receivers with a "MacroVision" video encoder fitted. MacroVision is a form of copy protection which prevents recording on a VCR. MacroVision Corporation have managed to get this implemented for DVD (Digital Video Disc) & it's also likely to appear on Digital IRDs. It will help protect PPV screenings of films possibly screened before they appear in the video hire shops! ! As usual, Hollywood is again exerting its influence.

**The Pace DVR 500 & 501**

Poor for dx-ing. They only work on symbol rates of 15-30 Megasymbols/second (i. e. R/S of 15000 to 30000) due to the current Pace implementation of the QPSK demodulator. The chip set used (LSI Logic + Plessey ADC) is capable of 1-45 MS/sec as NTL use the same ICs in their (professional broadcast) MPEG receivers which cover the full range. I wasn't able to receive any clear MPEG channels with this IRD other than the Multichoice ones for which I had the card & Irdeto CAM module. It would recognise Kirch DF1 & other IRDETO-based packages but wouldn't decode even the clear channels within the Irdeto bouquets. There is a fast serial port capable of receiving MPEG data directly - basically a V35 interface.

Note: for most SCPC (single channel per carrier) transmissions, a symbol rate well below 15, 000 is used (e. g. 5, 632). The actual menu was quite easy to use (even before I acquired an English version of the original -Dutch- handbook). There are no scart sockets - just Phonos. Future generations will use scart & wider symbol rate ranges are planned - but much of this is in the hands of the operators for whom Pace build the boxes under contract.

**Pace DVR600/DVR601**

These are updated receivers using a later series of chips. Teletext will be provided on some of them. Still limited symbol rates - no SCPC. Scart sockets at last (on the European version only). Some variants will include a full V32bis modem.

**Pace DSR200**

Pace's first receiver sold as officially FTA (Free To Air). It supports teletext but not SCPC or C-Band reception. No CAM as it's only intended for FTA channels. Good instruction manual but not a receiver for the dedicated or "techie" dx-er. It does have 2 scarts as well as phono outputs. Future variants will include a new receiver using a different QPSK chip set which will enable Pace to make a box with SCPC capabilities fairly soon.

**The Sagem box sold for French TPS multiplex**

Comes with modem & 6-pin RJ11 phone socket, 9-pin serial port & 2 scart sockets (for TV & VCR). PAL/SECAM & RGB are all supported as is S-VHS (Y/C). It's easy to set up on TPS & will recognise AB Sat which uses the same Viaccess encryption standard. On AB-Sat it comes up with the French equivalent of the following message: "This chain is not part of your subscription, contact TPS". I would have expected it to suggest contacting AB-Sat myself -but I didn't write the message! This is like asking you to contact Sky when your Filmnet card stops working! ! It will receive other clear channels if they're MPEG2/DVB ones. I'm not sure about SCPC news feeds etc. though. There was a review of this IRD in February 1997 French "Tele Satellite" magazine.

### Digiskan KR888

I had some info on this from someone outside Europe. It appears only to cover Symbol Rates of 20-30 MSymbols/second; this makes it of no use for SCPC. I believe this is based on a Thomson design - it uses a lot of SGS-Thomson chips.
The KR777 seems to be similar. I've only heard of them being supplied in Australia.

### Panasat IRD520

From Panasonic. These were the original boxes sold for use in South Africa. Symbol Rate only 18-28 MS/Second so no use for SCPC. There's a version for the middle-East bouquets in C-band also. The Panasats do have 2 scarts & a switchable 12 volt output connector + a duplex modem. The Grundig DTR1100 is a rebadged version of the same box. The Panasat IRD630 seems to be similar but adds teletext.

### Echostar DSB9800

This is the first digital receiver I've come across from Echostar in Europe; they're a major supplier of digital IRDs in the USA already. Symbol rates covered from 18.5 - 30MS/sec but not SCPC nor PowerVu. Works ok in C-Band also. A useful feature is automatic FEC rate i.e. you don't have to input this manually in a search. Handles NTSC & inverted video. The auto-FEC is down to their QPSK demodulator implementation whilst the video-encoder control circuitry enables choice of PAL or NTSC (for SECAM, they would have to use a different video encoder IC). No teletext yet but this is planned soon. In the FTA version there's no modem (but the CAM socket is still there).

### Thomson box ( Mediasat for Canal plus).

I've read some reviews from summer 1996 (in French) & this receiver doesn't seem easily capable of receiving non-Mediaguard/SECA channels. It has serial & parallel ports, scarts for VCR & TV + PAL, SECAM &

RGB outputs (includes Y/C), integral modem + a second F-type antenna connector. As well as the card socket for a Mediaguard card, there's a socket for a French smart bank-card -presumably for PPV.

**The D-Box**
This is the Nokia DVB9500S modified slightly for use with the Kirch/ DF1 multiplex. It comes with Irdeto CAM & (normally) basic DF1 smart card & is the best box so far for Satellite enthusiasts or dx-ers. With the original version of internal software it wouldn't receive SCPC but could receive the Dutch Multichoice transmissions with the right smart card. Then an over-the-air software upgrade appeared which made 2 very interesting changes - SCPC was enabled whilst, on MCPC, it wouldn't decode MultiChoice anymore (it also improved the Electronic Programme Guide or EPG at the same time).

Who knows what future upgrades will bring ?? Apparently, the reason that SCPC became possible was that the new software enabled the PSI (Program Specific Information) part of the SI (service information) data stream. Now SI can have 2 parts; 1 is the DVB-SI which helps the box find the channels & set up the EPG (Electronic Program Guide). The other is the PSI which the D-Box had been ignoring. Since most SCPC transmissions don't contain the DVB-SI (not needed for SNG feeds etc. ) the channels weren't recognised. The new software decoded the PSI & so allowed reception of the SCPC feeds. Now a number of hackers have been finding ways of protecting the D-Box from future upgrades as well as re-enabling it for BOTH SCPC & all MCPC functions. One of the most interesting finds was the (now well known) "secret menu". Pressing the right buttons on the remote control accesses all sorts of configurable parameters. The relevant sequence is:

" Menu, 9, 9, radio, menu ". One can then enter frequencies (either L-Band or KU-band), R/S rates, enable BER display on front panel & much much more. To find out more, visit some of the D-Box Internet WWW sites which have sprung up in the last month or so. Of course this "secret menu" was originally meant just for Nokia engineers & authorised repair outlets for debugging and setup. This receiver uses a TV/Com (now part of Hyundai) QPSK demodulator, a Rockwell 2400 baud modem chip set & Philips 8-bit video encoder. It covers the full symbol rates needed for all known SCPC & MCPC reception as well as working with some other standards used for SNG links etc. like

PowerVu; used correctly, it also handles the inversion that occurs due to low side mixing with C-Band reception. It has a SCSI-2 port, serial port, RJ11 socket for the modem, 3 scarts AND phono sockets for video & audio; finally it has a phono which can produce 12 volts (enabled/disabled via the "secret menu") to power external equipment.

Although setting up channels in the secret menu is arduous (each channel will overwrite the previous one), there is another solution if you don't mind using a PC with it - connected via the serial port : You can then either use your PC keyboard directly or, more useful, run macros containing the relevant FEC, Symbol Rate, frequency etc. with a different macro for each channel (or a nested macros scheme if you prefer). This more or less automates your channel-hopping - at the expense of tying up a PC. Some D-Box sites have ready written macros that you can download. It is possible to write this information over one of the previously stored channels so maybe you could store 200 of your own chans.

Use the Internet to find various sources of modified D-Boxes & more information. Also watch the relevant Usenet News groups for information, adverts, hints and so on. Some of these sites also explain how to enter audio & video PIDs (Program Information Data) which are needed to decode some channels. Referring to my points on the System Information (SI) stream above, I assume that the channels needing manual entry of PID via the secret menu aren't already sending the correct SI information with their signal. I expect to see a variant with more memory - hopefully enough to store several SCPC channels & several that can only be decoded using PID info.

**Mascom 9500 receiver**
Has been mentioned in Doctor Dish questions & answers (I have never seen the actual receiver). It is billed as a "digital free-to-air" receiver. This is a professionally modified Nokia 9500 with lots of features for Satellite dx-ers. It has been reviewed on a 1997 show by Doctor Dish. There is a Mascom Internet web site (see list below).

**Nokia 9200S**
This is the only Nokia digital receiver officially available in UK - i. e. with support/guarantee from Nokia in UK. There's no CAM supplied but otherwise it looks like the D-Box/ 9500. 1 MByte Ram memory, 2 MByte expansion memory & 1 MB flash.

### Nokia 9300S
Became available around late summertime '97. It appears to be a 9200 but with proper PCMCIA CAM interface conforming to the DVB Common Interface Standard. As such, it should accept any CAM (Irdeto, SECA, Cryptoworks & others) & relevant valid smart card. The preliminary spec. which I saw at April 1997 CabSat Show indicates that it does not have a SCSI port. It has 1 Mbyte RAM memory + 1 MByte flash. The same remote control is used for all the Nokia receivers. They're all manufactured under license from TV/Com - which is a company that Hyundai bought last year.

### Nokia 9600
Sold as a free-to-air box but with a CI compliant CAM socket &, in latest version or with software upgrade, fully CI compliant.

### Nokia 9602
I have seen this advertised in German satellite magazines. It appears to be very similar indeed to the 9600 but with a modem fitted.
This is a copy of the text of a letter which Nokia (UK) sent to all dealers. I don't think Nokia will mind my breach of copyright, since it contains information that they clearly want everyone to know:

*"Due to the continued and growing interest in the new digital services now available, we are once again facing unofficial "Grey" imports of Nokia digital receivers into the UK.*

*Despite these boxes being manufactured under licence for specific broadcasters and their own markets, some dealers have decided to purchase them to capitalise on demand.*

*Dealers should recognise however, that many of the boxes entering the UK are unauthorised reworked German d-boxes (designed for Kirch's DF- 1 service) where the software has been reprogrammed to operate as the Italian Telepiu box.*

*In addition we are starting to see the DVB 9602S Common Interface receiver appear in some areas. This receiver is designed for the Nordic market with different software options built in, and as such cannot be upgraded in the same manner as our authorised 'Free to Air' receivers the Nokia Mediamaster 9200S and 9600S Common Interface version.*

*It should also be noted that many of the non-authorised receivers include an in-built modem, which is illegal to use within the UK. Additionally, these digital receivers operate differently via EPG (Electronic Programme Guides) on screen displays. These menus are constantly updated by data fed down the relevant channel's signal path.*

*Many consumers and dealers are now reporting problems with these boxes, e.g. the software either locking up or reverting back to German menus etc.*

*This is primarily due to the receiver intercepting data from an Astra channel as used by DF-1 while the system is being set up, or customers realigning their dish away from HotBird to Astra to see what else they can receive.*

*Nokia in the UK are not importing or supporting any of these grey imports and dealers will need to refer back to their original supplier in case of faults or any other issues with these boxes.*

*However, on a positive note, Nokia will continue to offer you fully authorised "free to air" receivers in the form of the Nokia Mediamaster 9200S and the Nokia Mediamaster 9600S that will receive all DVB compliant "clear" digital broadcasts."*

### Nokia 9610

Version produced for Scandinavian market. Supposedly (according to Nokia's web site info) "top of the range" ; has DiSEqC, SCSI & serial ports + a V32bis modem. There are also boxes called 9500C & D-Box-C but these are digital CABLE receivers though using the same basic chassis & back end. During 1998 Nokia are due to launch their "3rd generation" receivers with 8xxx model numbers. As an example, the 8400 will be their FTA digital satellite box.

### Philips MediaBox / "Canalsatellite" IRD

Available for hire in Germany for the Premiere multiplex as well as for Canal Plus/CSN in France. Unfortunately not currently sold directly for cash. It has 3 scart sockets, SCSI port, RS232 & telephone socket for its modem. There is capacity to store 500 channels. The CAM supplied is the SECA/Mediaguard one but it will also receive clear MPEG channels; I don't believe it will receive SCPC transmissions - but maybe a later version or software upgrade might allow this (the original D-Box began as a MCPC box only). For a review of this box see Tele-Satellite magazine 3/4, 1997. Very quick at searching/finding Ku-band bouquets. It automatically finds the correct FEC & symbol rates. The official model number is 96514D.

### Galaxis Sat 500
Another free-to-air box with common air interface. From the info on their web site (http://www. galaxis. com) it seems to have 2 PCMCIA CAM slots; this would allow the user to have, for example, both an Irdeto & a SECA CAM in the box at the same time -assuming you could actually purchase the CAMs & smartcards. Launched at Cable & Sat Show April 1997 & taken up by Telenor according to press release. Only capable of 15-30MS/sec. so no SCPC or PowerVu.
It has an RF loop through for use with an analogue receiver as well as an S-VHS socket + 2 scarts. Samsung's first European DVB box.
It has DiSEqC and a good instruction manual.

### Galaxis FTA2
With the FTA 2, Galaxis presents a Digital Receiver for the reception of all free-to-air digital programs (SCPC/MCPC). Manufactured by Samsung and marketed in continental Europe by Galaxis.
Features: 2 Scart sockets; Serial data port; 950 - 2150 MHz tuner; DiSEqC switching; Sat IF loopthrough; SCPC/MCPC reception; FEC rate - ALL; Symbol Rate 2 - 36000. Available in the UK from Satellite Scene.

### Grundig DTR2000
Flexible design with plug-in modules to allow upgrades. Grundig have already announced 2 versions, one for digital cable & one for Dig-TV; cable needs a QAM (Quadrature Amplitude Modulation) demodulator whereas TV needs QPSK. If they produce a version for terrestrial digital TV this would use a COFDM demodulator (Coded Orthogonal Frequency Division Multiplex).

A future version will be CI compliant & so will work with any CI encryption system. The cable version will eventually allow Internet access.

This is a case of "watch this space" as the modular design will allow Grundig to come up with different versions & hardware as well as software upgrades.

### Hyundai DBS3001

I have an Italian report about this receiver ; I have come across it only in Italy. It has 3 scarts, uses a Motorola processor & will not work for SCPC. There is a 14K4 modem, serial port & fast 25-way service port.

### Lemon Volksbox

A German combined analogue AND digital receiver. Has DiSEqC, tone & voltage switching with 2000 channel memory. Also 3 scarts & RS232. Clever 3 LNB socket with loop through allows you to connect a separate LNB to the analogue input. The RS232 port can handle the full official EIA spec of 115KBits/s duplex. Has an optical digital audio output for loss less connection to suitable hi-fi equipment. PID codes can be entered in hex or decimal (saves using a converter or calculator). This unit, in addition, receives ADR (Astra Digital Radio) transmissions. This receiver sounds very interesting, particularly for those who want analogue AND digital without losing out on features or taking up too much space.

### RSD ODM300

A British (Scottish) designed FTA receiver (at last). Has 999 channel memory & SCPC with naming of the channels. Initially English menus with other languages to follow. Uses a fast Motorola Coldfire 33MHz processor which results in fast response to user instructions. The QPSK demodulator & the MPEG decoder use Hyundai "Odeum" chips - from a totally separate design group than the TV/Com QPSK chips used by Nokia - although Hyundai own both concerns. Symbol rates covered from 2-45 MS/s. I found the menu (on a prototype receiver at the factory) fairly intuitive & far better than Nokia's - although this will, in part, be a matter of personal taste.

Has DiSEqC, RS232, manual PID support, tone or voltage LNB control & 2 scarts.

This receiver is FTA only; i.e. no CAM or PCMCIA socket & is due for official launch in the first quarter of 1998. Looks like a good dx-er's receiver.

### Seleco SMB1900 /Emme Esse DRX900

These are the both same unit, apparently produced by Italtel (which is 50% owned by Telecom Italy & 50% Siemens).

This receiver has the usual scarts & also a modem but only works with signals that have Symbol rates between 18. 5-30MS/s. Thus it's no good for SCPC reception. It's auto download is quite fast (10 seconds for Telepiu bouquet). The menus are available in English, Italian & German.

**XSat CDTV200**
Interesting IRD made for simple reception of Pay-TV channels from Arabesque, AB-sat & TPS. Has Viaccess CAM. Has RS232, 2 scarts & an S-VHS port.

The remote control is subject to user mis-keying due to its use of 40 identical-looking keys, equally spaced. Slow in response to user commands but robust in terms of being very hard to crash. Although not mentioned in the manual this IS an SCPC capable box (2-30. 5 MS/S symbol rates); you just have to remember to add 10MHz to the nominal receive frequency, key in Symbol & FEC rates & away you go. There's a PID menu - although again not covered in the manual.

The OSD can be set for English, French, German, Italian, Spanish & Arabic. It also runs cool. A good alternative to the various Nokia boxes for the FTA dx-er.

**The BSkyB Digital IRDs**
Sky awarded 3 manufacturers with a contract for this receiver to a specification supplied by Sky. Early information from various sources indicates the following features : Proprietary built-in (non replaceable/hard wired) CAM with Sky's own encryption system. This will be from another Murdoch subsidiary (NDC). Scart sockets, fast modem & it will receive some non-Sky FTA transmissions - probably only those within a very restricted FEC & Symbol Rate range (e. g. 27, 500 & 3/4). The contracts were awarded to Pace, Amstrad & a consortium led by Grundig. These will be sold/rented only to those within Sky's subscriber area (just like existing Sky analogue) along with a smart card. The price will be subsidised to kick-off interest in BSB Digital.

**7) Channel Listings**

Good listings are published in Tele-satellite magazine each month. Internet site to check is :- http://www.satcodx.com

## 8) Further Info

DVB FAQ (from Markus Kuhn):-
ftp://ftp.informatik.uni-erlangen.de/pub/multimedia/tv-crypt/dvb.txt
MPEG FAQ & links (technical):-
http://www.spectra-media.com/mpegres.htm
MPEG/QPSK technical description:-
http://www.coolstf.com/mpeg
Irdeto web site - http://www.irdeto.nl
Nokia Web site - Mediamaster 9500 :-
http://www.nokia.com/products/multimedia/9500s.html
Mascom Web site -http://www.satshop.com/dvbcompa.htm
(comparison chart of various Nokia digital boxes)
Pace Web site - http://www.pace.co.uk
Doctor Dish : http://www.sat-net.com/drdish/
email queries to Doctor Dish - drdish@cuci.nl
Doctor Dish - General satellite TV questions. Dr. Dish has quite a lot of
knowledge about digital satellite TV. He also hosts a useful program
every month covering satellite TV topics. Recent programmes have contained a lot of info about digital TV & D-Boxes in particular. It can be
found on DFS2 Kopernikus, 28. 5 degrees East 11. 548 GHz. V. Audio
subcarriers: 6. 65 MHz, 300KHz bandwidth, 50µSecs de-emphasis. See
web site which archives the questions & answers & gives the time/date
of next Doctor Dish TV Show.
TurboSat's digital section - http://www. turbo. demon. co.uk/#dbox
Mueller Communications:-
http://subnet.virtual-pc.com/~mu449890/dbox.html
Another D-Box site:-
http://www.awihg-sat.de & http://www.sat-soft.com
Defiant Digital - http://www.eurosat.com/eurosat/index.html
Swiss Digital Site - http://www.eurosat.com/swiss/digital.html
CNJ Electronics - http://www.cnj-electronics.com/infobase

Recommended reading: Tele-Satellite International, published with joint
German & English text every 2 months. Available in most European
countries (but you will probably have to order it specially).

# Nokia Digital Receivers

*© 1998 Chris Heaton*

The main Nokia Digital receivers are the 9200, 9500 and the 9600. The main difference between them is that the 9200/500 comes with an IRD-ETO CAM. (The bit that decodes scrambled signals). The 9600 has no CAM but comes with a slot to insert one of the new open access CAMS. No CAMS are available yet for this receiver. This means that if you want to watch scrambled stations, such as the Italian package you need a smart card (either pirate or real) and a 9200/500. If you want a future proofed receiver that theoretically can handle all the future scrambling systems but at the moment you are happy watching the Free to Air stations then buy the 9600.

As I do not have a 9600 all the following relates to the 9200/9500.

The original software in these receivers are rubbish but if you are buying one now you should have the latest version of the software which is 1000% better. I will not dwell on using the old software. Suffice to say, if you have a receiver that has not been upgraded yet, then do it straight away. There are three ways to do this:-

1/ Use a program such as Transbox to upgrade the software via the RS232 port on the back of the receiver to either the latest Nokia software or others such as Dream 5.1.

2/ If Transbox will not work then you have an old D-Box with a boot-loader that will not allow RS232 upgrades. In this case you need to use a BDM interface. This is a small interface that connects between your computer and a socket inside the D-Box. There is also a small jumper within the D-Box which must be removed to allow the old boot-loader to be overwritten. Once the boot-loader has been changed all future upgrades can be done via the RS232 socket.

3/ Contact me for an upgrade.

chris@gb89.demon.co.uk

# FINDING STATIONS

## The Hard Way

Unlike an analog receiver you cannot just tune around to find stations. If you do not know the frequency etc then all you get is a blank screen. When you first turn on the receiver it should scan for stations. This works well but it does NOT find all the stations. To do this you have to put in the details manually. First bring up the Menu onscreen. Select Installation then Channel search. You will be given two options. Channel search and Advanced channel search. At this point you only need the Normal Channel Search. Fill in the details asked for on the screen, ie Satellite, Frequency, Polority, SR and FEC. There is also an option marked Network Search. To find the most number of new stations leave this option ticked. If you just want the one station you are looking for and you want to save time by not looking for any other new stations then uncheck the box. Now if you select OK the receiver will find and store the new stations. If all goes well the stations will be assigned numbers which put them next to other stations on the same satellite. (This does not always work, but there is an option in the Installation Menu which allows you to delete or renumber stored stations)

## The Easy Way

You can obtain a settings file containing ALL the stations available (including feeds). This settings file can be uploaded via the RS232 port using Transbox. Saves Days of work!!!!

The settings file is available from the Internet or I will e-mail the latest version if requested. (My e-mail address is: chris@gb89.demon.co.uk

## SECRET MENUS

You have probably heard of the RED Menu. This is a secret menu that can be accessed by pressing the following key combination [Radio] [99] [Radio]. With the new software it is now not necessary to use this menu. However there is ANOTHER secret menu which is the main Service Menues. Access this by bringing up the Main Menu, select Installation, then highlight System Settings but DO NOT press OK. Instead press 0000 (or in some cases 1234).

There are many things to play with in these menus including shifting the picture left or right when using RGB or changing settings in the Advanced Tuning Menu to see what happens. Most of these changes are not permanent BUT be careful it is possible to erase ALL your stored stations if you select the wrong option.

## USING WITH AN EXISTING ANALOG RECEIVER

This is possible but I recommend changing the LNB to a Universal LNB. You can obtain one with a flange which can be bolted onto your feed-horn. Although the skew control no longer works it makes little difference to the quality. Between the LNB and the receivers you need to fix a Global Smart Switch. This selects which receiver controls the LNB. When the digital is turned to standby the analogue receiver controls the LNB in the normal way. Once the digital receiver is switched on it has full control of polarity and band switching.

## USING THE DIGITAL RECEIVER ALONE

The digital receiver can be used with a fixed dish but it is not recommended because of the number of stations you could not see. There is now a H to H available that the D-Box will control by sending DiSeq commands through the normal LNB Co-ax. The H-H can handle dishes up to 1.2m in size and only needs the one co-ax between the dish and receiver. Up to 40 satellites can be stored. However at the moment the D-Box only has capacity for 8 satellites but this may change with future software releases.

## SPECIAL FEATURES

These features are not documented anywhere.

When watching a TV Station if you press the Radio button a small option box is superimposed on the screen. By using the Left and Right keys you can switch between different languages. Sometimes you may have a station with no sound. Try switching to another sound channel and it works fine.

To listen to Digital Radio Stations press the Radio button TWICE.

When listening to some radio stations such as La Radio 1 from Astra press the Radio button as mentioned above and the same option box will allow you to switch between many stations broadcasting in the same package. If this is the only station in the package pressing the Radio button will return you to TV viewing mode.

Pressing the HILFE button (the bottom button on the remote control) will bring up a subtitles option box. If subtitles are being transmitted you can select them in various languages or turn them off completely.

Pressing HILFE twice will bring up the teletext pages if any are being transmitted.

# Galaxis FTA2

A Digital Receiver for the reception of all free-to-air digital programs (SCPC/MCPC). Manufactured by Samsung and marketed in continental Europe by Galaxis.
Marketed in the UK by Satellite Scene (see appendix).

Comprehensive menu system
Modulator with loopthrough
2 Scart sockets
Serial data port
950 - 2150 MHz tuner
All functions accessible via remote control
An ideal match for the Galaxis "Future 1 Plus" flat digital antenna
DiSEqC switching
Sat IF loopthrough
SCPC/MCPC reception
FEC rate - ALL
Symbol Rate 2 - 36000
And much more ...

# Galaxis SAT500

Earlier version with limited symbol rate range.
Setup PIN 9949
UK models were modified by the addition of a diode next to the tuner to give LNB power for I.F. loop through, allowing the use of an analogue receiver in tandem. Marketed in the UK by Satellite Scene.

# Repairing Digital Receivers

Since all digital receivers are still under guarantee at the time of writing, there is no specific fault information available. However discussions with manufacturers indicate the following:

Faults generally fall into three categories.

1. Power supply failure or broken copper tracks.
2. Software bugs or user error (lack of understanding of the setup procedures, especially for "grey imports" which were not designed for the purpose for which they are now being used).
3. Component failure requiring expensive equipment to repair.

In respect of the latter, a minimum requirement is suggested as:

1. Desoldering station costing approximately £1200.
2. Oscilloscope costing approximately £3000.
3. Computer interface and software for diagnosis and uploading.
4. Model-specific training.

It seems likely that servicing of these receivers will take place as follows:

1. Simple (e.g. power supply) faults can be repaired locally.
2. Programming faults will be fixed by those with training and computer software and interface.
3. Other faults will require the unit to be returned to the manufacturer or a well-equipped authorised workshop. You can hopefully still make some profit by acting as an agent.

Since on-line banking may be one of the facilities offered by some receivers, it is possible that confidential information may be stored in the receiver. This might require that repairers obtain special authorisation to carry out work on these units.

Further information will be made available to those who subscribe to the "Satellite Round Robin" newsletter (Email only). For details send your Email enquiry to satcure@netcentral.co.uk

# Beginners Start Here

# Mains Plugs in the U.K.

No book about satellite receivers could be complete without a mention of mains plugs and I make no apology for including this section.

Mains plugs have been responsible for many, many receiver faults and have also contributed to death and injury.

Some years ago, a friend was drilling a hole in his kitchen wall when the metal casing of his old power drill became "live". The shock he received caused his muscles to contract and he fell from the metal step ladder, still clutching the whirring drill.

The continuing shock made him dance like a puppet, leaving a trail of gouges around the kitchen, until finally he managed to kick the switch on the plug socket. It transpired that the earth wire inside the plug had come loose and touched the live pin, thus passing the live mains through the "earth" wire to the drill body.

You may laugh at this little anecdote because my friend survived, but the story serves to illustrate the importance of correct and secure mains plug wiring. So, even if you *think* you know how to wire a plug, please read on.

Your choice of plug is very important from the point of view of safety and ease of fitting. There are several cheap plugs on the market which are at best fiddly to assemble and, at worst, downright dangerous. The plugs which have been approved as safely designed and manufactured now carry the designation BS1363 (or BS1363A for the type which will withstand knocks), so avoid those which do not.

Don't be ashamed to take a plug apart in the shop to inspect it. Ask to borrow a screwdriver, if necessary, and tell the shopkeeper where to put his plug if he is unhelpful. (However, if he is serving someone who is buying a £500 electrical gizmo, be patient and wait a couple of minutes). The features to look for in a plug are as follows:

1.     Fuse clips which are rivetted or welded securely to the other metal parts. Beware flimsy rivets and screws which can work loose and cause serious overheating. Fuse clips which are silver plated will be more reliable than those which are not.

2.     Cable sheath clamp which will hold the cable firmly. The best ones use a springy plastic flap which bites into the cable sheath and prevents it from pulling out. The worst are those with a thin fibre bridge held with two screws. Bridges moulded from plastic with tubular ends for the screws are good but fiddly; they are often reversible – to cater for thick or thin cable. Be sure to fit them correctly.

3     A captive cover screw. While this feature is not essential, it saves much scrabbling on the floor!

4     Correct value fuse. Sometimes the shop will swap the fuse for a more suitable value. (Sometimes they will offer to sell you a pack of ten).

## Fitting the Plug

Use a knife to remove about 40mm of sheath from the end of the cable. Do not saw with the blade but bend the cable over your finger so that when you touch it with the blade the stretched sheath splits. Continue the split around the circumference by turning and bending the sheath while touching it with the blade. Avoid nicking the individual coloured wires, or your own pinkies!

Once the end portion of sheath is removed, fit the cable into the plug, securing the remaining sheath with the clamp. Allow 10mm extra for connection and cut the brown and blue wires to reach the Live and Neutral terminals, respectively.

Any green-yellow wire should be cut with at least 25mm to spare.

Use pliers or wire strippers to remove 10mm of insulation from the end of each wire. (You may need to remove the cable from the plug while you do this).
The strands of each wire should be twisted tightly and doubled over to fit into those brass pins with a hole and clamp screw or else hooked clockwise around terminals which use a screw and clamping washer.

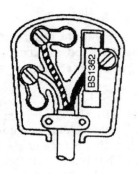

The green-yellow earth wire (if present) is deliberately left long so that, if someone should trip on the cable or tug at it in such a way as to pull the sheath out of the clamp, the safety earth will always be the *last* wire to be disconnected, thus ensuring that the appliance is earthed while there is a possibility of its becoming "live".

Ensure that no loose strands of wire are left, fit the fuse and replace the cover.

Since many appliances are "double insulated" you will find that only two core cable is used, with no green-yellow. Wiring the plug is simpler but do still make sure that the brown wire goes to the live pin via the fuse and the blue wire goes to the neutral pin. Since the cable will be thinner than three-wire cable, be sure to check that the clamp is tight and holds the sheath firmly.

Britain (& parts of Ireland) is the only country in the world which uses mains plugs fitted with a fuse. Other countries rely on the fuses at the main fuse-box or, sometimes, on a fuse in the socket. The fuse in the mains plug, therefore, while not being absolutely essential, does give an added degree of protection from the risk of fire. If the appliance itself has a fuse then the fuse in the plug will prevent the mains lead from catching fire in the event of a short circuit in the lead. It is also a useful backup in case the appliance fuse does not melt quickly when a fault occurs.

Fuses for use in mains plugs are manufactured to a British Standard BS1362 which should *always* be printed on the fuse cartridge.

Some appliances are now fitted with moulded plugs. The fuse is accessible for replacement but the wires are not. You should not remove this plug unless it is essential to do so. If you do need to remove the plug, take it out of the mains socket and cut the cable as close to the plug as possible. Remove the fuseholder and fuse. Destroy the fuseholder clip and dispose of the plug so that no child might plug it into a mains socket and receive an electric shock.

# Basic Tools

Here are some of the tools which are commonly used for satellite receiver repair.

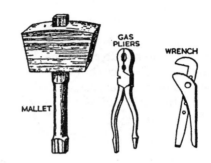

The heavy mallet is ideal for bending the wires of components after insertion in the holes.

Gas pliers can be used to remove components without the need to de-solder.

Use a wrench to undo stubborn tuner nuts, when a spanner is unavailable, and a rasp to smooth the threads.

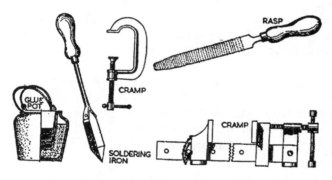

A heavy duty soldering iron is ideal for use with surface mount components.

(Get it nice and hot over a gas burner).

A variety of cramps will be needed to secure the board during hammering and soldering operations.

Finally, no tool kit would be complete without a glue pot. Absolutely indispensable for fixing those lifted pads and tracks after somebody else messed it up!

*No, I'm not serious, but some people do actually appear to use these tools when attempting repairs!*

# The Proper Tools

Before you embark upon any repair or modification work you should have an understanding of the basic use of tools used in electronics.

You really can not do better than to take an electronics course at college, if only to get accustomed to using the tools and terminology used in electronics.

## DANGER!

Once you remove the cover screws on a satellite receiver you expose yourself to a real danger of electric shock or burns. The intention of this section is to make you aware of some of the methods by which receivers can be repaired and modified and, while you might be encouraged to "have a go" yourself, please consider the risks involved – not only to yourself but to others if you are doing a "favour" for a friend.

Inside the receiver is a section which carries mains voltages. That is the good news. In a receiver which uses a "switch mode power supply" there are even higher voltages present. This power supply is extremely dangerous. Keep your fingers and tools away from it! You will find that it is almost always marked with a warning notice or symbol.

*You are recommended to take the receiver to a time-served repair engineer*
*if you are in any doubt at all.*

First, you need a set of basic tools. You are definitely *not* going to be successful if you use hedge cutters for cutting wires and a poker for soldering!

### Screwdrivers

The most common screwdriver is the flat-blade one used for slot-head screws. People don't seem to realise, however, that this comes in different sizes. Use the one which fits the slot exactly. The blade should be square-ended – NOT sharpened to a chisel point or rounded off because you tried to use it on a cross-head screw!

Cross-head screwdrivers come in two different types and several sizes. One type is called "Phillips" and the other is called "Pozidriv™". If you use the wrong one it will slip and damage the slots. The two most useful sizes are #1 and #2, although you might also need #0 for very small screws.

An unusual type of screwdriver is needed for receivers manufactured by Nokia. It is called a "Torx" driver and has a star shaped end. It is almost impossible to remove Torx head screws with anything other than the correct size Torx driver. The most useful size is a number 10 but some receivers used a number 9.

### Pliers

Pliers come in all shapes and sizes. For handling electronic components you will need a very small pair of needle-nosed pliers. A larger pair of snub-nosed pliers will be useful for holding a nut while you tighten the screw.

### Cutters

One of the tools most people think they can do without – until complaints arise from your spouse regarding misuse of the kitchen scissors! For cutting leads on components you need very small cutters. However, DO NOT use these for cutting thick cable or fence wire.

## Soldering Iron

You can buy a very low-cost soldering iron which will be satisfactory if you seldom use it. Such irons usually take a long time to reach the usable temperature and lose their heat rapidly when used to heat up anything other than the smallest solder joint.

A better choice is a high wattage, thermostatically-controlled iron. The one which I have used for twenty years is rated at 45 Watts and I use a number 8 tip which keeps the temperature above 400°C. The tip is iron-coated and lasts a long time. (Iron-coated tips must not be cleaned with anything other than a damp sponge or the iron will peel off and the tip will be useless). The tip size you choose should be tiny – about 1mm.

## Solder

You need fine solder of 0.7mm diameter *or less* for soldering modern electronic components. The solder should contain cores of flux. The percentage of flux will be marked on the solder bobbin. You will see that the solder is a mix of tin and lead in 60/40 proportion and the flux percentage should be about 5%. A higher percentage might make soldering a little easier but leaves a residue on the printed circuit board which looks messy and makes it difficult to inspect your work. A lower percentage may be acceptable and leaves virtually no visible residue but is not recommended for a beginner. (I use 2.2% rosin cored flux class 5A, grade KP, 0.7mm diameter 60/40 tin/lead solder from Maplin).

The reason for having flux is that it melts and flows over the metal which you are soldering. In doing so it excludes air and prevents the metal from oxidising (which would make it impossible for the solder to stick to the metal). Flux also has a slightly acidic action and dissolves any oxidation which is already present.

The most common flux is a resin called "rosin" which comes from trees. However, a number of synthetically manufactured fluxes (such as X32 made by Multicore) are also used. These fluxes leave either less residue or a clear residue, which makes inspection of the solder joint easier and may result in a more reliable circuit, since flux is known to cause problems if left on the board. However, your eventual choice may be influenced by the *smell* of the flux and its action on your nose and eyes!

## Soldering

To remove a suspect or faulty
component from a printed circuit board
is easy – once you know how!

Many people swear by pump-action
solder-suckers. These are like miniature bicycle pumps with an internal

spring. You prime the sucker by pushing
the plunger down until it locks. Pressing a
button releases the spring-loaded plunger
and it sucks up anything close to its
nozzle. Great for zits! Not so great for
printed circuits. The usual effect is that it
sucks the copper pad right off the board, leaving you with nothing to
solder the new component lead to.

By far the best method is to use a
product which goes under various
names such as "Solder wick" or
"Desoldering braid".
This is very fine braid – like the
screening braid found inside coaxial

cable. The difference is that it is impregnated with flux.
Simply place the braid on top of the solder joint and press the tip of the
iron onto it. When the braid is hot it will melt the solder which will be
drawn up the braid by capillary action, aided by the flux.

Sometimes you will need to "prime" the braid by melting a spot of
solder into it – called "tinning" – just to get it started.

When the solder is gone, use the tip of the iron to heat the component

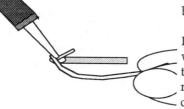

lead and push it upright so that it can
be removed easily from the hole.

In the case of "plated through holes",
where the copper goes all the way
through the circuit board, you must
make sure that ALL of the solder has
come out of the hole.

If it hasn't, resolder the joint with fresh solder then use the desoldering braid again.

Repeat this process for every lead or leg of the component then lift it out of the holes.

To solder a new component in, bend the leads (if necessary) to match the hole centres. Push the leads through the board, taking care not to lift the copper pads off the board. Bend each lead in the direction of the copper track, making sure that the component is flat on the board (unless the original was spaced higher to dissipate heat). Hold the end of the solder on the copper pad and press the tip of the iron onto the solder. Rotate the tip left and right while pressing and feed more solder in as it melts.

### Common Soldering Problems

Amateurs tend to put too much solder on the joint (and everywhere else, too!) and leave nasty big stains of flux so they can't see the track breaks which they have left.

A common mistake of the amateur is to melt the solder on to the tip of the iron then carry it to the joint.

It is easy for an expert to tell when an amateur has attempted a repair!

Broken copper pads and tracks are common. Amateurs tend to put too much solder on the joint (and everywhere else, too!) and leave nasty big stains of flux so they can't see the track breaks which they have left.

The solder joint should have a bright, shiny appearance and the component lead should stick out of it and not be submerged. The solder meniscus around the lead should be concave (curved inward) like a volcano. It should *not* look like a ball. If it does, then the solder has probably not made a good connection to the component lead.

Components should sit flat against the board, or be pushed down as far as they will go. Otherwise, when you touch them, the copper pads to which they are soldered will snap away from their copper tracks to leave an open circuit or an intermittent (on/off) connection. Even if you do not touch the badly mounted component, there is every possibility that vibration or a knock will cause it to move and damage the copper track. The only exception is that a component which may run hot, either normally or under fault conditions, may be required to be spaced away from the board. In such a case, the component legs should be kinked to hold it in place or heat-resistant sleeves or beads should be fitted to the leads. Always copy the mounting method of the original component.

When you bend a component wire underneath the board it should always lie along the attached copper track, if possible – never away from the track. This position ensures that, if you need to desolder it, the copper pad will not be damaged.

A common mistake of the amateur is to melt the solder on to the tip of the iron then carry it to the joint. The problem is that the flux has evaporated by the time the solder gets there so a bad joint is inevitable.

Always put the iron tip onto the component lead and copper pad then apply the solder to the opposite side of the pad, forcing the solder on to the component wire and around the copper pad.

Feed in just enough additional solder to encircle the joint then take the tip away immediately. Hold the component still for a few seconds until the solder has solidified.

Movement of the component lead while the solder is still molten will cause a "dry" joint. The solder will be greyish rather than shiny silver and the connection may be no good. If this should happen, remove the solder with braid and re-solder the joint, carefully.

The problem is that, by the time the solder carried on the tip is applied to the joint, the flux has evaporated and a bad joint will result.

When you bend a component wire underneath the board it should always lie along the attached copper track.

Movement of the component lead while the solder is still molten will cause a "dry" joint.

Always press the iron tip against the component lead and the copper pad then apply the solder to the opposite side of the pad.

# Surface Mount Components

Here is a brief summary of the components you will see. The most common component is the resistor. Made by depositing a film of conductive material on a little chip of ceramic, the resistor has tinned ends and the value printed on one surface in ordinary numerals. The first two digits represent the numerical resistance value and the third digit gives the number of noughts to be added.

The left hand example, above, is 68000 Ohms or 68k while the right hand one is 4700 or 4k7. There is no way to determine the tolerance or the Wattage. The uncoated part of the ceramic body is usually white.

The resistor shown on the left is 10k. On the right is a capacitor. These have no markings so the only way to determine the value is to measure it. Capacitors are usually uniformly coloured brown or green. Unlike the resistor, the capacitor has no coating on the surface. If you break one in half and examine it under a magnifying glass you will see that it is constructed like a multi-layer sandwich. Layers of metal (silver or lead) are separated by layers of insulating ceramic. Odd layers of metal are connected to one end and even layers to the other.

Transistors and diodes are usually found in the SOT23 type package which is small and fiddly to handle, even with tweezers. To add to the difficulty, the legs are usually made of tinned iron which is attracted to metal tweezers if these become magnetised.

The device is too small to accommodate the part number so the manufacturer prints his own code on the top surface — usually a single letter and a number only.

In the case of a diode, the middle leg is usually the cathode (striped on conventional diodes) and the other two legs are both connected to the anode. In the case of a transistor the middle leg is the collector, top right (in the picture) is the emitter and bottom right is the base.

The end terminations of resistors and capacitors are very delicate. Most manufacturers recommend a maximum cumulative soldering time of 5 seconds. When you come to remove one from a PCB, remember that 3 seconds were used up to put it there in the first place! Don't expect to remove one of these devices and to re-use it. Always fit a new one.

Remove the existing component by applying the soldering iron tip to each end alternately, several times in quick succession, and flicking the component away. This is not always easy because the component is often glued to the board. Get rid of the solder from the copper pads by using desoldering braid. Blob a tiny amount of new solder on the right hand pad (or left if you are left handed). With a pair of tweezers, position the new component and melt the solder blob to secure it. Solder the opposite end.

Use a 1.6mm tip (or smaller) and 26 gauge solder (0.5mm). Thicker solder or tips give enormous problems. Do the soldering as quickly as possible to avoid separating the end contact from the component. Don't worry about what the solder joint looks like. The strength of joint is unimportant.

## Recognising Components

Resistors come in various sizes but usually look like the illustrations, with three or more coloured bands to indicate the resistance value and tolerance (accuracy %).

Capacitors come in all shapes and sizes.
One of the most common is the ceramic disc.

Some capacitors may be fitted only one way round. This Tantalum Bead capacitor has its positive lead marked.

Electrolytic capacitors usually have the negative lead marked. The ones on the right are called "Radial lead" electrolytics. The one below is an "Axial lead" electrolytic.

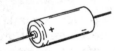

Transistors may be recognised by their black bodies and three legs – a bit like my mother-in-law!

The sketch shows three common types: The TO92 type is a low-power device and you will see lots of these everywhere. The TO220 is designed to cope with fairly high power and is often bolted to a piece of metal which helps to keep it cool (a "heat sink").

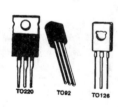

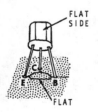

It is important to fit transistors the right way round. the three legs have names – Emitter, Base and Collector. The Collector is usually the middle leg on Japanese transistors but, with European made ones, the centre leg is often the Base. Amstrad receivers use some transistors where the middle leg is the Emitter so you *must* replace a transistor with an identical type.

This trimming potentiometer is a variable resistor. Its slider can be rotated to alter its resistance. NEVER adjust a trimmer without:
1. marking its original position and
2. understanding its function.

Diodes almost always have one end marked with a band. This end is called the "cathode". The diode will pass current only when this end is more negative than the "anode" end, so it is important to fit diodes the correct way round.

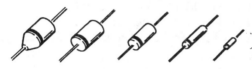 Higher power diodes are called "rectifier diodes" and are usually found in power supplies where they convert alternating current from the mains into direct current (D.C.) which the circuitry needs.

Another type of diode which looks identical is the Zener diode. This is used to prevent a voltage in the circuit from rising higher than a particular value. The value is often marked on the diode. For instance a BYX88C5V6 is a zener diode which works at 5.6 volts.

You will often see "bridge rectifiers" in power supply circuits. The "bridge rectifier" is simply a convenient way to house four rectifier diodes all connected together.

  Although they do not look much like ordinary diodes, these Light Emitting Diodes (LEDs) work in much the same way and must be connected the right way round. In this case, the "cathode" can be seen inside the LED as an anvil shaped wire.

The seven-segment displays used to indicate the channel number often contain LEDs.

Hopefully, you can recognise a fuse!

What you may not recognise is that there are several
different types of fuse. The fuse rating is marked on the
end cap or, in the form of coloured bands, around the body.

A fuse marked "T1A" is a one amp fuse with a Time-delay action.
A fuse marked "F1A" is a one amp fuse with a Fast action.

*You must not substitute one for the other!*

Always replace a fuse with one of an identical rating and type.
The rating should be marked next to the fuse holder (this is a safety
requirement which most manufacturers observe) so there should never
be a problem in determining what fuse to buy.

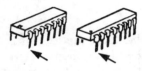

An Integrated Circuit (I.C.) can have any
number of pins. Pin 1 is indicated by various
methods – usually by a dot or notch near it.

The pins are counted anti-clockwise from pin 1.

The printed circuit
board is marked to
indicate the position of
either pin 1 or of the
notch near pin 1.

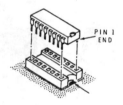

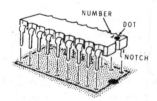

If you ever need to
replace an I.C. it is a
good idea to fit a socket, just in case you need to put the old I.C. back in;
much easier than desoldering all over again!

Sockets can be unreliable, however, so beware of intermittent faults
caused by them. Always ensure that every I.C. pin is inserted correctly
and pushed fully home. It is worth paying a little extra for a high quality
socket.

I.C.s are prone to damage by static electricity. You should make sure that
the receiver is disconnected from the mains. Touch the receiver

metalwork, to ensure that you are at the same voltage potential, before removing an I.C.

A mains transformer converts high voltage mains to safer low voltage which is required by the satellite receiver. It has one or more "primary" windings (hundreds of turns of fine insulated copper wire) connected to the mains and one or more secondary windings (thicker wire) which are isolated from the mains and should (in theory!) be safe to touch.

Some receivers use a switching relay to switch current from one point to another. A small coil of wire forms an electromagnet and pulls the switch contacts together when the coil is energised by an applied voltage.

Because relays have moving parts, it is not uncommon for them to fail in old age. Sometimes the contacts stick open and sometimes closed. A click from the relay indicates that the coil is working but does *not* guarantee that the contacts are all right.

SCART connectors (also called PERITEL) are used to make connections between the receiver and external equipment. Amongst other connections, the SCART carries video-in and video-out signals. It also carries left- and right-audio channels in and out.

## Quick Diagnosis

This section gives general fault-finding advice to those with some technical knowledge. You will need a test meter which can be used to measure fuses, voltage and resistance. A good fuse will measure short-circuit (almost zero Ohms on the resistance scale).

A receiver which is apparently "dead".
Check the fuse in the mains plug and all fuses in the receiver. If an internal fuse has melted then something is short circuit. If the fuse is intact (measure it!) then look for broken copper tracks or bad solder joints — often found under a board-mounted mains transformer or any component which is heavy (e.g. heatsink) or any components which can be subjected to strain (e.g. connector).

A receiver which "lights up" but produces no output.
Bear in mind that most TV sets are designed to mute the audio unless a recognisable picture is present. Use the RF output and put the Test Signal or Menu on. If audio is then present the fault is limited to the video section or decoder (but the tuner module is probably all right). Make sure that someone has not selected an external loop-through video path in the menu or by means of an internal selection link.

If the TV screen is blank, you can check to see if the video is being sent *out* to a decoder socket by connecting video out and video in with a suitable connector on the back panel of the satellite receiver.

Sometimes the video sockets are labelled "Baseband out" and "Baseband in". Sometimes there is just one socket labelled "Decoder". If this is a SCART socket, connect pins 19 and 20 together with a piece of wire. If it is not a SCART then you will have to check your handbook to find the video in/out connections.

Bypass any internal decoder by means of a wire link. Some receivers automatically bypass when the decoder board is removed (e.g. Pace) and some need a physical link wire (e.g. Amstrad). Where a link is used, the picture may flicker because the video signal is "unclamped". If the video appears when the decoder is no longer in line then the decoder is often at fault.

If no audio is present then check the Video output. A signal here indicates a faulty RF modulator or a disconnection to the modulator unit. No signal at the Video output often indicates a faulty tuner or a faulty circuit controlling the tuner. Check the voltages on the tuner pins. Make sure that the tuning voltage (VT) steps up as the frequency is increased (by pressing tune or channel buttons while you measure it).

If a picture is available at the decoder socket but not at the TV socket then the tuner is obviously OK and the fault lies in circuitry inbetween. Check *all* available outputs to pinpoint the fault.

Picture but no sound.
Audio circuits *can* be traced by using just an audio amplifier, provided that you have a circuit diagram and can read it. However, without an oscilloscope, you have very little chance of tracing the fault.
Some common audio fault causes are listed and you may be successful in curing the fault by replacing components without any testing knowledge whatsoever.

Horizontal "fuzzy" bar moves slowly up or down the picture — sometimes accompanied by buzzing on the audio.
*One* bar indicates mains frequency interference which is almost always caused by a faulty bridge rectifier. If there are *two* bars visible then 100Hz interference is present. This can indicate a healthy bridge rectifier and is usually caused by a faulty electrolytic capacitor on the DC output side of the bridge. The problem can also be caused by a faulty transformer or by mains voltage which is too low (e.g. a UK model used on the continent). The third possibility is a partial short circuit which draws excessive current from the power supply.
Similar interference can be caused by a problem with the DC supply to the LNB.

No horizontal **or** no vertical channels
In receivers which use a 13/17 volt switching LNB then, if the LNB itself is OK (check by substitution), the receiver is not switching the voltage which it sends up the cable to power the LNB. You need to measure the voltage coming out of the LNB input port on the receiver. A short cable with an "F" connector on one end and a resistor connected to the other end is useful in order to simulate the load presented by an LNB. Use a 100Ω resistor rated at 3 Watts (or more) which will draw 150mA with 17

volts applied. (Resistor gets HOT!) This is about the worst case that a receiver will see with a single LNB (but a twin output LNB can draw twice as much current). Measure the DC voltage across the resistor when first vertical (13v) then horizontal (17v) channels are selected. Take care not to short circuit the receiver input. If either voltage measurement is incorrect, the receiver is faulty. Note that most LNBs switch at 14.8 volts so the 13v or 17v setting is not very critical and +/- 0.5 volts is generally acceptable. Also note that most LNBs draw less than 180mA.

In receivers which use a magnetic polariser you will need to measure the current through the polariser by connecting a milliameter in series with one of the wires. Alternatively, you can connect a 100Ω 1 Watt resistor across the polariser terminals on the receiver and measure the *voltage* across the resistor. The voltage should vary as the skew is adjusted. Since each make and model of receiver gives a different reading, you should compare your reading with that of a known good receiver but *no* voltage change indicates a fault.

If the receiver polariser output appears to be OK then measure the resistance of the polariser itself and compare the reading with that of a known good polariser.

The reading may be anywhere in the range 47 to 110Ω but two identical polarisers should give the same resistance measurement +/- no more than 5Ω (see list of polariser resistances in the appendix).

In receivers which use a mechanical polarotor you will need to connect a polariser interface to the receiver and connect the test resistor to the interface output in order to carry out the checks, above.

The control pulses may be viewed with an oscilloscope. Some receivers provide the control pulses for just long enough to move the mechanical polarotor then cease. In addition, the 5 volt supply may be provided only for a short period before it is turned off.

Bear this in mind when you use an interface (most of which are designed to store the pulse information and continue to supply the current after the pulses have stopped but may not cope with the disappearance of the 5 volt supply!).

# Fault Finding

Most of this book relates to particular known faults and modifications for a number of different receivers. If your receiver is listed you can skip straight to that section. If your receiver is not listed, it may be one which was made by a manufacturer who then put another company's name on it (called "badge engineering").

If it was designed by Pace, you will find it listed at the beginning of one of the Pace sections. Otherwise you will have to look at pictures in magazines to see if it was made by somebody else. Pace manufactured for Ferguson, Grundig, Nokia, Philips and others in the past.

If your receiver is not listed then it must be either very uncommon or one which I have never had for repair (sorry!)

Even if your receiver is listed, you will find it of great benefit to read *every* section in the book. Some symptoms are so common that I may have forgotten to include a description in every section. You might find the problem mentioned for one receiver but not another. Decoder problems, in particular, tend to have similar causes in every make of receiver since the Videocrypt™ circuitry is basically identical, although component numbers may be different.

### A final word of caution

The dangers of working on satellite receivers must be emphasised:
*There is a risk of electric shock and a risk of burns from hot components. There is also some risk of cuts from sharp edges.*

There is a very real risk that you will nullify your warranty if you poke about inside your receiver.

There is a risk that, in attempting to repair it by yourself, you will eliminate all hope of repair by a qualified engineer.

### IF IN DOUBT, DON'T ATTEMPT TO REPAIR IT.
Simply use the information to learn about the possible cause and cure, in order to estimate the likely cost of repair, *then take it to a shop.*

# Let's Get Technical!

### Capacitors

Aluminium Electrolytic capacitors are used extensively in electronic equipment and are frequently responsible for equipment failure. The service engineer needs a working knowledge of these, and other types of capacitors, in order to do his job effectively.

An electrolytic capacitor is based upon a ribbon of aluminium foil which is first etched to increase its effective surface area. Imagine a pyramid; its surface area is much greater than the area of the square on which it stands. Now imagine millions of pyramids side by side, making up a long ribbon. This is the effect of etching and you would see it under a powerful microscope. The reason for increasing the effective surface area is to minimise the size of aluminium ribbon, thus reducing the size of the capacitor when the ribbon is rolled up.

The etched ribbon is made to oxidise by the application of a voltage. A very fine layer of oxide covers the etched surface. This oxide is called the "dielectric". It is an insulator. The eventual voltage rating of the capacitor depends on the thickness of the oxide layer. This etched, oxidised aluminium ribbon is the "anode" of the capacitor.

The cathode of the capacitor is a conductive liquid called the "electrolyte". It needs to fill the "etched valleys" in the anode in order to make the most efficient use of the surface area. The greater the contact area, the higher the capacitance value. The electrolyte is held in an absorbent ribbon of paper.

In order to make an electrical connection to the liquid cathode, a second aluminium ribbon is pressed against the impregnated paper. This second ribbon does not need to be etched since the liquid itself forms the shape of the etched valleys in the anode.

Finally, a wire is welded to each aluminium ribbon and the ribbon "sandwich" is rolled tightly and put inside a housing, the end of which is sealed with a rubber bung.

The capacitance value depends upon many different factors but most importantly:
The effective area.
The thickness of the oxide dielectric layer.

A capacitor can be damaged by:
Prolonged exposure to heat.
Some cleaning solvents.

Exposure to solvents can damage the aluminium anode.
Exposure to heat can evaporate the electrolyte liquid which will escape past the rubber seal.
This is expected and manufacturers give a capacitor a temperature-time rating. For example, a general purpose electrolytic capacitor might be rated at 85°C for 4000 hours. This also translates approximately to 105°C for 1500 hours. The expectation is that, after exposure to the rated temperature for the stated number of hours, 40 percent of the electrolyte will have evaporated. By this time the capacitor will be virtually useless.

Note that a temperature rating is meaningless without a stated lifetime in hours. A manufacturer could mark a capacitor as a 105°C type (1500 hours) or an 85°C type (4000 hours) but it would be exactly the same component.

The ESR (Effective Series Resistance) is the resistance which the capacitor presents to an alternating current. It is largely determined by the way in which the capacitor is constructed.
A low ESR is important in a switch-mode power supply where the capacitor will be subjected to fast-risetime high-current pulses. If the ESR is too high in value, the capacitor will become hot and will quickly vent its electrolyte. The ESR measurement is often a better guide to the state of health than the capacitance value of an electrolytic. If the ESR is too high, the capacitor will be unable to shunt fast-risetime pulses effectively to ground and interference will radiate from the power supply.

The physical size of an electrolytic is important. As a general rule, the larger the capacitor, the cooler it will run. Larger capacitors tend to have a lower ESR and a higher voltage rating, both of which will improve reliability in circuit. However, mechanical considerations may take precedence: while you might like to fit a 100µF/63 volt capacitor in place of a 100µF/25v device, if the hole spacing on the printed circuit board is not designed for the larger component or if there is simply insufficient space, you could be heading for disaster. A larger component is inevitably heavier and more susceptible to knocks and vibration which can crack the copper solder pads beneath the board. Worse - it might actually cause a danger if it comes too close to a high voltage source.

On the other hand, be suspicious of a circuit which uses, for example, a 2200µF/35v electrolytic across a 5 volt supply. You might be tempted to fit a 10 volt capacitor in its place but wait! Why did the manufacturer choose a higher voltage which is inevitably more expensive? The reason is probably twofold:
The power supply 5 volt output is producing high-current fast-risetime pulses which might peak at 25 volts and 2 Amps. To withstand this, the capacitor will need a very low ESR, a high "ripple current rating", a voltage rating higher than 25 volts and a physically large size to keep it cool.

# What sort of LNB ?

What sort of LNB ?

1) "FSS" LNB 10.0 GHz L.O.
Normally bolted to separate polariser and feed horn. Works in 1 band:
10.9 - 11.7 GHz. Receiver with standard 0.95 - 1.75GHz tuner may be
used. Noise figures vary. Very old ones can be 3.0 dB! Later types used
"High Electron Mobility Transistors" (HEMT) typically 1.3 dB orbetter.

2) "DBS" LNB 10.75 GHz L.O.
Normally bolted to separate polariser and feed horn. Works in 1
band:11.7 - 12.5 GHz. Receiver with standard 0.95 - 1.75GHz tuner may
be used. Noise figures vary.

3) "Telecom" LNB 11.0 GHz L.O.
Normally bolted to separate polariser and feed horn. However, Marconi
made a voltage-switching version with integral feed horn*. Works in 1
band:11.95 - 12.75 GHz. Receiver with standard 0.95 - 1.75GHz tuner
may be used. (* identified by a serial number label with a red corner,
although some were incorrectly marked). Noise figures vary.

4) Dual band LNB
Normally bolted to separate polariser and feed horn. Works in 2 bands
10.9 - 11.7 and 11.7 - 12.5 GHz. Receiver with standard 0.95 - 1.75GHz
tuner may be used. Bandswitching achieved by supply voltage of either
14 volts or 18 volts. Noise figures vary.

5) Tripleband LNB
Normally bolted to separate polariser and feed horn. Works in 2 bands
10.9-11.8 and 11.8-12.75 GHz. Receiver with 0.95 - 2.0 GHz tuner should
be used. Noise figures vary.

6) Quadband LNB
Normally bolted to separate polariser and feed horn. Works in 2 bands
10.7-11.8 and 11.7-12.8 GHz. Receiver with 0.95 - 2.05 GHz tuner should
be used. Noise figures vary.

**7) Enhanced LNB 9.75 GHz L.O.**
Works 10.7-11.7 GHz. Noise Figure usually 1.0 dB or better. Integral feed horn with 40mm neck.

**8) Universal LNB 9.75 and 10.60 GHz L.O.**
Works in 2 bands* 10.7-11.8 +11.6 - 12.7 GHz. (22 kHz tone switched). Voltage switched polarisation. Noise Figure usually 1.0 dB or better. Integral feed horn with 40mm neck.
*If your receiver tuning range is less than 2.15GHz you will have a gap between high and low bands. Refer to calculations, below.

**9) Twin output LNB**
Currently available in Standard, Enhanced and Universal form, the twin output LNB provides two outputs to feed two separate receivers. Each output can be switched by 13/17 volt input by the individual receiver to change polarisation.

**10) Dual output LNB**
Currently available in Standard, Enhanced and Universal form, the twin output LNB provides two outputs to feed two separate receivers. Each output has a fixed polarisation; one horizontal and one vertical. This type of LNB should be used with switching boxes such as the ÒMini MagicÓ which will feed four separate receivers.

**Explanation of Local Oscillator Frequency:**

Suppose a signal comes from the satellite at a microwave frequency of 12 GHz but your typical receiver tunes up only to 1.75 GHz? (Also bear in mind that most cable will NOT happily pass frequencies much above 2GHz).

The function of the LNB is to reduce the frequency of the satellite signal. It does so by subtracting a frequency figure from the satellite signal frequency.

This figure is called the "Local Oscillator" frequency ("LO") of the LNB.

So an LNB with a LO of 10.25GHz will send a 12GHz satellite signal down the cable at 1.75GHz (just within range of your old receiver).

12GHz - 10.25GHz = 1.75GHz

Working in reverse, if your highest satellite frequency is 12.6 GHz then you will need an LNB with a LO of at least

12.6 - 1.75 = 10.85GHz

in order to reduce the satellite signal to a frequency that your receiver can "see" (1.75 GHz).

Now let's reverse the process again:

A "standard" LNB has a LO of 10.0GHz. So the highest satellite program frequency that your standard receiver can *see* is

1.75 + 10.0 = 11.75GHz

An "enhanced" LNB has a LO of 9.75 GHz

1.75 + 9.75 = 11.50GHz

A "universal LNB has TWO LOs. One is 9,75 (same as "enhanced") The other is 10.6 which is selected if it "hears" a 22kHz (just above audible) tone.

1.75 + 10.6 = 12.35GHz

Of course, if your receiver can accept signals up to 2.0 GHz then the highest acceptable signal frequency becomes

2.00 + 10.6 = 12.60GHz

And a receiver with a tuner that extends to 2.15GHz achieves

2.15 + 10.6 = 12.75GHz (which happens to be the top of the "Telecom" band!)

Now, you are still puzzled about the DBS LNB

This has a LO of (typically) 10.75GHz

So an old 1.75GHz receiver will get up to

1.75 + 10.75 = 12.50GHz

A final consideration has to be the LOWER limit on tuning:

Most old receivers can tune no lower than 0950 MHz (= 0.95GHz) whereas later ones might go down to 0.70GHz.

Check out the above calculations with these lower tuning range limits to see the overall tuning bandwidth for any receiver.

This is all very basic "sums" - nothing complex - so once you have a "picture" of what is happening, you can sketch little band plans for any combination of receiver annd LNB.

Once you know the value(s) of the LO(s) in the LNB and of the upper and lower tuning limits of the receiver in question, you can quickly figure out what can be received.

NOTE:
Older receivers *expect" an LNB with a 10.0 LO and the frequency display is arranged just for this. However, you can use an LNB with a different value LO. It just means that the *displayed* frequency will be incorrect.


**What is a Feed Horn?**
A feed horn is a piece of microwave "plumbing" which sits at the focal point of a dish and collects the signal that is reflected by the dish. The dimensions and shape of the horn are critical: if the horn is too wide, it will collect noise reflected by the wall or sky outsie the boundaries of the dish; if too narrow, it will not collect signal reflected by the full area of the dish.

```
Transponder   - LNB Local   = tuner frequency
Frequency       Oscillator


12750 MHz
|
|
|   Telecom/Astra 1F
|
|
|   DBS/Astra 1E
|
11700 MHz   - 10000 MHz = 1700
|                            |
|   Astra 1B                 |
|                            |
|   Astra 1A     Receiver tuning range without ADX
|                            |
|   Astra 1C                 |
|                    950  + 500 = 1450
|   Astra 1D                      |
|                        Tuning range with ADX
|                                 |
10700 MHz   - 10000 MHz = 700   + 500 = 1200
```

An old standard receiver usually tunes from 950 to 1700 MHz.
The map above shows the limited tuning range of an old standard
receiver with an old standard 10.0 GHz LNB. The addition of an ADX
Channel Expander moves the Astra 1D frequencies up by 500 MHz into
the tuning range of the receiver.


To receive all Astra channels from satellites D to B without using an
ADX, a receiver would need a tuning range of 700 to 1700 MHz.

```
Transponder      LNB Local
Frequency        Oscillator


12750 MHz  - 10600 MHz = 2150
 |                         |
 |                         |
 |  Telecom/Astra 1F       |
 |            Receiver tuning range for Hi band (22kHz
on)
 |                         |
 |  DBS/Astra 1E           |
 |          - 10600 MHz = 1100
11700 MHz  -  9750 MHz = 1950
 |                         |
 |  Astra 1B               |
 |                         |
 |  Astra 1A               |
 |            Receiver tuning range for Lo band (22kHz
off)
 |  Astra 1C               |
 |                         |
 |  Astra 1D               |
 |                         |
10700 MHz  -  9750 MHz = 950
```

An Enhanced LNB has a local oscillator frequency of 9750 MHz.
The receiver now needs a tuning range of 950 to 1950 MHz as shown in the map above.

If a Universal LNB is used, its local oscillator can be switched from 9750 to 10600 MHz by sending a 22kHz tone up the cable. Some receivers have this
facility built inside. Some will need an external tone-inserter box connected into the cable.

If the receiver has a range of 950 to 2150, it will be able to receive programmes on both Hi and Lo band.

Another possibility is to use an ADX-Plus. This has an internal switch which, when moved across, makes the ADX-Plus move the frequencies DOWN by 500 MHz instead of up.

So a channel at 12750 MHz is moved down like this:

12750 - 10600 - 500 = 1650 MHz (with an ADX-Plus)

which is well within the tuning range of an old standard receiver.

And the lowest channel receivable will be:

950 + 500 + 10600 = 12050 MHz (with tone ON and ADX-Plus)

Note: MHz (MegaHertz) = GHz (GigaHertz) x 1000
So 9750 MHz = 9.75 GHz

**What is a Polariser?**
A polariser is used to alter the polarisation of the signal to match the physical polarisation of the LNB. A polariser can be either a magnetic type (a simple coil of wire) or a mechanical type which uses a tiny motor to rotate a stub of metal. Of the two, the magnetic one tends to be more reliable but also wastes more signal than the mechanical type.
Modern "switching" LNBs have two internal antennas opposed at right angles. The signal from either one of these can be selected by the LNB for amplification and down conversion so no external polariser is required.

**What is an "OMT"?**
OMT stands for Ortho Mode Transducer. This is a simply a piece of microwave "plumbing" in the shape of a "T". It allows you to fit two LNBs onto flanges. The leg of the "T" can be bolted to a feed horn on a dish. You can fit either a single polariser between the feedhorn and the OMT or you can fit two polarisers – one for each LNB. An OMT use to be used to achieve reception of two frequency bands before dual-band LNBs became available. An OMT might still be useful even now, since one LNB could be used for circular polarised signals and one for v/h polarised signals.

# Sparklies

Many installers have asked my advice about "sparklies" on Astra pictures and, although not an installer myself, I've tried to advise as best I can.

### Signal Too Weak

A weak signal can have many different causes. The most common are:
- Heavy rainfall
- Obstruction such as trees
- Buckled or rusty dish
- Cable fault (water inside, kinked or bad connection at LNB or a joint or connection in the cable)
- Faulty LNB or water inside
- very infrequently, a faulty tuner module inside receiver

The effects of rainfall and trees are all too obvious but they fool some people! If the picture is bad when it rains then a sparkly picture can result directly from the rain itself (because it reduces the signal coming from the satellite) or from water getting into the LNB or cable. The effect of trees is more obvious in summer when the leaves are present. The interference will vary as the branches move in the wind.

Dish faults are quite common. Even a brand new dish straight from the box can be twisted, bent or buckled. Even a slight amount of distortion is sufficient to move the focal point away from the LNB feed horn. You may be able to correct the distortion but the best answer is to change the dish.

To determine the exact cause of your problem, it's best to change each element, one by one. Try a different receiver first. The next, simplest step is to run a new length of cable alongside the old one. Connect it at each end and test the system. While you are there, check the old cable and LNB for corrosion at the connectors - a sure sign that water has crept inside. Occasionally an LNB can be dried out and will work perfectly again but, if it's difficult to reach the dish, my advice would be to renew the LNB. Be sure to use self-amalgamation tape to make a waterproof connection. It's also a good idea to fasten a polythene bag over the LNB, although this looks unsightly.

If you fit the new cable permanently, DO NOT KINK it by bending it tightly around a corner or by hammering a clip too hard.

## Signal Too Strong

My advice has always been that to point a large dish feeding a low threshold receiver at Astra is just asking for trouble because the combined signal strength of all the transponders is likely to overload the tuner input of the receiver.

Recently, I was contacted by Bert Dahlstrom of Sweden who suggested that his tests indicate an additional problem. It seems that most people will combine a large dish with low threshold receiver *and* a high gain LNB. According to Bert, much of the problem arises *inside* the LNB. He says that the high signal input from Astra, collected by a large dish, can overload the output amplifier inside a high gain LNB and cause "sparklies" on pictures.

Fitting an LNB of lower gain (around 45dB) solved his problem. Bert continues, however, by saying that it does not help to reduce the input level to the receiver if it is *not* overloaded (and normally it isn't if you have a reasonably long run of coax cable). However, if a short cable run is used, the input level to the receiver *can* be too high and must be reduced by introducing an attenuator.

Another problem, he points out, is the AGC (Automatic Gain Control) circuitry in the tuner, that reduces the level when you have strong signals coming in, making it difficult to get a low level signal among the strong ones. That is apparently the case in Stockholm with CNN from Astra. It is about 10 dB below the other transponders.This could be helped with a band pass filter at the input, say 200 MHz wide.
You can end up with sparklies in saturated colours when you have too narrow an IF filter. For example, looking at Eutelsat with an Astra receiver. Even if the filters are 36 MHz wide, you can have a signal with a low absolute level into the IF block. Then you use only the tip of the

filter (the response is not square in reality) and get a signal that is effectively wider than the filter.

Sparklies on saturated colours is called truncation noise, meaning that the signal is truncated (cut) by the filter. Another place where signal truncation occurs is in the video path; one or more of the video amplifiers is overloaded with signal, e.g. in a decoder. Amplifiers may truncate on the high or low end, (or both!!!!)
In some designs, amplifiers can't handle more than 1 volt video p-p; in many cases not even that much. It should be all right with 1 volt but if some signals go higher, you get noise in the picture.

Of course the real answer to the problem is another question: "Why would anyone spend money on a really high-gain, sensitive system, just to watch programmes from Astra?" (Sorry Mr Murdoch & Associates!)
I've also heard of problems at the output end of the receiver. The effect is often described as "sparklies" on saturated colours. From the reports I've heard, it seems to occur with certain makes of TV because they can't tolerate high video levels. The answer is to fit resistors in the Scart plug to attenuate the signal.

To sum up: Sparklies on the picture are not necessarily caused only by a *weak* signal - the signal may be too *strong*. If you have a problem like this, first try an attenuator near the receiver input (use the correct type, not one intended for a terrestrial signal). Buy one and keep it in the van! If this fails to solve the problem, try reducing the amount of signal reaching the LNB (the famous "wet rag" on the LNB?) or fit a lower gain LNB temporarily. Again, you should keep one in the van. If the problem is limited to decoded channels, it may be a problem with the decoder itself. If the picture is better through RF than Scart, get a Scart lead with attenuator resistors in the video lead. If the problem is with the weakest signal amongst strong ones (UK Gold on Astra in the UK I think?) then there may be no workable solution.

...with thanks to Bert Dahlstrom.

# Interference Problems

This article applies to UK and European transmissions.

A lot of interference can be eliminated completely by replacing substandard satellite and TV cable with good quality, double-screened cable, including RF leads. You should also avoid wall plates because the tiny stub of exposed centre core wire will pick up interference. Run both TV and satellite cables directly into the satellite receiver without any joints. If a wall plate must be used, throw away the guts and glue a female plug in the hole. Fit the cable end into this plug and solder the inner core. In this way, you keep the core fully screened. This applies to both "F" wall sockets and UHF wall sockets and surface boxes.

Interference from Astra 1D occurs because a Standard (10.000GHz) LNB converts the 1D frequencies down to UHF frequencies in the same band as TV channels 49 to 69. Reception areas covered by these terrestrial channels will suffer interference.

If the receiver has a 2GHz tuner, the simplest remedy is to replace the Standard LNB with an Enhanced (9.750GHz) LNB. If this is not possible, you can eliminate the 1D channels by fitting a 1D filter in the satellite cable. The filter is most effective when fitted next to the LNB, since otherwise the satellite cable may radiate interference along its length - possibly into the TV cable belonging to a neighbour as well as the owner's. However, the 1D filter obviously prevents reception of any 1D satellite channels!

If reception of 1D channels is required with a receiver that has no 2GHz tuner then the only answer is to use a frequency convertor such as the ADX Plus "Channel Expander". This can be used with a Standard LNB but the risk of interference is still there.

To avoid the possibility of interference, use the ADX Plus with an Enhanced LNB. The disadvantage of this is that the Enhanced LNB moves all channels up by 250MHz and the ADX Plus moves them back down by 500 MHz. The result is that ALL channels will have to be re-tuned by either 250MHz down (Astra 1D with ADX Plus off) or 250MHz up (Astra 1A, 1B, 1C with ADX Plus switched on).

Interference on Satellite channels can be caused by too strong a terrestrial signal. Try fitting a UHF attenuator between the TV aerial cable and the satellite receiver UHF input socket.

Interference on Television channels can be removed or reduced by fitting a mast-head amplifier to the TV aerial. If the terrestrial signal is already strong, you should also fit a UHF attenuator as described above.

For all cases of interference, you should test the receiver in a different location before assuming that it is faulty.

If you are absolutely certain that the interference is within the receiver itself and that it has appeared gradually, then the most likely cause is electrolytic capacitors which have aged because of heat. All electrolytic capacitors have a limited life and need to be replaced periodically. The largest capacitors in the power supply are most likely to fail first, closely followe by those around the tuner.

RELKITs are available for several models to cure interference caused by old capacitors.

## Interference with Motorised Systems

Interference on motorised systems can have two main effects:

1. The positioner counts too many pulses and does not reach the satellite position. This is often blamed on the positioner as "loses its memory."
2. The motor causes interference on the TV picture and possibly on neighbouring TVs and radios.

The main cause of interference is the use of unscreened caravan cable or telephone cable.

The remedy is to use proper screened cable. The motor wires should have a screen as a minimum. The pulse wires and polariser wires should also be screened separately. All screening braids should be connected to ground at the receiver only. They should not be connected to the dish. The dish assembly should have a separate ground connection to a copper rod in the adjacent soil.

# Appendix

The following section contains (hopefully) useful information. In this edition, I decided not to include a list of satellite transponders since they would be well out of date by the time the book was printed.

In addition, with the recent moving of Astra 1D and the advent of digital programmes which share a single transponder, a list of actual satellite transponders is no longer very meaningful.

See the SatCure web site at: http://www.netcentral.co.uk/satcure/ Packed with "FAQ" information about common faults and cures for ailing satellite receivers and decoders. Repair kits, upgrade kits, spare parts, surplus components, hobby kits and links to other satellite information sites.

**Current drain of LNBs** (typical values) measured at 17 volts.

| LNB | mA |
| --- | --- |
| Blue Cap LNB | 120 - 210 |
| Cambridge AE21 | 120 |
| Grundig Universal AUN2S | 122 |
| Amstrad SLB1 1.2 | 143 |
| Continental Microwave 1.2 | 154 |
| Marconi Compact Bullet | 162 |
| | |
| Marconi Twin "F" | 251 |
| Marconi Twin "Z" | 273 |
| Cambridge Gemini Twin | 294 |
| Global Mini Magic™ switch | 318 |

Some receivers can't supply a lot of current so it's useful to see just how much an LNB will need before you install it.

Twin output LNBs take much more current than single output and this can cause various problems with certain combinations of receiver.

## Polariser/Feed-polariser resistances

| Manufacturer | Resistance (Ω) |
|---|---|
| Maspro | 90 |
| Grundig | 105 |
| Irte | 85 |
| Racal | 55 |
| Channel Master | 69 |
| Lenson Heath | 67 |
| Echostar | 67 |
| Swedish Microwave | 97 |

Polarisers are fairly simple devices, consisting mainly of a tube with a coil of wire.

Measure the coil resistance with an Ohm meter.

If the resistance is significantly different from the value given in the table, then the polariser is faulty. If the resistance is within +/- 5Ω of the table value then the polariser *may* be faulty but it is fairly unlikely.

Do check for spiders, dirt and water ingress! Check for corrosion of the terminations.

You can measure the coil resistance at the two wires as they enter the receiver (disconnect them first!) Add a few Ohms to the table value to account for the small resistance of the cable (10Ω maximum).

If the reading is incorrect then measure the polariser at the dish to make sure it is not the cable at fault.

It does not matter which way round you connect the meter.

# RESISTOR COLOUR CODE

The most common resistor has three coloured bands to denote its value:

Band 1 is the first digit.
Band 2 is the second digit.
Band three is the number of zeros. A metallic band here denotes a divider.
A fourth band may denote its tolerance range since no resistor has an exact value.
The colours are as listed: ........................................................................

So red red red will be 22 and two zeros or 2200 Ohms (Ω). Divide by 1000 to get kiloOhms = 2k2Ω. (Decimal points are not written because they disappear
during copying and cause much confusion and stabbing at calculators!)

If band 3 is gold, take the first two digits as the value then divide by ten:
so red red gold would be 22 divided by 10 which is two point two Ohms — written 2Ω2 or 2R2Ω.
If band 3 is silver, divide the Ohmic value of the first two digits by 100:
so red red silver would be 0R22Ω.

| BLACK | 0 |
|---|---|
| BROWN | 1 |
| RED | 2 |
| ORANGE | 3 |
| YELLOW | 4 |
| GREEN | 5 |
| BLUE | 6 |
| VIOLET | 7 |
| GREY | 8 |
| WHITE | 9 |

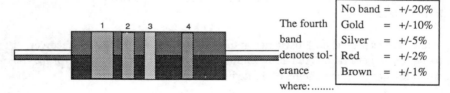

The fourth band denotes tolerance where: ........

| No band | = | +/-20% |
|---|---|---|
| Gold | = | +/-10% |
| Silver | = | +/-5% |
| Red | = | +/-2% |
| Brown | = | +/-1% |

Normally for 1% resistors the Ohmic value will be represented by three bands followed by a fourth band for the number of noughts and a fifth band for the tolerance. (Some have an extra band for temperature coefficient).

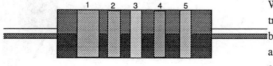

When you use resistors every day, translating the colour code soon becomes a subconscious exercise as you become familiar with the common values which you will recognise "on sight".

## Useful Contacts

I'm often asked "where can I get such and such a part" or "who can provide this information?" Although not by any means exhaustive, this list might help. Please note that some numbers may now be out of date although they were checked before going to press.

**Alba Plc** (Barking)
Tel 0181 594 5533, fax 591 0962, spares  0181 787 3010
Supplier of Alba and Bush equipment.

**Allicraft** (Poole)
Tel 01202 632211, fax 632453
Wholesale supplier of TV aerials and fixings.

**Alston-Barry UK Ltd** (Cambridge)
Tel 01353 669009, fax 669120
Importer of Drake satellite equipment

**Amstrad** (Brentwood)
01277 228888
Suppliers of Amstrad and Fidelity brand satellite products.

**Apex Equipment Care** (Manchester)
Tel 0161 793 1245
Repairer of satellite receivers and installation of IF & SMATV distribution systems.

**Bee Fast Fasteners Ltd** (High Wycombe)
Tel 01494 451227, fax 436270
Wholesale supplier of screws and Mungo Bolts etc.

**Calder Components** (Heckmondwycke)
Tel (01924) 411089, fax 411104
Supplier of Pace spares and other accessories

**Cambridge Industries Limited** (Reading)
Tel  01734 306699, fax 306633
Manufacturer of LNBs only.

**Cambridge Industries Limited** (Ayr)
LNB technical enquiries only 01292 284001, fax 288699
(For Cambridge spares see South Coast Technology and SatCure).

**Cardware** (Chesterfield)
Tel 01246 455150, 455945, fax 455650, email sales@cardware.ftech.co.uk
Suppliers of D2Mac conversion kits for Ferguson SRB1, Philips BSB, Nokia BSB.

**Channel Master Uk Ltd** (Blackburn)
Tel 01254 680444, fax 672299
Supplier of Channel Master dish products.

**Colourtrade** (Birmingham)
Tel 0121 359 7020, fax 359 6344
Wholesale suppliers of B grade satellite receivers/decoders and brown goods.

**Concentric Press Products** (Birmingham)
Tel 0121 551 4411, 523 4831
Manufacturer of dish products.

**Connexions (UK)** (Herts)
Tel 01707 272091, fax 269444
Computer networking products– NOT satellite any longer.

**Continental Microwave Satellite TV Ltd** (Dunstable)
Manufacturer of LNBs
01582 699664, 699129

**CPC** (Preston)
Tel 01772 654455, fax 654466
Major stockist of Satellite spares & accessories plus TV, VCR spares, etc.

**Economic Devices** (Wolverhampton)
Tel/fax 01902 773122, fax 29052
Suppliers of spare parts, accessories and kits for Satellite, VCR, TV, Audio.

**Echosphere** (Holland)
0031 5468 15122, fax  0031 5468 14691
Manufacturer of Echostar products.

**Electrotech (now Longreach Supervision)** (London)
Tel 0181 451 6766, fax 451 1834
Supplier of Maspro brand satellite products and most others.

**Express TV** (London)
Tel 0181 881 0764, fax 888 0397
Echostar service agent. Also Nokia, Grundig, Mitsubishi, Hitachi.

**Galaxy Communications** (Luton)
Tel 01582 452361, fax 487081
Suppliers Of Concentric Dishes

**Global Communications Uk Ltd** (Althorne, Essex)
Tel 01621 743440, fax 743676
Manufacturer of IF connection and distribution products.

**G J Electronics** (Ashford)
Tel 01303 814224, fax 814073
Supplier of RF connectors.

**Grandata Ltd** (Wembley)
Tel 0181 900 2329, fax 903 6126
Suppliers of spare parts, accessories and kits for Satellite, VCR, TV, Audio.

**Grundig** (Pontyclun)
01443 220220
Manufacturers of Satellite receivers and LNBs.

**Grundig International Ltd** (Rugby)
Tel 01788 577155, fax 562354

**Heathrow Systems** (Middlesex)
Tel 01895 431633
Supplier of Palcom products.

**Harrison Electronics** (Cambridgeshire)
Tel 01354 51289, fax 51416
Suppliers of Amstrad spares and accessories.

**Hills Components** (Watford)
Tel 01923 424344, fax 421421
Supplier of accessories, cables, connectors.

**HRS** (Birmingham)
Tel 0121 789 7575, fax 0800 212179
Major stockist of Satellite spares & accessories plus TV, VCR spares, etc.

**Insat** (London)
Tel 0171 354 8877
Satellite receiver Repairs

**IRTE International Ltd** (London)
Tel 01992 624777, fax 625522
Supplier of IRTE dish products.

**J D Electronics**
Tel (01245) 380226
Repairer of Echostar, Drake and Technisat receivers.

**Kesh Electrics** (Ireland)
Tel 013656 31449
Suppliers of "Pace Link" system. Repairers of satellite receivers.

**Lenson Heath Sat TV Systems Ltd** (Marlow)
Tel 01628 890820, fax 898268
Manufacturer of dish systems.

**Longreach Marketing Ltd** (Bath)
Tel 01225 444894, fax 448676
Supplier of satellite TV systems.

**Marconi** (Stanmore)
Tel 0181 954 2311, fax 954 3033
Satellite Dish Supplier

**Maxview Ltd** (Kings Lynn)
Tel 01553 810376, fax 811638
Supplier of TV aerial products.

**M.C.E.S. Ltd** (Manchester)
Tel 0161 746 8037, 746 8038, fax 746 8136
Repairers of Tuners, IF modules, RF boosters, Video heads and LNBs.

**Michael Black Plc** (Newcastle On Tyne)
Tel 0191 270 0772, fax 270 1239
Supplier of satellite TV systems.

**Mildenhall Satellite** (Newmarket)
Tel 01638 711220, fax 712202
Supplier/repairer of Amstrad receivers. Also Pace etc.

**Mimtec**
Manufacturer of Mimtec satellite receivers.
No longer trading. No spares available apart from PSU repair kit SATKIT 15.

**Nec Uk Ltd** (London)
Tel 0181 993 8111, fax 993 5215
Manufacturer of NEC products.

**Nokia** (Swindon)
Tel 01793 556000, sales 556001, spares 556002, technical (dealers only) 556003
Suppliers of Nokia and Finlux brand satellite receivers and spares.

**Northern Telecom** (Paignton)
Tel 01803 662000
LNB Manufacturer

**Pace** (Shipley)
Tel 01274 532000, spares orderline & technical fax 537128. Email service@pace.co.uk
Manufacturers of satellite receivers & modems.

**Philex plc** (West Hendon)
Tel 0181 202 1919, 202 1717, fax 202 0015
Suppliers of switches and remote control handsets

**Premier Video Productions** (Wolverhampton)
Tel 01902 26269
Design and manufacture of decoders Secam-pal transcoders, video switching units, etc.

**Procom Microwave Ltd** (Chinnor)
Tel 01844 54490
Manufacturer of satellite dishes

**Promax** (St Albans)
Tel 01727 832266, fax 810546
Supply/repair of Promax Meters

**Protel Distribution Ltd** (Finchley)
Tel 0181 445 4441, fax 445 5861
Wholesale Distribution/Repair of satellite products

**RSD Communications Ltd** (Stirling)
01786 450572, 446222, fax 474653 Web site at    http://www.rsd-communications.co.uk
Email    sales@rsd-communications.co.uk    technical@rsd-communications.co.uk
Design and manufacture of satellite TV decoders, receivers and accesories

**SatCure** (Crewe)
Tel 01270 753311, fax 761928, mobile 0589 355411. Email satcure@netcentral.co.uk
Mail Order Satellite repairs, spares & kits including Pace, Amstrad, Cambridge, Nokia.

**Satfix** (Swansea)
Tel 01792 897096
Repairers of satellite receivers and decoders. All models.

**Satellite Services** (London)
Tel 081 961 4662, fax 961 4682
Repairers of satellite receivers and Maspro LC2E Meters.

**Satellite Solutions Uk Ltd** (Northampton)
Tel 01604 787888, fax 787999 and Congleton branch 01260 299658
Supply and repair of satellite systems and accessories. Echostar agent.

**Satfinder Uk** (Henley On Thames)
Tel 01491 573390, fax 573380
Manufacture/repair of Satfinder meters.

**SCT Steve Chilver Trading** (London)
Tel 0181 566 7830, fax 566 7832

**SEME**
01664 65392
Stockists of spares & accessories for Satellite, VCR, TV, Audio.

**Sendz Components** (Shoeburyness)
Tel 01702 332992, fax 338805
Stockists of spares & accessories (new and surplus) for Satellite, VCR, TV, Audio.

**Sharp UK** (Manchester)
Tel 0161 205 2333
Wholesale suppliers of tuners and RF modules.

**Sky TV**
Smart Cards 0506 462000   Fax 0506 463000   Tel 0171 705 3000
Call Sky customer services on 0990 102030

**Sontec (electronics) Ltd** (Norwich)
Tel 01603 483675, fax 788937
Repairer of Nec Equipment

**South Coast Technology** (Portsmouth)
Tel 01705 650545, fax 01705 673647
Stockists of Cambridge satellite spares. Repairers of LNBs & tuners.

**Strong UK** (London)
Tel 0171 491 7474, fax 491 7575
Suppliers of Strong brand and Palcom satellite receivers

**Tandy** (Walsall)
Wholesale distribution centre Tel 0121 556 6101

**Tatung (uk) Ltd** (Telford)
Tel 01952 613111, fax 293564
Manufacturer of Tatung products

**Taylor Bros (Oldham) Ltd**
Tel 0161 652 3221, fax 626 1736
Manufacturers Of TV RF Amplifiers Etc.

**Technetix** (Royston)
Tel 01763 248555, fax 245338
Supplier of Satellite IF and SMATV distribution equipment.

**Telepart**: see Economic devices.

**Teleste Cablevision Limited** (Cambridge)
Tel 01223 66521, fax 316483

**Televes Uk** (Cwmbran)
Tel 01633 875821, fax 866311
Supplier of Televes brand equipment.

**Tonks Communications** (Walsall)
Tel 01922 646710, fax 644059
Installers, Repairers and suppliers of satellite spares and accessories (and CB Radio).

**Trackdown** (Oxford)
(01608) 678057, fax 677872
Suppliers of Remote Control handsets and accessories to the hotel trade.

**Transworld Satellite Systems** (Whitby)
Tel 01947 880016
Supplier of converted BSB-D2Mac decoders & most makes of satellite equipment.
See full advert on page 159.

**Unifix** (West Bromwich)
Tel 0121 609 0099
Wholesale supplier of cable clips.

**Volex Raydex** (Skelmersdale)
Tel 01695 33061, fax26017
Wholesale manufacturer of cable, mains cords.

**Webro (long Eaton) Ltd** (Nottinghamshire)
Tel 01602 730114, fax 461230
Wholesale manufacturer of coaxial cable.

**Webwel** (Braintree)
Tel 01376 550044, fax 550022
Wholesale manufacturer of coaxial cable.

**Wiltsgrove Ltd** (Birmingham)
Tel 0121 772 2733, fax 766 6100
Supplier of satellite TV parts, VCR etc.

**Wizard Distributors** (Manchester)
Tel 0161 872 5438, 848 0060, fax 873 7365
Suppliers of spares for Satellite, Audio, TV, VCR, Computer & Microwave.

**Eurosat Distributors** (wholesale only)

Eurosat Bristol
Tel 01272 820040, fax 822494

Eurosat Distribution Midlands Ltd (Walsall)
Tel 01922 39299, fax 39398, Email eurosat@brunel.co.uk

Eurosat Distribution Ltd (London)
Tel 0181 452 6699, fax 452 6777, Technical Line 830 5458

Eurosat Eastern Ltd (Borehamwood)
Tel 0181 953 9998, fax 953 9991

Eurosat Manchester (Urmston)
Tel 0161 747 2007, fax 747 2008

Eurosat Northern (Barnsley) (now called N.E.W.)
Tel 01226 290800, fax 243300

Eurosat Scotland (Glasgow)
Tel (0141) 552 2111, fax 0141 556 4273

Eurosat Southern
Tel 01483 730500, fax 730503, Email 101665.1155@compuserve.com

Eurosat USA   (Wisconsin)
Tel 00 1 608 846 5944  Fax  00 1 608 846 5945

Eurosat Western (Exeter)
Tel 01392 445111, fax 445110

**I live in Europe and want to subscribe to SKY.**
**They told me this is not possible. Why?**

The reason that Sky channels are encrypted and are not available outside the U.K has nothing to do with an agreement with other channels; it's to do with copyright.

Films and TV programmes are sold on the basis that the purchaser buys the rights to show that material in a specific country only. This is how the programme makers earn their money. (It would be no use, for example, if a film production company spent a million dollars to make a film, sold the rights to one cinema for 10,000 dollars and then allowed that cinema to sell copies of the film to all other cinemas.)

Sky, therefore, buy the rights to show the programmes only in the U.K. They then encrypt their transmissions and make their viewing cards available only to U.K. viewers.

The Film or TV company also sells the rights to other cinemas and broadcasters to show the same programme material in other countries.

The alternative would be to have to buy the rights for all of Astra's transmission area, which would be very expensive and not cost effective for Sky. Their transmissions would still have to be encrypted anyway, otherwise they would have no way of making any money. No company can afford to pay for Films and TV Programmes without getting a return on their investment.

Of course, many people get friends or relatives in the U.K. to subscribe to Sky channels then post the card to them for use outside the U.K. Although Sky might secretly be pleased to have the extra revenue, they are bound by the licence agreement to take all reasonable steps to prevent viewing outside the U.K. This means that your card will be turned off if Sky discover that you are using it outside the UK. If you take your card on holiday and get problems, *don't* ring Sky from abroad and complain! Of course, you won't be prosecuted if you have a valid subcription but they *will* turn your card off.

This is my opinion of how the system works. It may not be strictly accurate but it should be sufficiently close to explain the problems.

# Abbreviations

Abbreviations can be a nuisance but we all use them. Some of the meanings are obvious to those who have English as a first language. However, if English is your second language, you can have real problems in understanding the text (as I have found out when trying to read German language text myself!) So, to help both beginners and non-native English speakers, I have looked at my text and found the following confusing words.

I hope this list will make it easier for you to understand this manual!

Abbreviations:

| | |
|---|---|
| Aux | Auxiliary |
| BER | Bit Error Rate (D2Mac) or Beyond Economic Repair |
| B+W | Black and white |
| Chans | Channels |
| CPU | Microcontroller or microprocessor |
| Chip | Integrated Circuit |
| Graphics | On-screen graphics (text) |
| Gibberish | Nonsense, silly (Gibber = to chat like a monkey) |
| Hor or Horiz | Horizontal |
| I.C. | Integrated Circuit |
| Intermit | Intermittent |
| L | Left |
| Mains | 230 volt power connection |
| Menu | On-screen adjustments page |
| Micro | Microcontroller or microprocessor |
| N/a | Not available or not applicable |
| NC | No connection |
| No. | Number |
| o/c | Open-circuit (disconnected) |
| On-screen graphics | text messages on the TV screen |
| OSD | On-screen display (text) |
| OSG | On-screen graphics (text) |
| Pics | Pictures |
| Quid | UK pound sterling |
| R | Right |
| Sat | Satellite |
| s/c | Short-circuit |
| Scope | oscilloscope |
| VCR | Video cassette recorder |
| Vert | vertical |
| Syncs | synchronisation pulses |

# Fault Index

## Amstrad SRD510/520

## Fault Index

## MSS100/Prima

## Apollo/MSS200/300

## Grundig GRD150/250 etc

## BT-SVS250